From the Finca
to the Maquila

From the Finca
to the Maquila

Labor and Capitalist Development
in Central America

Juan Pablo Pérez Sáinz

Westview Press
A Member of the Perseus Books Group

Copyright © 1999 by Westview Press, A Member of the Perseus Books Group

Published in 1999 in the United States of America by Westview Press, 5500 Central Avenue, Boulder, Colorado 80301-2877, and in the United Kingdom by Westview Press, 12 Hid's Copse Road, Cumnor Hill, Oxford OX2 9JJ

Originally published as *De la Finca a la Maquila: Modernización Capitalista y Trabajo en Centroamérica* by Facultad Latinoamericana de Ciencias Sociales (FLACSO)

Library of Congress Cataloging-in-Publication Data
Pérez Sáinz, Juan Pablo.
  [De la finca a la maquila. English]
  From the finca to the maquila : labor and capitalist development
in Central America / Juan Pablo Pérez Sáinz.
    p.   cm.
  Includes bibliographical references and index.
  ISBN 0-8133-3519-1
  1. Labor market—Central America—History—20th century.   2. Labor
movement—Central America—History—20th century.   3. Structural
adjustment (Economic policy)—Central America.   4. Informal sector
(Economics)—Central America.   I. Title.
HD5733.A6P4713   1999
331.12'09728—dc21   98-34576
                                                                                                                          CIP

The paper used in this publication meets the requirements of the American National Standard for Permanence of Paper for Printed Library Materials Z39.48-1984.

10   9   8   7   6   5   4   3   2   1

Contents

5 Conclusions 143

Tables

Acronyms

ANACH	National Peasants' Association of Honduras
ATC	Rural Workers Association
CACIF	Coordinating Committee of Agriculture, Commerce Industry, and Finance Associations
CATD	Authentic Democratic Workers Confederation
CCTD	Costa Rican Democratic Workers Confederation
CCTRN	Costa Rican Rerum Novarum Workers Confederation
CENPRO	National Export Promotion Center
CGS	General Trade Union Confederation
CGTC	Costa Rican General Workers Confederation
CGTG	Guatemalan General Workers Confederation
CGTS	General Workers Confederation of El Salvador
CLAT	Latin American Workers Confederation
CNGG	National Guatemalan Peasants Confederation
CNT	National Workers Center
CNUS	National United Trade Union Committee
COCA	Central American Workers Confederation
COCTN	Somozist Organizing Committee for the Nicaraguan Workers Confederation
COPA	Panamerican Work Confederation
CPT	Permanent Workers Council
CRM	Revolutionary Mass Coordinator
CROS	Workers Trade Union Reorganization Committee
CSG	Guatemalan Trade Union Council
CST	*Sandinista* Workers Confederation
CTC	Costa Rican Workers Confederation
CTCR	Confederation of Costa Rican Workers
CTG	Guatemalan Workers Confederation
CTH	Workers Confederation of Honduras
CTN	Workers Confederation of Nicaragua
CUC	Peasant Unity Committee
CUS	United Trade Union Council
CUT	United Workers Confederation
FAS	Autonomous Trade Union Federation
FDR	Democratic Revolutionary Front

FECCAS	Christian Federation of Salvadoran Peasants
FECORAH	Honduran Agrarian Reform Cooperatives Federation
FRCT	Central Regional Workers Federation
FSG	Guatemalan Trade Union Federation
FUSS	United Trade Union Federation
FUTH	United Workers Federation of Honduras
GEXPRONT	Non-Traditional Exports Guild
IADSL	American Institute for the Development of Free Trade Unionism
MUSYGES	United Trade Union and Guild Movement of El Salvador
ORIT	Interamerican Regional Organization
SITRATERCO	Tela Railroad Workers Trade Union
SNOTS	National Labor and Wage Organization System
UASP	Trade Union and Popular Action Unit
UNSITRAGUA	Guatemalan Workers United Trade Unions
UNTS	National Salvadoran Workers Unity
UPD	Democratic Popular Unity

Introduction

And when I was eight I started earning money on the finca and it was then that I decided I would set myself the task of picking thirty-five pounds of coffee a day and they would pay me twenty cents, in those days, for the job. And sometimes I didn't make it in a day. If I managed thirty-five pounds, then I'd earn the twenty cents, but if I didn't, the next day I'd still be earning the same twenty cents. . . . Sometimes you have to shake the trees for the beans to fall off. And you have to pick the ones that are nearer carefully because if we pulled a branch off we'd have to pay for it out of our salary. So we had to pick bean by bean. . . .

And in the mornings we practically had to take it in turns to go into the woods to relieve ourselves. There are no latrines and there's no toilet on the *finca*. Instead, there was a place with lots of hills and that was where everyone went—all four hundred of us who lived there. Everybody went to the same hill, so it was like a latrine, all those people went to the toilet there. . . .

There's an office where all the work's taken to—when you hand your work in they weigh it and they make a note to keep track. . . . The weights were always fixed. . . . This is how it works, from the moment the people leave the towns where they're hired like animals, from the minute they get onto the truck, they start to be cheated out of their salary. They're charged money for everything, for lending them a hand to lift things onto the truck, or whatever. And when they get to the finca, right from the very first day, the men in charge start to rob the workers of their money. And right up until the very last day, even in the bar, they're all out to rob the workers.

This account was taken from the autobiography of Rigoberta Menchú, a Quiché Amerindian who was awarded the Nobel Peace Prize (Burgos, 1991). The excerpt recounts her experience when as a young girl she began working as a coffee bean picker on plantations along the southern coast of Guatemala. Although her recollection contains no mention of specific dates, she probably experienced the *finca* in the mid-1960s. The compulsory recruitment of workers had been abolished approximately two decades earlier, but work conditions were not that different from those described in the vivid account set down by Valentín Solórzano (1985) of Juan Tayún, also from an indigenous community, when he was working on the coffee plantations during the Ubico era.

Some thirty years later, on September 21, 1994, Lesley Margoth Rodríguez Solórzano, a worker at a factory located in one of the free trade zones in Choloma, Honduras, testified before a United States Senate committee to the following:

I am from Honduras and I turned fifteen on 5 August 1994. I started working in a *maquila* factory making Liz Claiborne sweaters when I was thirteen years old. I work for a Korean company called Galaxy Industries, located in the ZIP Galaxy Industrial Processing Zone. There are several girls in this park the same age as me and some who are thirteen—the same age I was when I started work. I would like to tell you about our working day. It begins at seven thirty in the morning and we work until seven in the evening. During the week we sometimes work until nine or ten at night. We are allowed half an hour for lunch. Sometimes we work eighty hours a week. The bosses have very high production quotas that we can never meet. If we manage to meet the quota, the next day they increase it, so we are always struggling to keep up with production. . . .

During the day we have no breaks apart from the half an hour for lunch. If you want to go to the toilet you have to put up your hand and ask permission. The toilets are locked. We can only go to the toilet twice a day, once in the morning and once in the afternoon. They keep a check on the time we spend in the toilet and if we take too long they punish us. . . .

My salary is 188 lempiras a week—I've been told that's equivalent to twenty one and a half dollars. . . . I'd like American workers to know how much we suffer to produce one of these sweaters. They tell me that in the United States each one of these Liz Claiborne sweaters costs ninety dollars. I earn thirty eight cents an hour making them.

This account has much in common with the earlier one—despite the fact that the first refers to the coffee economy, which has influenced the history of Central America during the greatest part of the twentieth century, whereas the second deals with one of the major effects of the current process of globalization taking place in the region. Work begins at an early age; the pace is intense and exhausting; salaries are low and inadequate; conditions are so hazardous that it is not difficult to imagine the exploitation endured; and in both cases, despite formal differences, the difficulties encountered in carrying out basic bodily functions are brought to light. It seems that the past and present are very much the same.

Indeed, this similarity has inspired the present text. I herein propose that a certain logic, which has constructed a vulnerable world of labor in Central American countries, has persisted over time. My aim in the following pages is to reveal and identify this logic. In order to carry out this exercise, a specific period of development in the history of Central America has been analyzed. This period begins around the middle of the twentieth century. The term "capitalist development" in the book's subtitle refers, in effect, to the period that started in the 1950s and witnessed modernizing changes that also affected the world of labor. In this sense, it is important to explain—albeit briefly—the historical significance of the period in question.

It can be said that the economic recession of 1929 and the early 1930s shook the material foundations of the oligarchic establishment in Central America, thereby shedding light on its historical limits. The belief that the oligarchic crisis was only partially resolved has a certain measure of consensus in the interpretations of the period. On the one hand, from an economic point of view, the primary-export model based on coffee and bananas was redefined; this change initially came about due to a diversification of agricultural and livestock products and was later due to the substitute industrialization of imports within a framework of regional integration. The result was the formation of more heterogeneous societies; within this context, the issue of modernization can begin to be discussed. Politics, on the other hand, evolved in the direction of authoritarian regimes, thereby sustaining the oligarchic pattern of dominance.

In a similar manner, it would be reasonable to suggest that the crisis in the 1980s, which in Central America's case was essentially political, offered some solutions for the pending problem of the oligarchic crisis. The recent upsurge of democratic governments illustrates this, and although we cannot yet benefit from sufficient historical hindsight, it would be difficult to argue that the likelihood of a return to oligarchic dominance is still a reality. This by no means signifies that the problems associated with governing Central American societies have been resolved. Following this line of reasoning, it could be said that the current restructuring of production processes, within the context of the globalization process, constitutes a second redefinition of the economy's modernization plan. But what of social issues during the second half of the century?

In this regard, it may be argued that the dependency (a very common term in past decades and nowadays largely ignored) of Central American economies made it difficult for the modernization process to benefit the majority of the population in the region. However, this fundamentally external condition did not constitute an insurmountable obstacle. Internal political resources existed: This involved action on the part of the state. Without entering into the discussion—by no means trivial or irrelevant—on whether the strategy for modernizing the economy could have been better implemented or even redirected, the state could have taken on a compensatory role by using social policy to its advantage. The problem, in this case, was the perpetuation of the oligarchic mode of domination, which limited this possibility. Thus, differences, which can be explained by the political resolution of the oligarchic crisis of the 1940s, arose between countries. Guatemala, El Salvador, and Nicaragua adjusted perfectly to that mentioned above: They set up authoritarian regimes that eventually degenerated into state terrorism. Costa Rica, in contrast, chose the path of democracy, and its ruling classes had the good sense to uphold the social achievements of the 1940s and expand them, thereby offering compensation on the part of the state for the detrimental effects of the accumulative model in the form of an authentic response. From this point of view, the well-known Costa Rican exception is a reality that cannot be ignored. Honduras occupied an intermediate position for two reasons: On the one hand, there was a predominance of bananas enclave, the oligarchy was less structured, and the army in the 1970s was hoisting reformist flags; on the other hand, due to the magnitude of the bananas enclave, the majority of the population found themselves on the fringes of the modernizing process, and their integration in the same took longer than in the rest of the region. Thus, despite the fact that Central America's modernization process has, in a Latin American context, been late, that of Honduras has been doubly so. Consequently, the process that took place in Honduras can neither be compared to that of Costa Rica nor linked to that of the other three countries.

It may be concluded from the previous paragraph that in social terms, modernization can only be discussed to any significant degree with regard to Costa Rica and, to a very limited extent and at a much later date, with reference to Honduras. In the rest of the region, scant and irresolute social policies did little to compensate for the regressive effects of the model of accumulation. Therefore, in these cases and from a social point of view, the modernization process was synonymous with impoverishment. Honduras too failed to escape this phenomenon. In effect, it had the highest level of poverty in the region during these decades, although this was due more to the inertia of the traditionalist structures of its society than to the damage caused by the modernization process. In other words, the type of impoverishment underwent fundamental changes, although it is measured similarly to that generated by capitalist modernization. The crisis in the 1980s, with its economic and, above all, political repercussions, aggravated the decline in social conditions. More importantly still, it seems that rather than rectifying this decline, the reordering of production, which is currently underway and was induced by structural adjustment programs, is more liable to exacerbate it. Furthermore, this tendency is also affecting Costa Rica, whose social model is currently being questioned. As a result, this exception to the rule is being considered within a relative context—it is, in effect, being "Central Americanized."

One could hazard a general hypothesis based on these brief considerations, which would form the basis of the present study: Social issues constitute the main problem pending resolution in the Central American modernization process, and the short-term and mid-term perspectives do not appear very promising. The modernization process, then, is not yet over, despite the fact that the accumulative basis is being redefined and political democracy is no longer an exception in the region.

In order to analyze this aspect of social issues, one must realize that the world of labor represents a privileged scenario. It constitutes the main link between the economy and society. The labor market thus constitutes the most effective mechanism for expressing the inequalities, generated by accumulative factors, present in households and their respective impoverishment. As a result, the employment structure sheds light on both the dynamics of accumulation and forms of development, and domestic reproductive logic. The establishment—whether it be a company or another form of economic unit—and the household interact through work. Furthermore, the state also partakes in shaping the world of labor. A well-known characteristic of Latin American development, which can also be applied to Central America, is that there has been no emergence of actors from purely social backgrounds. Instead, sociopolitical actors, in whose goals the political system has played a fundamental role, have appeared in their place. In this respect, the problems related to the subjects and actors of the labor world link employment to the state.

It is in light of this virtue of a privileged environment that capitalist development must be understood. In other words, although the following pages analyze the development of the world of labor in Central America during the period of modernization, the study's ultimate focus is on matters of social relevance. To identify the continuing historical logic that shaped this world, as demonstrated by the two opening accounts, is to attempt to partly explain why the social aspect of the modernization process still remains an unsolved problem in the region.

Before making explicit reference to the way the text is structured, its academic nature must be justified. "Academic nature" in the context of Central America's current developments in the field of the social sciences, as in other parts of Latin America, is very underrated. If we limit ourselves to the region, it could be said that with the exception of history, production is marked by a considerable degree of empiricism and emphasis on a short-term approach. Research that cannot be applied to practical situations in a reasonably prompt fashion is not accredited, and funds are therefore not forthcoming for this type of work. This is not to say that academic knowledge should be divorced from practical use, and in this sense, the fact that social scientists have had to force themselves to relate their findings and thoughts to models of intervention is indeed healthy. However, a certain amount of scientific work demands respect for its own particular logic, which cannot depend on its immediate practical value. It is precisely this kind of work that is needed to systematize and accumulate knowledge, thus allowing interpretative frameworks to progress. Unfortunately, the situation affecting the social sciences in Central America hinders this activity enormously. The great danger is that reports and documents containing valuable empirical information are piling up and cannot be analyzed in a serious and systematic manner. In other words, not only is theoretical and methodological progress not being made but this mine of information also runs the risk of being overlooked. Thus, the present text, regardless of its possible analytical contribution, vindicates the work of the social sciences outside the commercial and political funding criteria that the work of the academic community is currently subjected to.

Chapters 1 through 4 of this book focus on specific periods of the modernization process. Chapter 1 also attempts to explain the background to this process. This firstly entails reviewing the excellent bibliography available on the historical context of coffee and banana production, which sheds light on work-related aspects. A comparative analysis of national censuses from 1950 follows, in which greater attention has been paid to key aspects in order to illustrate the extent of traditional factors implicit in work structures on the eve of the early stages of modernization. The rise of the labor movement in the region is the third aspect dealt with in this first chapter, illustrating the type of actors that emerged from the world of labor at that time.

Chapter 2 considers the information provided by the censuses and focuses on three moments in time: 1950, the mid-1970s, and an intermediate milestone in the 1960s. Modernizing trends in employment are analyzed in order to see how labor markets were transformed during these decades. An in-depth analysis is also carried out on labor relations conceived within the new process of accumulation resulting from the modernization process—namely, new agricultural exports and import industrialization substitution coupled with its induced urbanization. The chapter concludes by once again analyzing the development of the labor movement that had already acquired a clear trade union–based identity and direction.

The crisis in the 1980s constitutes the historical context within which Chapter 3 is set. Thus, the first aspect discussed is how labor markets in the region have adapted to this situation. Due to problems of data availability, only two countries, Guatemala and Costa Rica, are analyzed in detail. However, both represent sufficiently diverse cases to be able to illustrate the range of situations that have resulted throughout the region. Along the same lines, one problem that has benefited is urban informality. This is due to the fact that it is precisely this kind of work that has constituted the main labor adjustment mechanism in the region. The chapter ends by offering an interpretation of how trade unionism faced the economic and political challenges presented by this crisis.

Chapter 4 is structured differently from the first three. It is set within the current restructuring of production and analyzes its effect on occupational heterogeneity. In this sense, some of what are considered to be the most significant changes are discussed. In short, two phenomena are studied. On the one hand, the dynamics of employment, labor relations, and work processes in the *maquila* industry are discussed; the latter represents one of the most important examples of the new emerging accumulative model based on the production of tradable goods and services within the globalization process. On the other hand, a combination of three case studies are presented on the new scenarios for informality. I should point out that as in the section on informality in Chapter 3, this chapter is based on rewritings of my previous works—these concerns have continued to be the target of my research during the past few years.

The text's conclusions, presented in Chapter 5, are primarily intended to highlight the most relevant analytical elements of the previous chapters. However, my aim in this chapter goes far beyond this unifying objective: I attempt to identify the structuring logic that, having remained unalterable with the passing of time, has shaped a vulnerable world of labor in Central America. This leads me back to the interpretative suggestion, induced by the accounts of Rigoberta Menchú and Lesley Rodríguez Solórzano, which inspired the present text.

This work has benefited from the comments of Victor Hugo Acuña Ortega, Victor Bulmer-Thomas, Edward Funkhouser, and Rafael Menjivar Larin. They are in no way responsible for any errors, and I thank them all for their contributions.

1

Coffee and Bananas: The World of Labor on the Eve of Modernization

This chapter seeks to explain how the region's world of labor was structured during the early 1950s. This period is important both from an economic and sociopolitical point of view. In the first case, it represents the end of the second phase of the primary-export model imposed on the region since the end of the past century, which was characterized by the overwhelming predominance of coffee and banana production. During the following decades, a certain measure of economic diversification meant the modernizing process made its mark on the region's economies. Moreover, this period represents the termination, at the political level, of the oligarchic crisis that began in the 1930s. The different ways in which each nation tackled this situation were to influence Central America's sociopolitical development until the late 1970s.

The analysis thus covers three sets of problems. The first reverts back to the earliest historical references dealing with the kind of labor relations that were established in the context of the two main production activities Central America centered on in the first half of the twentieth century: coffee and bananas. The second section analyzes the employment structure that existed in the region in 1950 based on the information in the corresponding national censuses and identifies the productive and reproductive logic that shaped this structure. The chapter concludes by offering a profile of the type of labor actor that emerged and developed in the 1950s; this is done in order to determine the former's situation and to realize what plans were being made to face the process of modernization.

Coffee, Bananas, and Labor

There is a consensus in Central American historiography that the coffee-farming milieu varied from country to country. The differences were brought on by a combination of factors, among which the following are worth noting: socioproductive elements inherited from the colonial era; a period of growth and expansion for this export product,[1] localization and transport facilities; land availability; production systems; the state's capacity for promoting policies in favor of this sector; and the manpower available at the time. The latter—the most relevant in this case—may be divided into three types of work systems within the Central American coffee economy during the first few decades of the twentieth century: the coercive system, the wage system, and the family system (Samper, 1994b: 19–20).[2]

The first of these originated in areas where indigenous communities provided seasonal labor. The strong divisions between different ethnic groups permitted the use of economic and directly political coercive methods, aided by the state itself along with its local representatives, for obtaining an abundant supply of labor that was very poorly paid. This type of situation occurred in Guatemala and Nicaragua during the late nineteenth century and early twentieth, but work relations eventually evolved into more modern forms of wage labor, although these were still characterized by the ethnic factor, especially in Guatemala.[3]

Coffee production developments in Guatemala were based on the use of two coercive labor recruitment mechanisms. The first of these consisted of reviving the colonial *mandamientos* system, which involved the direct intervention of the state to guarantee that manpower was supplied by the communities to coffee plantations. This model was legally enforced in an inconsistent manner. However, it was complemented by state labor force discipline policies involving compulsory participation in work on infrastructure development programs.[4] The second mechanism, known as *habilitaciones*, was based on obtaining labor in exchange for debt payments. Workers were given advance payments that they were forced to repay in the form of work on the coffee plantations. Although the compulsory recruitment of labor was widespread around the 1880s, a variety of factors (the landowners' payment of road taxes, the threat of military service, etc.) meant the peasants' debts escalated, thereby undermining the *mandamientos* system (Williams, 1994: 116–117). Thus, the *habilitaciones* model gradually took over and witnessed the rise of the *enganchador*, an agent of proletarianization at the service of the landowners who was the linking element in this labor system's operational logic. Naturally, the state, with its coercive power, guaranteed this mechanism's operations. In Nicaragua, an attempt was made to imitate the Guatemalan model by using a similar method of seasonal labor in exchange for debt payments; however, the Nicaraguan state system was not as powerful or efficient as that of Guatemala (Williams, 1994: 133–138). Most importantly, these mechanisms not only sought to control and supply labor but were also based on the payment of artificial salaries that fell short of basic subsistence costs (Samper, 1993: 88). In other words, they did not constitute authentic labor markets because extraeconomic coercion was the key element in this system's operating force. Moreover, even when during the late 1920s and early 1930s, Guatemala recognized the need to increase the salaries of indigenous peasants due to the accumulated decline in their reproductive conditions, the conservative mentality of the large landowners prevented them from proposing the abolition of these coercive methods. The solution, implemented by the Ubico government, was an intermediate measure involving the enactment of two, sadly, renowned laws: the Vagrancy Law and the Highway Administration Law. The former made it compulsory for peasants (especially indigenous peasants) on land that did not produce enough to generate an "adequate" income to work between 100 and 150 days per year for a salary. The second law made two weeks unpaid work on road construction obligatory for all adults unless they paid two quetzales; this amount was equivalent, in those days, to two weeks' work on the coffee plantations (Bulmer-Thomas, 1989: 91; McCreery, 1995: 217–225).[5]

The communities initially showed open resistance to these coercive mechanisms, and they later evolved into a less collective and more silent approach. Thus, in Matagalpa, Nicaragua, reference has been made to the laborers' search for loans from several bosses as well as the former's desertion (Gould, 1994); and in Guatemala they apparently fled to other towns or farms, uninhabited areas, or even to Mexico and Belize, and it is said that they also addressed written petitions to the political authorities (McCreery, 1990, 1994a). Nonetheless, it is important to stress the fact that as long as this resistance involved indigenous laborers, it took on an essentially ethnic dimension that transcended class. As Gould (1994: 327) points out, in Matagalpa's case, which may perfectly well be extrapolated for that of Guatemala, "It was a form of resistance against full proletarianization, against directly submitting to power and to the ladino landowner's discipline. It was not a reaction against working for a salary but rather it expressed the refusal to work for a salary under conditions dictated exclusively by the coffee-growing élite, which restricted the freedom of indigenous workers to determine the rate at which their own work and lives progressed."

These forms of labor had serious repercussions for the indigenous reproductive sphere—that is, their own communities. With respect to Guatemala, reference should be made to the fact that initially, wage labor, albeit seasonal, injected vast amounts of money into the communities and played havoc with their economies, especially in that which concerned the trading of their lands. Internal social differentiation resulted, making the poorest and most traditionalist indigenous members the losers while ladinos and certain indigenous members of the community benefited (McCreery, 1994a: 268).[6] In the same manner, attention has been drawn to the fact that in Matagalpa, forced labor meant lands were lost and the towns' indigenous military chiefs became agents of the state responsible for enforcing the coercive labor legislation. This led to a loss of respect for authority at the heart of the communities and the rise of violence within the same (Gould, 1994: 329).

It was the system of wage work that prevailed on Salvadoran and Costa Rican *haciendas*.[7] This type of system implied a high level of mobility of the rural population who had no ties. Furthermore, these types of labor relations were more suited to top-level production systems where the labor component was fundamental. In El Salvador, the existence of a greater sector of the population unable to obtain land—due to the high concentration of inhabitants and the absence of an agricultural frontier—meant that the abundant labor supply was poorly paid and salaries had to be supplemented by food rations. In contrast, the Costa Rican context (geographically located east of Cartago) was characterized by a more reduced population and, above all, by the existence of an agricultural frontier, which led to work being better paid (Samper, 1993: 85).

Within this wage-earning labor force it should be noted that those with a permanent status tended to be paid by the day. These individuals were predominantly male, though primarily female participation occurred at specific periods such as during harvesting and, above all, when the processed coffee beans had to be selected. In addition to a certain degree of division of labor in terms of gender, practices that clearly discriminated against women, whereby the latter were paid less than men for similar work, were also common (Samper, 1993: 85).[8] In relation to the permanent labor force, reference should be made to the *colonato* phenomenon, which was an attempt to secure labor in particular. Those of interest were largely workers who lived on the fringes of their native communities (McCreery, 1994a: 270). In Alta Verapaz, Guatemala, and in parts of Nicaragua the laborers were granted plots of land that were not used for coffee growing in order that they be used for subsistence purposes. Thus, the link between salaries and land usage was reinforced.[9]

Finally, the family labor system developed in relation to different forms of access to land: individual ownership, communal farms, or different types of smallholdings and tenant farming. Northern Nicaragua and Masaya,[10] as well as a number of areas in Costa Rica, were the most paradigmatic examples of this type of system.[11] These individual producers have been portrayed in Costa Rica's case as subordinates in a position similar to that held by wage workers in relation to commercial capital: Their annual delivery of produce was equivalent to being paid by the piece, and their autonomy was reduced to organizing the crops grown on their plot of land with few technical or institutional options (Pérez Brignoli, 1994b: 108).[12] In Nicaragua, this phenomenon is associated with the process of moving the coffee production sector from the Pacific region to the central northern region. In the latter, small- and medium-sized farms predominated during the 1950s. The unstable economic conditions of the small coffee farmers meant that members of the domestic unit often had to work for wages on large farms, which adversely affected maximizing the use of the family work force for their own plot of land (Dore, 1994: 427–428).

In regard to this third system, it should be noted that labor was exchanged between family units, and that kinship and neighborhood ties governed these exchanges. This phenomenon, known as "changing hands," was not exclusively based on solidarity and equal terms because it occurred in areas where processes of farm laborer differentiation were being developed (Samper, 1993: 91–92).

The three banana-producing countries that reached a higher level of development in this area (Costa Rica, Honduras, and Guatemala) adopted the enclave system.[13] This meant that in contrast to the coffee-producing sector, a much more homogeneous environment existed, allowing it to be considered in terms of a wage work system as a whole. Three aspects should be highlighted in this respect: the source of the labor force employed; the labor process in effect on the plantations; and the reproduction of the labor force.

With regard to the first aspect, it should be pointed out, first and foremost, that banana-producing activities were initially developed in farming areas on the Atlantic coast. This meant the population was scarce, and consequently there was an insufficient supply of labor. Despite this, as was the case with coffee and the indigenous communities (especially in El Salvador), lands belonging to local inhabitants, such as the *bribris* in Costa Rica's Talamanca and Sixaola districts, were expropriated (Bourgois, 1994: 59–63). The inadequate labor supply was aggravated by the fact that living conditions on the Atlantic coast were very harsh (particularly in the early stages, when the jungle had to be cleared and a minimum of infrastructure established), making it difficult to lure laborers from other parts of the respective country. Furthermore, the banana companies had to endure the coffee farm owners' opposition whereby they offered higher salaries. Faced with this situation, foreign labor, namely Antillean, had to be brought in, thereby making this activity's labor market international.[14]

The use of Afro-Caribbean labor introduced an ethnic, and specifically racial, dimension that played a central role in this labor environment.[15] The greatest presence of this type of labor occurred in Costa Rica, where it is said that at the turn of the century almost 75 percent of workers employed by the United Fruit Company were of Jamaican origin. In Honduras the respective governments restricted this kind of immigration, but the American companies argued against this, highlighting precisely the advantages of ethnic factors: previous experience, strength and resistance to tropical diseases (especially malaria), and knowledge of English. One should also bear in mind that this labor force had experienced slavery in the not-so-distant past, suggesting the more ready acceptance of a strictly disciplined work routine; moreover, it had internalized a prevailing racist culture in its country of origin under British colonial rule (Bourgois, 1994: 93). The linguistic advantage meant that Jamaicans[16] in particular often served as intermediaries between managers and workers, thereby adding racial overtones to the labor dispute (Acuña Ortega, 1993: 266; Posas, 1993: 141–142; Bourgois, 1994: 101ff.). In other words, the banana companies introduced a racial dimension to labor force management with a view to impeding class solidarity.

As regards the division of labor, it must be remembered that the banana enclave essentially comprised three kinds of activity: the cultivation of the fruit as such; its transportation by rail; and its storage for export at the ports. In this manner, three types of workers existed concomitantly: plantation workers, railway workers, and dockers. These made up a pyramid of occupations in which the latter constituted the apex and the former the base (Acuña Ortega, 1993: 265). However, all of them were wage workers and comprised the proletariat, in the traditional sense of the word. The plantation workers were the most numerous group, comprising almost three quarters of the sector. The workers in this group were organized on the basis of specialized tasks: cutters; gatherers (those who carried the stalks on their shoulders to the mules); muleteers (those who carried them to the railway); packers (who loaded them onto freight cars); and others in charge of tasks related to the plantations' maintenance. The work was undertaken using cooperative methods based on teamwork (Posas, 1993: 142–143).

With regard to the reproduction of the work force, it should be pointed out, first of all, that the workers lived in the so-called company towns, where a dozen families were hoarded into each large hut. Let it be said in passing that ethnic distinctions extended to the reproductive sphere, where the pattern of residency in effect sanctioned racial differences (Acuña Ortega, 1993: 265). It also should be noted that salaries were initially paid on a monthly basis, meaning any advance was obtained in the form of coupons that could be used for purchasing goods in the companies' own stores. If they were used outside these stores their purchasing power was rendered void. Consequently, this work force's reproductive sphere was set within the company's own economic sphere of influence, thus reinforcing the nature of the enclave.

In short, during the late 1920s, it can be said that wage work combined with family labor was predominant in Central American coffee production sectors, whereas in the bananas enclave the labor force was clearly proletarianized. Nevertheless, the 1929 economic crisis severely affected both the coffee and banana sectors, although the latter were, in addition, suffering from problems caused by plagues that had been affecting the plantations since the mid-1920s. In terms of labor, the consequences were typical: a reduction in employment and a lowering of salaries.

It appeared that the former consequence had a greater impact on the bananas enclave. The geographical mobilization of labor was restricted, as was the case with the black workers in Costa Rica, despite new plantations being opened on the Pacific coast. Thus, the importance of the ethnic factor in relation to this labor market was manifested. As for the coffee sector, the adjustment of the labor system provoked by the crisis seemed to be more evident in the reduction in salaries. Hence, attention has been drawn to the fact that prior to the depression, the average wage varied between US$.25 and US$.30 a day. During the crisis years, the coffee producers attempted to reduce it to US$.15 despite strong opposition from the laborers (Bulmer-Thomas, 1989: 75). The type of labor system in force allowed for different kinds of salary adjustments: On the large farms, as in western El Salvador where wage costs were fixed, the laborers' salaries were lowered; in situations where salaries were paid partially in kind, as in certain areas in Guatemala, the adjustment was not as drastic because products such as corn were reduced in price; and in regions where the family system prevailed, such as in Costa Rica's Central Valley, the farming economy itself underwent a process of self-adjustment (Bulmer-Thomas, 1993: 346–347). Nonetheless, unemployment also affected the coffee sector's labor force, although differences between the Salvadoran and Costa Rican situations have been pointed out. As mentioned earlier, it was in these countries where wage-earning systems of labor were more firmly established. The Salvadoran day-laborers' greater dependence on their salary meant that open unemployment reached higher levels than in Costa Rica, where laborers often combined their work on the large farms with self-sufficiency activities on their own plots of land (Samper, 1994a: 162–163).

With the exception of the coffee sector's coercive system and its evolvement into more modern forms of wage labor, postwar recovery does not seem to have modified the kinds of labor systems that existed in these two production sectors, which were essential to Central American economies. However, they acquired key significance in light of the modernizing alternatives being proposed at the time and, in particular, with respect to the economy's tendency toward integration. Bulmer-Thomas (1989: 166) has presented a convincing argument regarding the coffee sector:

In addition to all the conventional reasoning against the monoculture, the dependence on coffee in particular constituted a considerable obstacle to economic integration. Coffee not only has a markedly seasonal demand for labor, it is also a very labor-intensive product. Given world prices, increases in monetary salaries paid to hired laborers reduce profits due to the difficulties encountered in adopting labor-economizing techniques; thus, a policy of higher salaries was improbable as long as coffee remained an important source of export earnings.

The Employment Structure in 1950

In order to obtain a global image of the structure of employment in the region, reference will be made to information held in censuses taken in 1950. A series of indicators that deal with both the supply of and demand for labor will be referred to. The analysis of these indicators aims, above all, to give an idea of the level of modernity, or rather traditionality, present in Central American labor markets at that time. This same type of analysis will be used in the following chapter, although in a different historical context: that of the modernizing process. In this manner, the present interpretation advances a view of the point at which this process began. Furthermore, these indicators will allow us to identify the reproductive logic of households as well as the productive logic of establishments (firms or other forms of economic units).

Table 1.1 in effect allows us to observe the structure of employment in the five countries in the region. The upper half of the table focuses on the labor supply, and the lower section illustrates the demand, which is linked to basic job characteristics

One of the first phenomena to be analyzed is the rate of employment. This can be done by associating the economically active population (EAP) with the inactive population,[17] thus providing a global view of the similarities and differences present in the region. In this regard, in almost all of the countries, approximately half of the population of working age were either employed or actively seeking employment at the beginning of the 1950s. These rates vary between 45.0 percent for Guatemala and 52.8 percent for Nicaragua.[18] Clearly deviating from this pattern is Costa Rica, where the rate of activity is 34.0 percent; in other words, only one out of every three people of working age were active in this country. Thus, it appears that conditions for the reproduction of the work force were less precarious in Costa Rica, and as a result, there was less of a need to enter the labor market.

In terms of the labor supply, two aspects of modernity have been taken into account. The first of these is the inactive population's schooling. This indicator shows the type of strategy implicit in the mobilization of the

TABLE 1.1   State of Employment in Central America (1950)

Indicators	Guatemala[a]	El Salvador[b]	Honduras[c]	Nicaragua[d]	Costa Rica[e]
Inactive population	1,184,055	663,276	721,212	294,820	528,891
% of students	12.4	16.2	n.a.	4.2	20.1
Rate of female participation	11.8	16.2	41.8	14.1	10.4
Total EAP	967,814	653,409	647,393	329,976	271,984
% of wage workers	40.0	55.5	31.4	55.0	66.5
% of self-employed laborers	38.9	25.7	30.0[f]	25.0	10.4
% of agricultural workers	68.2	63.2	83.1	67.7	54.7

NOTES:
[a] Population aged 7 and over
[b] Population aged 10 and over
[c] Not refined
[d] Population aged 14 and over
[e] Population aged 12 and over
[f] Includes owners

SOURCES: DGEC (1952) for Honduras 1950; DGEC (1954) for Nicaragua 1950; DGEC (1953) for Costa Rica 1950; DGEC (1953) for El Salvador 1950; DGEC (1957) for Guatemala 1950.

work force on the part of households. Thus, a high rate would imply that domestic units adhere to a strategy based on maximizing future incomes by training their work force in the education system. Low percentages would mean households are forced to follow a strategy that focuses on maximizing current incomes by including as many members of school age as possible. In terms of levels of modernity, this implies that the higher the relative importance of this inactive population category, the higher this level would be, and vice versa. Naturally, this indicator can only offer a partial view of the modernizing phenomenon of schooling because the education system's development and geographical coverage would have to be taken into account; at that time, these societies were predominantly rural.

The second indicator refers to women's participation in the labor market. It may be postulated that the more women involved, the greater the level of modernity.[19] The underlying reproductive logic is naturally that which concerns the division of labor within the domestic unit in terms of gender. The participation of women in the labor force gives rise to conditions that question traditional models without necessarily implying a redefinition of this division.

From this analytical perspective, the figures show that with regard to the first indicator (percentage of inactive population involved in some form of study), no two countries were alike. In this sense, it is worth noting that on the one hand, in Costa Rica there was a greater display of labor mobilization strategies that sought to maximize future incomes, while on the other hand, in Nicaragua this type of strategy was minimal. With respect to Costa Rica, it should be pointed out that there were more possibilities for integration into the school system in this country than in any other due to the greater geographical coverage of the education system and, thus, also a greater degree of modernity in this area.

The same table demonstrates that in all countries the level of female labor participation was very low. In other words, it may be assumed that women were consigned to the reproductive sphere, and that a division of traditional domestic work predominated. The exception is in Honduras, which presents an interesting methodological paradox. The creation of a labor market where paid work becomes predominant tends to facilitate the development of labor representations where a distinction is drawn between employment and work.[20] This distinction is placed in the context of the processes that separate the productive/public sphere from the reproductive/private sphere. One of its effects is the well-known underrepresentation of women's participation in labor. We thus venture to propose that this Honduran exception should be understood in view of the high level of traditional factors in the labor market at this time. Furthermore, in the other countries a certain degree of underrepresentation of women's integration in the occupational structure was already being brought to light.[21]

The lower half of this same table demonstrates the two facets of the labor force's incorporation in production: the occupational and the sectorial in terms of fields of activity. From the point of view of modernization, a higher incidence of wage work and less emphasis on agricultural work would indicate less traditionality. The payment of wages would also indicate that surplus labor was accumulated directly. Moreover, the prevailing branch of activity would denote the type of development in progress.

Two kinds of situations can be observed from the table in terms of occupational entry. First, there were those in which wage work prevailed; these included the Salvadoran, Nicaraguan, and Costa Rican contexts, already showing signs of widespread proletarianization. In contrast, both Guatemala and, in particular, Honduras experienced the opposite—family production units (farming or urban) were clearly more abundant.[22] In contrast, the importance of agriculture, within which most employment occurred and which, in the majority of cases, absorbed two thirds of the work force, was apparent. Two countries diverged from this reality: Honduras, where the extent of agricultural employment was overwhelming; and Costa Rica, where almost half of the work force was employed in

TABLE 1.2   Population Employed in the Agricultural Sector According to
Country and Job Category (1950)

Job Category	El Salvador	Honduras	Nicaragua	Costa Rica
Owners	2.9	—	16.6	15.0
Wage workers	49.5	25.2	47.8	59.8
Self-employed	28.1	30.0[b]	26.6	9.1
Unpaid family workers	19.0	44.8	9.0	16.1
Total	100.0	100.0	100.0	100.0
	(412,646)[a]	(537,982)	(223,426)	(148,837)

NOTES:

[a] 2,166 workers have not been classified

[b] Includes owners

SOURCES: DGEC (1952) for Honduras 1950; DGEC (1954) for Nicaragua 1950;
DGEC (1953) for Costa Rica 1950; DGEC (1953) for El Salvador 1950; DGEC
(1957) for Guatemala 1950.

other activities. Among the latter, worth mentioning is the service industry, in which 14.8 percent of the total EAP were employed.

It is possible to relate these two aspects of labor, particularly in the
case of agricultural employment, which, as mentioned above, was the
most significant. Table 1.2[23] shows a predominance, with the exception
of Honduras, of wage work, which at that time was common in Costa
Rica. Second, Salvadoran farmers appeared to have a greater concentration of land. In addition, the peasantry demonstrate three kinds of situations: It has been suggested that Nicaraguans' participation in the
family labor force was restricted whereas in Costa Rica and Honduras
the opposite appeared to be the case; El Salvador occupied an intermediate position

As a result and as was to be expected, the predominance of an agricultural pattern of development in terms of production tendencies can be
confirmed. This pattern naturally encompassed a variety of sectors such
as that related to exports or domestic consumption, which were governed by different production rationale. However, in terms of accumulative logic, situations varied. In El Salvador, Nicaragua and, above all, in
Costa Rica the direct accumulation of surplus labor predominated; in
contrast, indirect accumulation prevailed in Guatemala and Honduras
in particular.

A more detailed study of the employment structure can be made by taking into account the characteristics of labor force according to sex. The first
point to be observed in relation to Table 1.3[24] is that as the low rates of
women's participation had already indicated, Central American labor markets in the early 1950s were largely male-dominated. More than eight out
of every ten workers in 1950 were men. However, the figures also demon-

TABLE 1.3   Job Profile According to Country and Sex (1950)

Sex and Job Characteristics	Guatemala	El Salvador	Nicaragua	Costa Rica
Males	843,582	544,862	283,644	230,149
Job category	Self-employed (40.2%)	Wage workers (53.6%)	Wage workers (53.1%)	—
Branch of activity	Agriculture (76.0%)	Agriculture (73.3%)	Agriculture (76.9%)	Agriculture (54.7%)
Females	124,232	108,547	46,146	41,835
Job category	Wage workers (55.6%)	Wage workers (65.2%)	Wage workers (67.2%)	—
Branch of activity	Services (43.0%)	Services (43.8%)	Services (53.8%)	Services (61.3%)

SOURCES: DGEC (1952) for Honduras 1950; DGEC (1954) for Nicaragua 1950; DGEC (1953) for Costa Rica 1950; DGEC (1953) for El Salvador 1950; DGEC (1957) for Guatemala 1950.

strate that wage labor was common to both categories, although rates were higher for women, and that activities differed: Men were involved in agricultural work whereas women's activities centered on services. In short, the most common occupations within each sector were agricultural worker and domestic worker, respectively.[25] Thus, the male work force centered on what was the Central American economies' main branch of activity at that time; women were relegated to a secondary branch and, in short, to an occupation that was merely an extension of housework

In addition to these general observations, two diverging aspects are worth mentioning. In Guatemala the variety of sociodemographic profiles was the most marked because it had not experienced wage labor; furthermore, the percentage of women wage workers was the lowest in the region. As for Costa Rica, on the one hand, the percentage of the male EAP working in agriculture was the lowest, and on the other hand, the percentage of women working in the service sector was the highest. In other words, men were employed in a diverse array of sectors, but women were highly concentrated in a limited number.

In brief, according to the figures provided by the respective national censuses, Central American labor markets in the early 1950s had three features in common. First, these spheres showed a high concentration of male workers; the exception to this is Honduras (although a methodological explanation has been formulated in order to hazard a possible explanation for this anomaly). Second, there was a significant presence of young labor, indicating the limited schooling of the same. Third, agriculture provided the greatest source of employment, with a high sectorial concentration and a spatial organization that meant labor markets were largely rural. Only Costa Rica proved a relative exception to these last two traits. Thus, employment structures did not demonstrate any significant level of modernity. Costa Rica was the only country that partially contradicted this image, of which Guatemala and Honduras were the prime examples.

The Origins of the Labor Movement

In the first section of this chapter it was suggested that at least until 1929 conditions were not yet ripe for the creation of labor organizations within the coffee economy, given the relations that existed within the sphere of production. The main factors determining this situation were the lack of firmly established wage links and the seasonal nature of the work. Furthermore, in the case of the indigenous work force, they already formed part of another type of social organization—the community—in spite of the internal divisions mentioned earlier, which were caused by the commercialization brought about by the coffee sector. In effect, the result was a worker marked by a mixture of temporary proletarianization and relative community ties.[26] As for the banana-producing sector, although more clear-cut, stable wage relations were established, the hard line adopted in work control—a key feature of this type of enclave—meant it was very difficult for labor organizations to be set up. It was, on the contrary, in an urban context—and more specifically in the realm of the handicrafts sector—that workers' organizations in Central America were first conceived.

Table 1.4 illustrates the organizational development of Central American workers for the period from 1870 to 1929 as well as the initial strife encountered

As was to be expected, the first examples of organizational models appeared in the form of *mutualidades* (mutual benefit societies), the last to develop being those of Nicaragua. The existing bibliography identifies a series of features linked to this phenomenon. Thus, in Guatemala the lack of concern for demanding better work conditions and for the shift from apoliticism to transitory and circumstantial political positions has been emphasized (Balcárcel, 1985: 13; Witzel, 1991: 36–47). In Honduras, the aim was to secure mutual aid and savings as well as to develop cultural activities. Furthermore, it has been pointed out that these organizations were tolerated and even promoted and subsidized by the state (Posas, 1977: 7). Similar features are highlighted with regard to Nicaragua: the emphasis on savings and education, the inability to keep economic and political interests separate, and its weakness in succumbing to the ideological influences of both conservatism and liberalism (Gutiérrez Mayorga, 1985: 198–199). With respect to Costa Rica, where two further examples (Catholic handicraft circles and the league of workers) are identified in addition to the *mutualidades* and cooperatives, the handicraft workers' three guiding principles were association, savings, and education (Oliva

TABLE 1.4   Organizations and Worker Mobilization in Central America (1870–1929)

Organizations and Mobilizations	Guatemala	El Salvador	Honduras	Nicaragua	Costa Rica
Founding year of the first *mutual*	1877	1872	1884	1904	1874
Founding year of first handicraft and workers federation	1918	1918	1921	1918	1913
Number of handicraft and workers associations	138	85[a]	34	n.a.	51[b]
Number of strikes	22	n.a.	22	12	32[c]

NOTES:

[a]The information is limited to 2 associations for the period 1870–1899, 45 for the year 1918, and 38 for the year 1929.

[b]The information is limited to 19 associations for the period 1879–1899 and 32 for the year 1914.

[c]The information is only available up to 1919.

SOURCE: Acuña Ortega (1993, tables 4.2–4.5).

Medina, 1985: 106).[27] Thus, the *mutualidades'* objective was to unite rather than confront. This unification was to be achieved by securing both the members' material well-being by means of savings and mutual aid, and their cultural well-being mainly through schooling in the workplace. These types of standards, which did not clearly define social interests, meant that organizations such as these could be manipulated at the political level.

The historical significance of the *mutualidades* has been very clearly stated by Acuña Ortega (1993: 273), who argued that the following three processes combined to produce this phenomenon:

the formation of an identity and a way of life based on the world of urban employment, with no apparent regard for economic differences; the foundation of a public springboard for projecting liberal goals, as, while the handicraft workers discovered their group identity they were also being formed as citizens or, in other words, members of an emerging political arena, and as patriotic members of a new concept also in its initial stages: the nation; finally, the handicraft workers association movement constituted the starting point for the simultaneous and interrelated emergence of the working class and the urban middle classes; at the heart of the *mutualidades* the contradiction inherent in the process of establishing a sector comprising both persons offering labor power and those acquiring it within the realms of handicraft and manufacturing activities in the cities, became clear.

Consequently, as this third development process suggests, the *mutuali-dades* movement led to the formation of genuine workers' organizations. In effect, on certain occasions the *mutualidades* themselves began to con-template proposing demands, thereby indicating a move toward trade unionism, as was the case in Guatemala (Balcárcel, 1985: 22).[28] In the same manner, the mutual benefit movement in Nicaragua was divided into two branches: the Organized Labor Movement, which adopted a clearly mutualist line; and the Nicaraguan Workers Federation, which at-tempted, unsuccessfully, to redirect its actions toward trade unionism (Gutiérrez Mayorga, 1985: 199). In addition, at the end of the 1910s Costa Rica registered only three organizations (the General Workers Confeder-ation and the bakers and cobblers trade unions) undertaking trade union duties (Acuña Ortega, 1986a: 39).

The first trade union–based organizations began to appear during the 1920s. Two types of causes for this situation have been proposed: on the one hand, a certain measure of openness on the part of the political sys-tems in the region; and, on the other hand, external ideological influences based on recent revolutions such as those in Mexico and Russia (Acuña Ortega, 1993: 277). In terms of ideological influences, reference should be made to both anarchist and Communist principles. The existence of the former has been mentioned in relation to Guatemala, where its apoliti-cism (Balcárcel, 1985: 25) and introduction to handicraft sectors threat-ened by the modernization of manufacturing has been highlighted (Witzel, 1991: 219).[29] It was also observed in El Salvador in the early 1920s with the rise of the first trade unions (Menjívar, 1985: 73). Moreover, its influence in Costa Rica at the beginning of the present century has also been noted (Rojas Bolaños, 1985: 256). Nonetheless, communism was, without doubt, the most significant and lasting influence, making itself strongly felt starting from the 1930s, as will be seen further on.

With regard to the emergence of trade unionist workers organizations, three kinds of situations occurred within the region. The first of these is its virtual nonexistence during the 1920s, as was the case in Nicaragua. In other words, the historical delay in terms of mutualism was accumu-lated, thereby hindering the emergence of trade unionism.[30] The second corresponds to both Costa Rica and Honduras, where, although they were seen to emerge, these new types of organizations were not consoli-dated during these years. Thus, despite the fact that Costa Rica witnessed the first example in the region of an organization defining itself as a trade union, the true launching of the trade union movement did not take place in this country until the following decade.[31] In the same manner, de-spite the creation of the Honduran Workers Federation, its institutional logic was still marked by mutualism, and the year 1929, in which the Honduran Trade Union Federation was founded, is considered the benchmark date for the rise of trade unionism there (Acuña Ortega, 1993: 277–279). The third situation, concerning Guatemala and El Salvador, demonstrated the most resolute emergence; however, it was to be aborted in the following decade due to the repression of respective dictatorships. In regard to Guatemala, this development took shape in the form of the Regional Workers Federation of Guatemala, founded by the Communists and noted for its high level of trade unionist activism (Balcárcel, 1985: 24–27; Witzel, 1991: 203–211). In 1929, the Regional Workers Federation of El Salvador had joined together thirty-one urban, four rural, and three mixed trade unions. To this quantitatively significant aspect, estimated at a fifth of the urban labor force, must be added the qualitative change in class orientation (Menjívar, 1985: 74–78).[32]

The last aspect to be analyzed in this section deals with the dispute factor—in short, the strikes. In this sense, the protagonist was the enclave system rather than the urban context. Thus, in Honduras, 1916 is identified as the year in which the first significant strike movement took place in the banana plantations.[33] As of that moment, this type of action, in which demands—including the questioning of the coupon—were essentially related to salaries, became frequent (Meza, 1991: 21–30); in this regard, one should bear in mind the role played by the company stores in terms of controlling the labor force's reproduction. The state tended to use force in response to these cases, as mentioned in relation to the Guatemalan banana enclave strike in 1924, which was suppressed in an manner unprecedented in that country (Balcárcel, 1985: 23). On the whole, in countries where the presence of the banana enclave was more notable, such as Honduras and Costa Rica, labor disputes focused on this sector rather than on urban society. Moreover, demands varied according to this distinction. As Acuña Ortega (1993: 289) points out:

> The key issue in urban strike movements was wages, along with regulating the working day, night work and Sunday closing. In addition to wages, the banana workers raised the issues of payment in the form of coupons, ill-treatment by foremen, inconsistencies between salaries paid to nationals and foreigners as well as racial problems linked to this; in the miners' strikes demands were also made in relation to health and occupational hazards.

As mentioned above, it was in the two countries where trade unionist labor organizations had experienced a more promising start that they were aborted in the early 1930s. Thus, in Guatemala, the crisis in 1929 meant labor disputes began developing in coffee-growing areas. These were quelled in a response that culminated in the rise of the Ubico dictatorship (1930–1944). Despite the fact it had reached its peak in the 1920s, the workers movement was disbanded, limiting not only Communist and anarchist-based organizations but also independent groups (Witzel, 1991: 270ff.); only a small number of *mutualidades* managed to survive this dictatorship (Balcárcel, 1985: 28). One must bear in mind that Jorge Ubico imposed a system of labor force control during this time, which was referred to in the first section in this chapter. El Salvador was the scene of bloodshed in 1932 in the Izalcos region located in the country's main coffee-growing area. Added to the crisis suffered by this export product, with its familiar social consequences (wage reductions and unemployment), a less circumstantial and more far-reaching conflict—that of the confiscation of indigenous communal and public lands—arose. The outcome on the one hand involved the suppression of the labor movement, which took several years to recover, and on the other hand held more tragic consequences for the indigenous population.[34]

In contrast, Costa Rica witnessed the consolidation of the trade union movement under the leadership of the Communists. In this regard, one cannot ignore the famous banana workers strike in 1934. Faced with dire work and living conditions in the Atlantic region, the workers' demands were varied, ranging from wage-related issues (elimination of piecework, a minimum wage, fortnightly pay, etc.) to demands for health clinics and the recognition of the trade unionist organization itself. The strike, which ultimately mobilized approximately ten thousand workers, developed in two stages. The first ended in an agreement with national businessmen who acceded to the workers' demands. Nonetheless, action was, once more, taken up due to the United Fruit Company's refusal to accept this agreement. During this second stage, action was confined to the multinational companies' plantations, and although the strike committee was arrested, putting an end to strike action, the majority of the workers' petitions, including the legal recognition of the trade union organization, had to be accepted (Rojas Bolaños, 1985: 263–265). However, the banana companies' almost immediate move to the South Pacific meant these measures became merely symbolic and failed to signify the organizational strengthening of the trade unions. The latter was to be found, rather, in the urban context, and in particular in the cobblers' sector, which constituted the most sound social basis for Costa Rican trade unionism during the period (Acuña Ortega and Molina Jiménez, 1991: 183).

The rise of the Honduran trade union movement also took place in the early 1930s under the direction of the Communists. Numerous strikes within the banana sector, especially in 1932, illustrate this. Nevertheless, the setting up of the Carías dictatorship eradicated this development (Meza, 1991: 49ff.). In this regard, it is worth mentioning one of the main conclusions of Bourgois's analysis (1994: 291) on the labor strategy employed by the banana companies (in particular that of the United Fruit Company at its Bocas del Toro division, located between Panama and

Costa Rica): During moments of conflict the key factor was not so much the ethnic aspect, as has been argued earlier, but rather that of the laborers' work experience.

It was within the context of World War II that the world of labor in Central America experienced a period of peak progress, demonstrated by three phenomena. First, considerable organizational development took place. In Guatemala, for example, immediately after the fall of Ubico, the workers' movement reorganized itself and founded the Guatemalan Workers Confederation (CTG), which later suffered two divisions, resulting in the creation of new organizations: the Central Regional Workers Federation (FRCT) and the Guatemalan Trade Union Federation (FSG) (Balcárcel, 1985: 30–34). The struggle for the labor code reversed this dividing process and led to the founding of the National United Trade Union Committee (CNUS), which resulted in the formation of the Guatemalan General Workers Confederation (CGTG) as the sole trade union center (Witzel, 1992: 136–142; 156–160). In Nicaragua, the Workers Confederation of Nicaragua (CTN) was set up and had to compete with the Somozist Organizing Committee for the Nicaraguan Workers Confederation (COCTN) (Bulmer-Thomas, 1989: 175). Two principal organizations emerged in Costa Rica: the Confederation of Costa Rican Workers (CTCR), based on Communist ideals; and, the Costa Rican Rerum Novarum Workers Confederation (CCTRN), organized by the Catholic Church to counteract the influence of the former and put into practice the social doctrine it had been preaching since the end of the nineteenth century (Rojas Bolaños, 1985: 271; Aguilar, 1989: 32).

The second phenomenon consisted of the upsurge of political parties linked to the labor movement. Examples of these include the following: the Revolutionary Action Party and the National Revolution Party in Guatemala; the Nicaraguan Socialist Party, which established close links with the CTN; and the Costa Rican Communist Party, which, in 1943, changed its name to Popular Vanguard and which controlled the CTCR.[35] Even in Honduras, reference must be made to the emergence of the Honduran Democratic Revolutionary Party, on whose political platform the legal recognition of trade unionism was a priority issue (Bulmer-Thomas, 1989: 175).

Finally, the worker as such is recognized by the state, and this recognition is consolidated in the regulation of work relations through the proclamation of labor legislation. In this regard, three examples should be referred to. In Costa Rica this process took place in 1943, whereas in Guatemala it coincided with the year 1947.[36] In this case, emphasis must be placed on the pressure exerted by the above-mentioned CNUS illustrating, as Witzel (1992: 159) has pointed out, that the enactment of this code was due more to the trade unions' struggle than to a mere concession offered freely by the government. In the same manner, in Nicaragua, Anastasio Somoza established the most advanced labor legislation in all Latin America during this period, which was subsequently never applied.[37] Along this same regulatory line, the two social security programs in Guatemala and Costa Rica must be mentioned, as must the chapters on "social benefits" that were gradually included in the constitutions of the countries throughout the region (Bulmer-Thomas, 1989: 175).

However, these circumstances were later dependent on the manner in which the oligarchical crisis that had begun in the former decade concluded. In this sense, it must be remembered that three proposals regarding the 1930s have been put forward: the oligarchic system of domination was not questioned; the prolonged effects of the economic crisis were due to political causes resulting from the ruling classes' orthodox and conservative conduct; and the end of the recession reestablished the productive action of the oligarchy. It is important to point out that the antidictatorship struggles of the 1940s, in which the demand for democracy became almost synonymous with the independent vote, were not seen through to the end in any of the Central American countries apart from Costa Rica (Torres-Rivas, 1987: 23–28). In effect, the way in which the oligarchic crisis arose explains the subsequent development of each Central American society (Torres-Rivas, 1984: 33). The outcome of the 1930s and its epilogue in the late 1940s led to a double transition. The political arena developed toward an authoritarianism that degenerated into state terrorism, and in the economic context, the redefinitions of the primary-export model gave rise to more heterogeneous socioeconomic societies (Torres-Rivas, 1987: 23–30). Thus, the economy witnessed partial change while methods of political control remained the same (Torres-Rivas, 1984: 26–27).

This general prognosis was fulfilled unequivocally in three cases (Guatemala, El Salvador, and Nicaragua) and partially in Honduras; only in Costa Rica did the end of the oligarchic crisis lead to the establishment of an effective democratic regime and the constitution of a less socioeconomically polarized society. Nonetheless, the consequences for the trade union movement were not strictly the same, thereby demonstrating the specific nature of this field of social action. In this regard, three types of situations that marked the development of the workers' movement in the following decades may be identified.

First of all come the cases where the movement was disunited and would take some time to reconstitute itself. Countries in this situation included El Salvador, where the effects of the circumstances that arose in 1932 have already been mentioned. For its part, Nicaragua presents an unusual situation in which the rise of workers' organizations was the slowest and weakest in the region. During the mid-1940s the workers' movement played an important role in politics, supporting Somoza through difficult times; this resulted in the granting of an advanced labor code as well as the offer of freedom to set up trade unions and carry out trade union action, which failed to be implemented later on (Gutiérrez Mayorga, 1985: 219). However, the most dramatic case within this first type of situation was that of Guatemala. The radicalism of the process begun in 1944 meant that with the election of Juan Jacobo Arbenz in 1950, the trade union movement in this country reached the highest level of development in Central America.[38] The reasons for this originated in the unification process mentioned above, resulting in the creation of the CGTG, which around 1954 was made up of an estimated 500 organizations and contained over 100,000 members (Balcárcel, 1985: 41). Furthermore, one must bear in mind the presence of the CNCG in rural areas; in this regard, reference has been made to the fact that in 1952, this organization claimed to have 215,000 members (Jiménez, 1985: 302). The tragic outcome of the Guatemalan process brought on by the invasion of Castillo Armas from Honduras and the installment of an anti-Communist government were harsh blows for the Guatemalan trade union movement. Both the CGTG and the CNCG were disbanded; 533 trade union memberships were canceled; and the labor code was reformed in what was, for the workers, a regressive manner (Bulmer-Thomas, 1989: 175). In the same way, the first postrevolutionary government attempted a "reorganization" of the trade union movement mainly through the Autonomous Trade Union Federation (FAS), whose Social-Christian leaders were politically co-opted. Therefore, Guatemalan trade unions were forced to face a second abrupt rupture in their development in 1954, whereby they were no longer a significant force in the country's sociopolitical life (Witzel, n.d.: 22–31).

Costa Rica presented a different kind of situation. As already mentioned, the workers' movement was a leading force in this country in the 1940s. However, the outcome of the 1948 conflict, in spite of the fact that it consolidated a democratic regime, caused the trade union movement to be suppressed. Thus José Figueres, the victor in this conflict, proscribed the CTCR and its appointed trade unions and pursued Communists.[39] During the Ulate government, although the social achievements of the former decade were maintained, trade unionism suffered considerable setbacks, including a decrease in the number of trade unions, which even affected the labor movement associated with the Catholic Church. In respect to the latter, several factors that may explain a weakening within this context include the lack of tradition and limited presence among the workers; the principal leaders' participation in government affairs; the lack of a political will on the part of this institution to promote trade unionism; and, faced with the proscription of the CTCR and the persistence of labor disputes, the fact that the CCTRN was forced to take charge of the latter (Aguilar, 1989: 78ff.).

Only Honduras witnessed a strengthening of the trade union movement. Reference has already been made to the fact that after a period of relative activity in the early 1930s, the labor movement was subjected to the demobilizing effects of the Carías dictatorship. Following this dictatorship, a comparatively tolerant climate was created for workers' organizations outside the bananas enclave, where the same repressive environment persisted. However, it was within the latter that, in 1954, the "Great Banana Workers Strike"—considered the most significant milestone in the country's social history—occurred. It took place amid unusual circumstances (economic recovery of the banana companies; considerable trade union development outside the enclave; and an election period) and originated due to management's refusal to pay the Tela Railroad Company's dockers double the daily wage for working on feast days. The dispute generated a widespread display of solidarity in different sectors of the population, and as a result, action was extended beyond the banana enclave workers' sphere.[40] A key event was that of the creation of a Central Strike Committee, whose first initiative was led by the Communists; the second was led by the Independents. It was with the second committee that an agreement was made, with the support of the government, which put an end to the conflict. Regardless of the evaluation that may be made of the achievements, with regard to the initial demands, the importance of this strike was twofold. On the one hand, it implied the recognition of the right of workers to join a trade union; on the other hand and as a result of the former, it led to the enactment, in 1959, of a Honduran labor code (Meza, 1991: 75ff.). An important precedent, which would have consequences for the future, was therefore set regarding the resolution of labor disputes. Thus, in contrast to the other countries in the region, the Honduran trade union movement was consolidated following the oligarchic crisis.

In brief, as in other parts of Latin America, Central America saw the rise of the *mutualismo* as the first example of a workers' organization. During the 1920s the first signs of trade unionist action appeared, acquiring a more powerful form in Guatemala and El Salvador. However, with the rise of dictatorships in the region within the context of the 1930s crisis, this activity, particularly in these two countries, was suspended. The exception was in Costa Rica, where the trade union movement was, in contrast, consolidated. The mid-1940s were significant with regard to the world of Central American labor for three reasons: organizational development, the rise of political parties with labor tendencies, and state recognition of the worker along with the enactment of labor codes. Nevertheless, the end of the oligarchic crisis implied, for a number of reasons, a weakening of the trade union movement in Central America, with the exception of Honduras. Finally, four fundamental events in the region must be highlighted. The first is that of 1932 in El Salvador, whose outcome implied that this country's labor movement would require years to recover, although the indigenous population paid a still higher price. The second is the Costa Rican banana enclave strike along the Atlantic zone in 1934, which had an important symbolic value for the consolidation of the trade union movement, although the results of the conflict in 1948 would weaken the latter, causing it to regress. The third concerns the fall of Arbenz and the suppression of the Guatemalan trade union movement, which, at that time, had reached the highest level of development in the region. Finally, the 1954 banana enclave strike in Honduras meant that country's strengthened labor movement was the only one in Central America capable of facing the era of modernization to come.

Notes

1. This explains why Honduras, whose development did not take place until after World War II, is not discussed in this chapter.

2. In a comparison between the three countries (Costa Rica, El Salvador, and Guatemala) that, thanks to coffee, made a "successful breakthrough" into the world market, Pérez Brignoli (1994a: 33) argues that two basic factors controlled the supply of manpower and work systems: population densities, in terms of the relationship between land and labor, and state action.

3. Along these same lines, Samper (1993: 90–91) raised the issue of the existence of more subtle coercive mechanisms, such as that of the godfather figure that was associated with baptism. This fictitious kinship implied reciprocal obligations—although these were obviously one-sided in the context of relations between landowner and worker. This phenomenon existed in Costa Rica and El Salvador as well as in other areas throughout Central America.

4. For an analysis on the historical development of this system see Castellanos Cambranes (1985: 265ff.).

5. These laws had varying effects within the indigenous communities—certain members had sufficient resources to avoid the farm work and could thus consolidate their agricultural status and even take part in commercial and transport-related activities (McCreery, 1994b: 320–321).

6. With respect to Guatemala, Smith (1990) argues that coffee production development gave rise to three social subjects: semi-proletarians, proletarians, and agents of proletarianization. These coincided with the new ethnic environment that was taking shape. Thus, the former were Amerindians and the latter two were ladinos. This author has proposed the hypothesis that it is this differentiation that gave rise to the structuring of interethnic relations in Guatemala in the twentieth century: the Amerindian versus ladino opposition.

7. The extraeconomic coercive element was also present in this system, particularly in the case of El Salvador, in legislation that sought to control and recruit members of the peasant community who had been dispossessed of their lands (Browning, 1975: 329–330). These type of practices were carried out until the 1940s, and an important distinction has thus been made between Costa Rica

and El Salvador that, as pointed out by Samper (1994a: 199), concerns the different ways in which power was exercised in these two societies. Nonetheless, Menjivar (1980: 152) claims that this type of legislation was applied unyieldingly in El Salvador up until the beginning of this century and that its later application was of a repressive rather than disciplinary nature. This contrasts with Guatemala, where as mentioned earlier, the latter objective was maintained until the 1940s.

8. For work carried out by women and children on coffee plantations in Guatemala, see McCreery (1994b: 278–281).

9. Williams (1994: 118) has referred to the fact that this system prevented large landowners from competing for labor during harvest time.

10. The exception this region represents has been discussed by Williams (1994: 132–133). The indigenous population was able to adapt to the new republican era while maintaining control of the local power that they had acquired during the colonial era.

11. This system also prevailed in Honduras, where it even developed into different types of suprafamily organizational units. Reference should also be made to the fact that in the woodlice-producing areas of Guatemala (around Lake Amatitlan and Antigua), which were later used for growing coffee once more, the small farm and, subsequently, this system of family work, prevailed (Williams, 1994: 121–122).

12. This dependence also helped mystify any hostility that may have existed between small farm owners and their respective wage-earning laborers (Gudmudson, 1995: 128). Moreover, Acuña Ortega (1986b) has argued that for the period 1900–1936, a social dispute between farm laborers and coffee processors arose in Costa Rica's coffee-producing sector in the absence of a formal mechanism for fixing prices. This antagonism became more pronounced between 1932 and 1936 due to the effects of the crisis. In 1936 a new stage, characterized by the intervention (both of a financial and exporting nature) of the state began, whereby mechanisms were institutionalized and hostilities were thus appeased.

13. Mining enclaves also existed in Honduras, although they were less significant from an economic point of view than was the bananas enclave.

14. It appears that in Honduras the presence of Salvadorean workers, recruited by the banana companies' own *enganchadores*, was considerable (Posas, 1993: 142). Similarly, in Costa Rica the number of Nicaraguans working on the clearing of lands was significant (Bourgois, 1994: 244ff.).

15. It must be added that there were ethnic groups of Caribbean origin on the Atlantic coasts of Guatemala and Honduras, such as the *garifunas*, who were also involved in work related to banana production (Ghidinelli, 1972). In contrast, the above-mentioned bribris did not participate in this kind of work due to their lack of involvement in the monetary economy, which made it difficult for them to be proletarianized (Bourgois, 1994: 87).

16. It is important to note that within the Antillean population there were internal differences in terms of place of origin: Creoles, Trinidadians, Jamaicans, and so on (Bourgois, 1994: 106).

17. Note that this rate represents the quotient between the working and openly unemployed population and those of working age (EAP plus inactive population).

18. This comparison is hindered by the fact that the age defined for the population old enough to work differs from country to country; the problem is more acute in Honduras because the rate of activity is not refined, given that it takes into account the entire population. In relation to this, it should be noted that the lower the age limit, the lower the rate of activity. In other words, Guatemala and especially Honduras would show higher rates if this limit had been higher or if it had simply been fixed.

19. However, as we shall see further on, traditionality can shape representations that are more advanced than those produced by modernity itself.

20. In the same way, it must also be mentioned that the high number of unpaid family workers registered in the Honduran census meant this job category within the EAP reached 38.0 percent. This failure to make a distinction between employment and work could have occurred either in the informants' perceptions or in those of the censors.

21. With reference to Guatemala, it may be considered that the public/private distinction, in the case of the indigenous communities, could have operated on the basis of ethnic factors: The men interacted in public areas, subjected to the effects of ladino domination, while the women, consigned to the realm of domesticity, set themselves up as the detainers of indigenous tradition and identity. This phenomenon has managed to influence perceptions of work and employment in a manner opposite to that of Honduras.

22. The percentages corresponding to unpaid family work must be added to those of self-employment. In Guatemala this was equivalent to 18.4 percent; in Honduras it was 38.0 percent.

23. In the publication of the results of the Guatemalan census there are no tables in which these two variables are combined. In the case of Honduras, the information is arranged according to provinces but has been reconstructed on a national scale.

24. This table contains the modal categories for each of the employment characteristics, for each country, with its corresponding proportion in brackets. This type of information, arranged by sex, cannot be found in the published results of the Honduran census. It should also be noted that there was a lack of data for Costa Rica on the distribution of the work force by occupational category according to sex.

25. With the exception of Costa Rica, a breakdown of information is available for principal occupations. In all cases, under the occupation "farmers," that of "farm workers" is the most common, varying between 52.9 percent in Guatemala and 67.3 percent in El Salvador. With respect to the "service workers" category, the most significant is that of "domestic service workers," with percentages ranging from 79.0 percent for Nicaragua to 89.7 percent for Guatemala.

26. Piel (1995: 97) clearly illustrates this in his reference to a group of youths from Nebaj (ixil Quiché municipality): "It can be said that, as temporary proletarians, they differ from the "traditional" industrial proletariat due to their linguistic and geographic isolation from the urban sector and their mere seasonal presence in the wage-earning world (their biological and socio-cultural reproductive environment remains indigenous and outside capitalist circles); however, as indigenous peasants they differ from others in that they have become familiar with

other parts, other authorities and other ways of earning a living unknown to those in their communities and towns caught up in an identical reproduction cycle and an economy of straightforward exchange."

27. It is worth mentioning that in 1911 the First Central American Workers Congress was held in San Salvador with a view to uniting the *mutualidades* in regard to basic labor issues (improving the economic situation of workers, regulating the working day, etc.). Ten years later, this time in Guatemala City and at the request of the governments of the region, the Central American Workers Congress was held to commemorate the first centenary of independence. The congress was sponsored by the Panamerican Work Confederation (COPA), giving rise to the Central American Workers Confederation (COCA).

28. In regard to this country, Witzel (1991: 63) refers to the founding, in 1918, of the Guatemalan Workers Federation for the Legal Protection of Labor as the outset of "positions that surpass the essence of the mutual benefit system and on which new methods of representing the interests of the workers are being based." Furthermore, as of this moment the artisans and workers began to distance themselves from the Estrada Cabrera regime; workers' groups were later involved in overthrowing it in 1920.

29. An analysis of how anarchism developed in Guatemala can be found in Taracena Arriola (1988).

30. However, its subsequent emergence did little to advance the development of the trade union movement. This is illustrated by the number of strikes held in Nicaragua between 1931 and 1959: fourteen, which was three more than in the previous stage (Gutierrez Mayorga, 1985: 219). Nevertheless, it is worth pointing out one exception: that of Chinandega, the only department in the country where, in the late 1940s, Somoza banned all trade union activity (Gould, 1988: 146).

31. Nonetheless, the importance of the strikes held in February 1920 must be pointed out. These gave rise to a new stage in the political orientation of the workers, who broke away from state protection by implementing more autonomous actions, as stated by Acuña Ortega (1986a:79–81). However, as this author also points out, they, moreover, represent the first important move toward regulating work conditions, whereby the eight-hour day was established; and, for the first time, implied the significant mobilization of labor, involving different groups of urban workers.

32. One of the effects of this upsurge of trade unionist organizations, coupled with the subsequent development of trade disputes, was the undermining of the attempt, instigated by the Pan American Federation of Labor, sponsored by the Central American governments, and that had materialized in the form of the Central American Labor Confederation, to organize workers on a regional scale.

33. In effect, this country's first strike in 1909 also broke out in an enclave—that of the miners (Meza, 1991: 5).

34. Adams (1993: 175–177) has argued that the 1932 massacre was the most notorious genocide to have taken place in the region during the twentieth century prior to the killings that took place in Guatemala between 1979 and 1984. Not only was the physical extermination of indigenous persons carried out but a stigma was attached to their ethnic condition, which had been linked to commu-

nism, for many years afterward. This meant the idea of recovering the expropriated communal lands was overlooked at the end of the past century and that the *nahuas* and *pipile* communities in El Salvador were subjected to a more rapid and complete process of ladinization than that which occurred in certain areas in the Guatemalan highlands.

35. However, it has been said that the Communists' entry into the alliance between Calderón and the Roman Catholic Church indicated a change in the way trade union disputes were handled, as demonstrated by its role as mediator during the banana strike of 1943 (Rojas Bolaños, 1985: 271). As Aguilar has pointed out (1989: 27), union action was determined by the line taken by those who governed this alliance.

36. In the case of Costa Rica, during the three years that followed the enactment of the code, organizations divided, resulting in an increase in the number of trade union organizations from 85 in 1943 to 213 in 1946 (Aguilar, 1989: table 3). For its part, the Guatemalan code initially excluded the majority of the agrarian work force, which constituted the largest sector in this country. This group was later included, and worth highlighting is its spectacular organizational development, which materialized in the form of the National Guatemalan Peasants Confederation (CNCG) (Balcárcel, 1984: 39).

37. Gould (1986) has argued that during the period in question, Somoza's political program had a populist slant inspired by Peron's experience, and consequently, its relation with the labor movement was not demagogic. In this respect, it took on the outward expression of the above-mentioned COCTN. However, the subsequent alliance established with North American capital led to the abandonment of this populist direction.

38. The workers' organizations were even able to develop in the bananas enclave, where it was estimated that during this period, a little over a third (35 percent) of the labor force were trade union members (Ellis, 1983: 240).

39. However, in 1953, several federations known as "independent trade unions" helped to set up the Costa Rican General Workers Confederation (CGTC), which gave organizational continuity to the Communist tendency within the country's labor movement.

40. An interesting aspect of this situation was the support the business sectors of San Pedro Sula showed for the strikers, thus illustrating its regional vocation (Euraque, 1996: 92–93).

2

A Time of Hope:
Capitalist Modernization
and Labor

In the former chapter an attempt was made to provide an outline of the world of labor both from a structural (the state of labor relations) and an action-related viewpoint (the development of the handicraft and workers movement), which was set within the oligarchic system that made its mark on the development of Central American societies during the first decades of the present century. This second chapter is set within the historical context that witnessed the process of redefining this system amid a period of modernizing change. By and large, this process was characterized by a series of traits that likened it to similar processes that occurred in other parts of Latin America. However, there were features unique to the Central American process, which should be emphasized—albeit very briefly—in order to outline the change in context.

Although this analysis covers a period of approximately twenty-five years, from the early 1950s to the mid-1970s, three different stages must be pointed out. The first focuses on the late 1940s up until the early 1960s. A significant diversification of agricultural exports occurred during this period, which, alongside coffee and bananas, witnessed the emergence of cotton, beef, and sugar. These new commodities were controlled by local capital, thereby making the importance of the banana sector's transnational capital a more relative phenomenon. For its part, the 1960s coincide with what has become known as "the illusion of a golden age." These are the years of an attempt at import substitution industrialization, involving three previously unfamiliar elements: This was a predominantly urban rather than rural activity; it developed within a protected environment, implying less resistance to wage demands on the part of the entrepreneurs; and its market had a more regional scope. Finally, in the 1970s, faced with the rapid decline of this industrializing experience, both agricultural and nontraditional manufactured exports were promoted, although this initiative was short-lived due to the onset of the crisis (Bulmer-Thomas, 1989: 366–367).

In terms of economic results, although considerable growth has been indicated, it proved insufficient in relation to demographic tendencies. This growth has been described as erratic due to the vulnerability of Central American economies, which were open as a result of a limited number of export products and, consequently, exposed to changes in external demand. Even so, the attempts at industrialization did not succeed in modifying this vulnerability to any great extent. Despite the level of openness of these economies, they were unable to satisfy the import requirements of either the industrial sector or that of the new consumer trends. The latter were one of the major causes of the low level of domestic savings. Along the same lines, although major efforts at investment had been made, these proved incapable of absorbing the growing supply of labor power. Moreover, in spite of the fact that poverty levels declined due to the migration induced by the urbanization process and—in Costa Rica, as a result of the implementation of social policies that had universal scope—this series of initiatives only served to maintain social inequalities (PREALC, 1986: 21–51).

This last observation leads one to consider the main social processes that materialized during this period of modernization. In the first instance, broad masses of peasants as well as wage workers suffered impoverishment. This phenomenon will be discussed in the present chapter from a labor relations perspective. Second, there was evidence of the rise of intermediate sectors linked to urbanization and the expansion of public employment resulting from the state's own process of modernization. This process had a greater impact on Honduras and, above all, on Costa Rica; the impoverishing tendencies ultimately affected the majority of these sectors in the remaining countries. Third, the new activities (agricultural and industrial exports and new services) provoked the rise of a new range of factions within the bourgeoisie that continued to maintain links with the traditional oligarchy. As Vilas (1994: 86) has argued, it was the land-owning oligarchy itself that initiated the modernization process and defined its form and scope.[1]

In political terms, the former chapter has already referred to the ways in which the oligarchic crisis, which began in the 1930s, was resolved: Authoritarian regimes evolved, then degenerated into state terrorism; however, from an economic point of view, the redefinitions of the primary export model gave rise to more socioeconomically diverse societies. In other words, partial changes were experienced in the economic field in contrast to methods of political control, which remained the same. As already mentioned, this general explanation was true, in every sense, in three cases (Guatemala, El Salvador, and Nicaragua), and it was partially true for Honduras; only in Costa Rica did the resolution of the oligarchic crisis lead to the rise of a democratic regime and a less socioeconomically polarized society.

It is within the context outlined above that the world of labor also underwent transformations, which this chapter will attempt to explain. Consequently, the first section offers a global view of the development of employment following the analysis of the occupations structure of 1950 that I presented in the previous chapter. On the basis of this global framework, the second section will make a more in-depth analysis of the two most significant modernizing processes: agricultural changes and the rise of an industrial manufacturing sector (and how the latter affected the urban economy). The chapter ends by referring back to the analysis of the workers' movement in order to illustrate its development and the changes that took place during these decades of modernization.

Modernizing Dynamics and Labor

In order to explain how the employment structure was transformed during the decades of modernization, an analysis that differentiates between the labor market's supply and demand will be undertaken, continuing on, with slight modifications, the previous chapter's interpretation of the level of modernity of the region's labor markets. However, this analysis will be based on trends rather than levels, for it is a diachronic rather than a synchronic analysis such as that of the previous chapter, which is limited to the year 1950. Precisely in relation to the impact of modernizing trends will an attempt be made to provide a global vision of the labor markets, by integrating both supply and demand perspectives. It should also be pointed out that the use of three time intervals, even though these are not the same for each country, facilitates a global interpretation by permitting a comparison between the different national contexts in terms of two stages within the modernization process: The first is related to the diversification of agrarian exports, and the second to industrialization.

Table 2.1 represents the labor force supply angle. Bearing in mind that the focus is on development, growth rates have been given priority. These serve to assess the type of respective modernizing trend; in this regard, three kinds of development have been identified: negative, when the growth rate of the corresponding variable is accompanied by a minus sign; moderate, when the rate is positive but below the global growth rate with which it is compared (EAP or inactive population); and high, when the rate is greater than the latter.[2] Moreover, the comparison between two census intervals also allows one to determine whether the tendency is sustained or, on the contrary, tends to become static or even decelerates.

TABLE 2.1 Labor Supply Indicators According to Country (Growth Rates)

Indicators	Guatemala[a]		El Salvador[b]		Honduras[c]		Nicaragua[d]		Costa Rica[e]	
	1950–64	1964–73	1950–61	1961–71	1950–61	1961–74	1950–63	1963–71	1950–63	1963–73
Total EAP	2.9	1.5	2.1	4.5	-1.1	2.6	3.4	0.8	3.5	4.8
Inactive population	4.2	0.3	3.1	3.6	-0.9	3.9	5.8	4.0	6.0	-3.4
EAP aged 65 and over	5.1	1.8	3.4	4.0	n.a.	5.2	2.6	0.8	17.7	5.5
Inactive student population	12.5	1.1	8.8	10.5	n.a.	8.9	75.1	7.7	n.a.	4.0[f]
Female EAP	2.5	3.3	3.0	7.5	-6.8	4.9	18.2	1.9	4.1	n.a.
Urban EAP	5.5	3.2	2.7	5.2	n.a.	6.0	1.9	8.8	3.7	n.a.

NOTES:

[a] Population aged 7 and over for 1950 and 1964; aged 10 and over for 1973.

[b] Population aged 10 and over.

[c] Not refined for 1950; population aged 10 and over for 1961 and 1974.

[d] Population aged 14 and over for 1950; aged 10 and over for 1961 and 1974.

[e] Population aged 12 and over.

[f] 1950–1973.

SOURCES: For the first census observation (in the 1950s), DGEC (1953) for Costa Rica 1950; DGEC (1953) for El Salvador 1950; DGEC (1957) for Guatemala 1950. For the second census observation (in the 1960s): DGEC (1963) for Honduras 1961; DGEC (1967) for Nicaragua 1963; DGEC (1966) for Costa Rica 1963; DGEC (1965) for El Salvador 1961; DGEC (1971) for Guatemala 1964. For the third census observation (in the 1970s): DGEC (1975) for Honduras 1974; DGEC (1974) for Nicaragua 1971; DGEC (1974) for Costa Rica 1973; DGEC (1977) for El Salvador 1971; DGEC (1975) for Guatemala 1973.

The relation between the development of the first two indicators allows us to evaluate tendencies in terms of the rate of labor participation, which, as in the former chapter, constitutes a starting point for identifying regional similarities and differences. The first census interval indicates that all the countries experienced a higher growth rate with respect to the inactive, as opposed to the active, population. That is, the rates of activity tended to decrease in the 1950s. Honduras had the lowest decrease (from 47.3 percent to 46.6 percent) whereas Nicaragua represented the highest (from 52.8 percent to 47.8 percent); however, both cases present problems regarding the refining of data, although in opposite directions, implying that the difference in Honduras's case should have been greater, and in Nicaragua's case, less acute. The lowest rate was still that of Costa Rica, with 29.6 percent. If we refer back to the comment made in the previous chapter, in which Costa Rica is compared to the rest of the region, it would not be unreasonable to argue that this decrease indicates that Central American households began to demonstrate less of a need to mobilize their labor resources. This could reflect evidence of improvements in living conditions due to the onset of the modernization process.

Within a context of modernization, from the point of view of the labor market supply, there are three processes that illustrate the most significant changes brought on by modernizing action. The first deals with the development of the higher age group (65 and over) of the EAP. One would expect this rate to increase at a slower pace than that of the total EAP, or even decrease, as a result of modern progress, implying that households (or actions carried out by a protective state—a less probable option in Central America) are capable of taking on the reproduction of an already depleted labor force unlikely to be able to reproduce itself. The second process focuses on the growth of the female EAP. It has been proposed, as a hypothesis, that the modernization process should induce a higher growth rate of this sector of the work force than that of the total EAP. That is, employment should become more female-orientated, which, in reproductive terms, should result in the conditions being created for questioning the traditional division of domestic work. Finally, a greater increase in the inactive population involved in study activities in relation to the inactive population as a whole is expected. Thus, modernization should imply the schooling of the potential work force and greater opportunities for domestic units to maximize their future, as opposed to their current, incomes.

The table illustrates that the EAP's rejuvenating trend was only applicable to Nicaragua. In contrast, El Salvador, Guatemala, and Costa Rica demonstrated that their households did not have the capacity to absorb the reproductive costs of the already depleted work force, which was forced to remain within the labor market.

Likewise, the countries for which data was available coincided with regard to the increase in schooling, which was, without doubt, the most dynamic trend.[3] Given Costa Rica's background, it may even be assumed that this country underwent the same phenomenon as Honduras, although perhaps in a more limited manner. In short, Central American households could begin to embark on strategies for maximizing their future incomes due to the higher level of schooling of their younger members.

In contrast, with respect to the circumstances surrounding women's participation in the labor force, two situations have been identified. On the one hand, in El Salvador, Nicaragua,[4] and Costa Rica the female EAP growth rates were higher than those of the total EAP; the opposite was true in the two remaining countries, especially Honduras, where this modernizing trend proved negative.[5] However, the overall decrease in rates of participation throughout the region must be taken into account. Although the feminization of employment tends to increase this rate,[6] it would be reasonable to propose a hypothesis arguing that despite evidence of the feminization of employment in El Salvador, Nicaragua, and Costa Rica, it does not appear to have had any significant impact on the distribution of labor within domestic units.[7] Consequently, the existing pattern of the division of labor within the household was maintained and, indeed, strengthened with regard to Guatemala and Honduras. Thus, Central American women continued to be discriminated against in terms of labor participation during this initial period of modernization.

As a result, this first phase of modernization demonstrates that, by and large, Central American households proved themselves more capable, on the whole, of successfully controlling their labor resources than they had been in 1950, when it had been suggested there was a need to incorporate half of their members in the labor market. This greater measure of control resulted, essentially, in an attempt to increase the schooling of the young labor force, presumably—in certain countries—in favor of men; however, this effort was not applied to older members, because their participation in the labor market increased. In contrast, feminization of employment took place, to a certain extent, although it was unlikely this had any major impact on reproductive behavior. Therefore, the evidence available suggests that the only hypothesis fulfilled during this first stage of modernization was that concerning an increase in schooling.

The second phase of modernization, which may be linked to the impact of industrialization, points to two different situations in terms of labor participation initiatives. First of all, Honduras and Nicaragua maintain the same downward trend regarding the rate of participation, registering 43.7 percent and 42.5 percent respectively. The remaining countries, in comparison, reversed this tendency, and the corresponding rates increased for Guatemala (from 42.0 percent to 44.3 percent), El Salvador (from 47.6 percent to 49.1 percent), and above all, Costa Rica (from 29.6 percent to 48.4 percent).[8] Furthermore, differences worth highlighting exist within these two groups. Thus, whereas in Nicaragua both the inactive population and, above all, the EAP decrease, in Honduras the opposite occurs. For its part, Guatemala shows a much lower increase in EAP than El Salvador and Costa Rica, who appear to have undergone more dynamic employment-generating processes.

Due to the broad range of situations, it is not easy to carry out a comparative analysis of these rates. Nevertheless, it seems there are two contrasting cases, which may, to a certain extent, facilitate an explanation and serve to illustrate the extremes between which this array of situations occurred within the region. On the one hand, it is thought that the historical delay experienced by Honduras implied that the same type of process was still occurring in this country. Moreover, it has been suggested that to demonstrate the difference, in the case of Honduras, between two instances of the modernization process would not be very logical because this country experienced a continuation of the initial stage of this process. In this sense, therefore, the decrease in the rate of activity could be interpreted in the same manner. On the other hand, it may be said of Costa Rica that the highest level of development in the field of labor was achieved in this country. In effect, the analysis of the entire range of modernizing trends confirms this, as we shall see further on. In this type of context, an increase in the rate of participation would not necessarily reflect a deterioration in reproductive conditions. The modernization of the labor market, especially in metropolitan areas, reconfirms a participation in the labor force that does not respond solely to reproductive needs. In other words, this type of labor market, which is much more structured and complex than those of rural areas, offers the possibility of multiple job opportunities, thereby making work not just a mere means of subsistence but also an end in itself. The rise of firms and public institutions as paradigms of the modernization process pointed toward the possibility that the reasons for employment were different to those related to the coffee-growing milieu or the banana plantations. Consequently, these changes are thought to have been more effective in Costa Rica than in the rest of the region, where it was more likely that reproductive logics of subsistence in terms of labor incorporation would predominate.

With regard to the three modernizing trends, it must first be pointed out that the EAP corresponding to older age groups showed a higher increase than the total EAP in Guatemala, Honduras, and Costa Rica. That is, in these countries the expected labor force rejuvenation hypothesis was not fulfilled, and the respective households did not prove capable of absorbing the reproductive costs of this labor. Only in El Salvador did the opposite occur; Nicaragua's situation was at a standstill. In other words, at the regional level the tendency toward nonrejuvenation persisted.

In contrast, all the countries showed a strong upward trend with regard to schooling.[9] Nonetheless, it is worth highlighting the differences between countries in the previous period. On the one hand, both in Guatemala and Nicaragua this tendency's momentum dwindled. Nicaragua's previous census interval presents methodological problems resulting in serious doubts as to whether such a decrease occurred. In Guatemala's case, however, there is clear evidence of a downward trend in this second phase of modernization. El Salvador, for its part, reflects the opposite; in other words, a strengthening of the schooling process along with a consolidation of the modernization process. As a result, it appears that Central American households continued to show evidence of reproductive strategies that sought to maximize future incomes, although at least in Guatemala's case this type of strategy began to show signs of constraint.

The tendency toward feminization also remained the same in all the countries for which information was available. It is once again worthwhile to compare the results from the two censuses. With the exception of Nicaragua,[10] in the remaining three countries, and presumably also in Costa Rica, this tendency was reinforced. It should also be pointed out that in Guatemala this process proved to be more dynamic than that of schooling. Thus, one could put forward the hypothesis that the increase in the rate of activity represented by Guatemala during this second stage of modernization demonstrated that the incorporation of women in the work force was significant.

Therefore, during this second phase of the modernization process, from the point of view of supply, two of the tendencies identified in the previous period were maintained: the schooling of the future work force, and the nonrejuvenation of the labor force. The opposite was true of the latter tendency only in El Salvador. The feminization of employment, for its part, was consolidated. However, these tendencies decelerated in some countries. This was the case regarding schooling in Guatemala and feminization in Nicaragua.

The last aspect considered in the present table deals with the urbanization of employment. This indicator refers to one of the key trends in the modernization process, and in terms of interpreting reproductive logics, it illustrates the spatial scope of the same.[11] It is only to be expected that the modernization process should result in an increase in the urbanization of the labor force. In effect, in all the instances for which data was available, the growth of this type of labor is higher than that of the total EAP. Nicaragua is the exception to this in the first census interval, although in the second interval this country registered the fastest growth rate in the region. It must also be stressed that this tendency's momentum weakened in Guatemala. This situation is important because it reminds us that this type of analysis, which places far too much emphasis on aggregates, conceals the development of urban systems of a different kind. In this sense, one must bear in mind that in Guatemala, the primacy of the metropolis (Guatemala City) was more marked than in any other Central American country. This implies that the primary focus of Guatemala's urbanizing process was on this city; in contrast, in the rest of the countries, it was distributed among other city centers. This, in turn, was significant in terms of the link between urban and nonagricultural areas. It was most probably in Guatemala where this connection was the most clear-cut. In other cases the development of certain sectors of the urban system, namely the lowest, could have constituted a response to developments in the field of agriculture. Thus, these smaller urban centers were, by and large, residential areas for agricultural workers.

Table 2.2 permits an analysis of the employment structure from the point of view of demand. In this case, three modernizing trends benefited: wage labor, professional work, and tertiary employment. The development of each of these alongside the consolidation of the modernization process has therefore been presented by way of hypothesis.

Three kinds of situations have been identified in respect to the wage labor trend. The first corresponds to El Salvador and, above all, Guatemala, where wage labor was present during the first stage of modernization, although this trend was reversed during the second stage. The opposite occurred in Nicaragua and, in particular, in Costa Rica, because the latter's growth rate in terms of wage work showed an increase in the second census interval with respect to the first. Moreover, Honduras presents a less dynamic wage labor situation, although it is more consistent over time.[12] That is, no standard tendency was identified for the growth rate at the regional level; indeed, the wage labor growth hypothesis was wholly fulfilled only in Honduras and partly fulfilled in Nicaragua and Costa Rica.

These tendencies show that on comparing the last census observation of each country with that of 1950, two kinds of processes occurred. On the one hand, there were the cases in which the importance of wage work increased throughout the entire employment structure. This was true of Guatemala, though this increase did not imply a more widespread process of proletarianization. The same occurred in Honduras, which registered the most marked variation.[13] Furthermore, only in Costa Rica did this increase reinforce the existence of an already widespread process of proletarianization, which by the mid-1970s affected almost three quarters of the labor force.[14] On the other hand, the two remaining cases—El Salvador and Nicaragua—show that this occupational category's relative importance declined. As a result, it has been noted that toward the end of

TABLE 2.2   Labor Demand Indicators According to Country (Growth Rates)

Indicators	Guatemala[a]		El Salvador[b]		Honduras[c]		Nicaragua[d]		Costa Rica[e]	
	1950–64	1964–73	1950–61	1961–71	1950–61	1961–74	1950–63	1963–71	1950–63	1963–73
Total EAP	2.9	1.5	2.1	4.5	-1.1	2.6	3.4	0.8	3.5	4.8
Wage work	7.3	-0.6	4.7	1.2	1.0	3.8	3.7	1.2	3.4	6.5
Self-employment	-0.6	8.0	0.3	6.7	0.7	1.3	4.8	0.3	11.0	3.9
Professional and technical	7.3	8.7	7.3	9.8	12.7	9.0	5.6	13.5	9.6	12.6
Agricultural	2.6	-0.1	1.6	3.0	-2.7	1.7	2.1	-2.0	2.6	1.0
Industrial	2.3	4.9	3.6	1.0	1.6	7.0	3.7	1.6	4.0	5.4
Commercial	4.3	4.0	4.0	5.9	21.0	9.1	9.7	4.6	6.2	7.5
Services	4.6	2.6	3.2	9.7	12.7	2.0	7.2	6.0	5.4	7.4

NOTES:

[a] Population aged 7 and over for 1950 and 1964; aged 10 and over for 1973.

[b] Population aged 10 and over.

[c] Not refined for 1950; population aged 10 and over for 1961 and 1974.

[d] Population aged 14 and over for 1950; aged 10 and over for 1961 and 1974.

[e] Population aged 12 and over.

SOURCES: For the first census observation (in the 1950s), DGEC (1952) for Honduras 1950; DGEC (1954) for Nicaragua 1950; DGEC (1953) for Costa Rica 1950; DGEC (1953) for El Salvador 1950; DGEC (1957) for Guatemala 1950. For the second census observation (in the 1960s): DGEC (1963) for Honduras 1961; DGEC (1967) for Nicaragua 1963; DGEC (1966) for Costa Rica 1963; DGEC (1965) for El Salvador 1961; DGEC (1971) for Guatemala 1964. For the third census observation (in the 1970s): DGEC (1975) for Honduras 1974; DGEC (1974) for Nicaragua 1971; DGEC (1974) for Costa Rica 1973; DGEC (1977) for El Salvador 1971; DGEC (1975) for Guatemala 1973.

the modernization process, proletarianization had not succeeded in becoming widespread either in Guatemala or Honduras, and in El Salvador and Nicaragua it lacked stability. Thus, in the majority of the region the different modes of surplus labor accumulation were forced to combine the direct accumulation of wage work with indirect accumulation. Only in Costa Rica did it appear that the modernization process had consolidated a form of direct accumulation.

In contrast, the tendency that proved unequivocal was that of professionalization. It increased in all the countries and for each period, reaching levels far in excess of the respective rates of the total EAP. There is only a slight exception—that of Honduras in the second census interval—that may be explained by the high growth rate of the previous period, due to the fact that the presence of this kind of labor force was minimal in this country in 1950.[15] Consequently, the modernization process appears to have induced the development of more complex forms of organizing work, as was to be expected.

In addition, the tendency toward tertiary employment was confirmed by higher growth rates than those of the total EAP for commercial and service-related activities and for each period with only one exception: Honduras in the second census interval. Nonetheless, two kinds of situations arose. The tendency toward tertiary work was constant in El Salvador and Costa Rica while it tended to decelerate in the second stage of modernization. However, the information provided by the present table allows us to observe developments that occurred in the fields of agriculture and industry. It is worthwhile to comment on these activities because they will be analyzed in more detail in the following section. With regard to agriculture, it must be stressed that this branch of activity had limited employment-generating capacity. Its growth rate was lower than that of the overall EAP in all the countries and in each of the periods discussed; thus, its trend can be described as moderate. Furthermore, between these two periods of modernization two types of situations arose. On the one hand, the creation of agricultural employment decelerated in Guatemala, Nicaragua, and Costa Rica; in this regard, during the second census interval Guatemala experienced a standstill, and in Nicaragua labor was even dismissed from this activity. On the other hand, however, the two remaining countries showed an increase—especially El Salvador, which appeared to be the country with the most dynamic agricultural sector in terms of labor absorption. For its part, the manufacturing industry presents two kinds of situations. Growth rates decelerated in El Salvador and Nicaragua between the two census intervals while the opposite occurred in the remaining countries. Nevertheless, both activities mask a variety of internal circumstances with different factors and effects on the labor market, which will be discussed in the following section.

These changes, in terms of branches of activity, implied that the model of development no longer centered almost exclusively on agriculture, as was the case in 1950. However, during the 1970s, in all the Central American countries—with the exception of Costa Rica—the majority of the labor force was still involved in agricultural work. This was especially true of Guatemala and Honduras, whose societies remained predominantly agrarian. From the point of view of employment, industrialization did not demonstrate any major influence on any part of the region. It was rather in the field of services that El Salvador, Nicaragua, and Costa Rica reflected a measure of diversification in modes of development.

Consequently, of the three employment-modernizing trends focusing on demand, only that which refers to professionalization shows a clear direction with respect to the hypothesis presented. Although there was also evidence of a tendency toward tertiary employment, this process was only consolidated in the second modernizing period in El Salvador and Costa Rica. In addition, Honduras was the only country in which a sustained process of wage labor took place. In the remaining countries, occupational heterogeneity prevailed; Guatemala and El Salvador even underwent a process of relative decline with respect to wage labor.

This last observation points to the formation of heterogeneous labor markets in the region, induced by the process of modernization. This phenomenon can be analyzed with the help of Table 2.3, which demonstrates employment generated in four different segments.[16]

These figures above all demonstrate that the growth of urban employment surpassed that of agriculture in all of the periods and in all five countries. However, the development of each of these components varies according to each specific case, thereby illustrating the particularities of each national context. In this regard, reference may be made to the fact that Costa Rica showed the most active and sustained growth of urban employment whereas the generation of agricultural employment experienced a gradual deceleration in its growth rate. In other words, this is the clearest case of labor urbanization in the region. Nicaragua should also be mentioned here, although more in relation to the reduction in growth of agricultural employment. The opposite was true of Guatemala, where the growth rates of city jobs remained almost the same while those of agricultural work increased. Thus, deruralization was less marked in this national context.

In terms of urban employment, two types of situations may be detected in relation to the first two decades shown in the table. On the one hand, Guatemala and Costa Rica[17] underwent more noticeable processes of employment formalization than those of informalization whereas in Nicaragua and Honduras the modernization process resulted in a greater relative importance of informality. An unusual situation developed in El

TABLE 2.3   Segmentation of Labor Market According to Country, 1950–1980
(Growth Rates)

Country and Period	Formal	Informal	Total Urban[a]	Modern	Traditional	Total Agriculture
Guatemala						
1950–60	4.0	3.6	3.4	2.5	0.8	1.4
1960–70	4.3	2.5	3.4	1.8	2.0	2.0
1970–80	3.2	4.1	3.3	1.1	2.9	2.2
El Salvador						
1950–60	3.9	1.9	3.2	3.5	–1.1	1.3
1960–70	4.1	4.9	4.3	0.8	4.1	2.2
1970–80	4.1	4.5	4.1	0.2	3.6	2.0
Honduras						
1950–60	6.1	6.3	6.3	–0.7	2.4	1.3
1960–70	4.7	5.8	4.3	3.2	0.2	1.2
1970–80	4.2	6.1	4.4	6.1	0.7	1.5
Nicaragua						
1950–60	3.8	5.2	4.1	–0.6	3.2	1.3
1960–70	4.7	5.8	5.1	0.4	2.0	1.1
1970–80	3.7	6.0	4.6	–0.5	1.9	0.8
Costa Rica						
1950–60	4.1	3.4	3.8	1.0	2.3	1.5
1960–70	5.3	3.5	4.8	0.6	2.3	1.3
1970–80	5.5	6.0	5.5	2.1	–2.3	0.4

NOTE:
[a] Includes domestic work.
SOURCE: PREALC (1986, table 12).

Salvador, where a more dynamic generation of formal employment became one in which informality prevailed.

In the case of agricultural employment, three situations are worth mentioning. In Nicaragua and Costa Rica the traditional sector was the most dynamic during the first two decades of modernization. Guatemala and El Salvador reflect changes in that the area showing most activity was the traditional rather than the modern sector. Moreover, this process was reversed in Honduras.

Furthermore, in contrast to the preceding tables, this one allows us to observe the trends in the 1970s that foreshadowed some of the processes that were to emerge later on in the heart of the crisis. Thus, in terms of agricultural employment, the same tendencies that occurred in the 1960s were maintained—with the exception of Costa Rica, where the modern sector took on added significance. This phenomenon could be linked to a successful process of agricultural diversification involving the export of nontraditional products. The higher level of activity in Honduras per-

sists; this phenomenon demonstrates the delayed process of modernization in this country, which has been highlighted on several occasions. As
mentioned earlier, the Honduran labor market reached a level of modernity in the 1980s similar to that which took place in Costa Rica forty years
earlier (PREALC, 1986: 77). Moreover, in relation to urban employment,
the informal sector's greater capacity to absorb labor in all the nations in
question during the last years of modernization is evident. Therefore, the
importance of this type of employment, which as discussed in the following chapter constituted the region's main adjustment mechanism for labor markets during the 1980s crisis, was already being anticipated.

This section concludes by offering a global view of the labor market,
taking into account both its supply and demand and starting from the
moment when the main modernizing tendencies in this area of exchange
began to materialize. This view is represented by Table 2.4.[18]

First, it must be said that all the variables in the five countries had
higher rates than those of their respective EAP or than the inactive population in the case of schooling. Therefore, one could claim (in the light of
the analytical perspective adopted herein) that the employment structures in the region were modernized. The only tendency that partially
contradicts this statement is that of feminization.[19] This is due to the case
of Honduras, in reference to which the methodological reasons already
mentioned several times before with regard to 1950 should be kept in
mind. Costa Rica is also worthy of mention in respect to a growth rate
equal to that of its total EAP, implying that the importance of women in
this country's labor market remained constant during the period under
consideration. In fact, this modernizing trend was the weakest, although
this statement must be modified with respect to El Salvador and, above
all, Nicaragua.

Schooling and professionalization were the two most dynamic modernizing tendencies in all of the countries, with the exception of feminization in Nicaragua. These two processes are not totally unrelated, though
their impact differs due to the significance of each one. Indeed, while the
incidence of professionalization toward the end of the modernizing
process remained marginal, with the exception of Guatemala, schooling
represented approximately one third of the inactive population.

With the exception—once more—of Guatemala, tertiary labor (related
only to the EAP in the service sector) proved itself to be a dynamic trend.
However, toward the end of the period under consideration, none of the
countries showed evidence of high levels of employment in this sector.
Thus, the tertiary labor trend was dynamic but did not have any significant impact on the labor market.

For their part, urbanization and wage labor—two trends that were not
entirely disassociated during the period under consideration—did not

TABLE 2.4 Employment and Modernizing Tendencies According to Country

Modernizing Tendencies	Guatemala		El Salvador		Honduras		Nicaragua		Costa Rica	
	1950–73	% 1973	1950–71	% 1971	1950–74	% 1974	1950–71	% 1971	1950–73	% 1973
Schooling	8.1	22.8	9.6	35.9	8.9[a]	29.1	49.5	31.5	4.0	32.6
Inactive population	2.7	100.0	3.3	100.0	1.7	100.0	5.1	100.0	2.0	100.0
Feminization	3.5	14.0	5.2	21.6	–0.5	15.7	12.0	21.9	4.1[b]	16.4[c]
Urbanization	4.6	39.0	3.9	42.5	6.0[a]	33.2	4.5	48.4	3.7[b]	37.0[c]
Wage labor	4.2	48.0	3.0	47.2	2.5	44.2	2.8	58.1	4.7	73.5
Professionalization	7.9	3.7	9.2	3.5	10.7	4.1	8.6	5.0	13.6	8.8
Tertiarization	3.3	12.5	6.3	17.8	6.9	11.5	6.7	19.8	6.3	20.3
EAP	2.4	100.0	3.3	100.0	0.8	100.0	2.4	100.0	4.1	100.0

NOTES:
[a] 1961–1974
[b] 1950–1963
[c] 1963

SOURCES: For the first census observation (in the 1950s), DGEC (1952) for Honduras 1950; DGEC (1954) for Nicaragua 1950; DGEC (1953) for Costa Rica 1950; DGEC (1953) for El Salvador 1950; DGEC (1957) for Guatemala 1950. For the second census observation (in the 1960s): DGEC (1963) for Honduras 1961; DGEC (1961) for Nicaragua 1963; DGEC (1966) for Costa Rica 1963; DGEC (1965) for El Salvador 1961; DGEC (1971) for Guatemala 1964. For the third census observation (in the 1970s): DGEC (1975) for Honduras 1974; DGEC (1974) for Nicaragua 1971; DGEC (1974) for Costa Rica 1973; DGEC (1977) for El Salvador 1971; DGEC (1975) for Guatemala 1973.

show any notable developments despite the fact that these two areas were the most significant at the end of the modernization process.

Consequently, it may be said that, by and large, Central American labor markets were modernized. The most dynamic aspects were those related to the qualification of the work force and, to a lesser extent, the development of the service sector. Nonetheless, urbanization and wage labor proved to be the most notable trends in this process. In contrast, feminization showed poor results. Certain particularities, in addition, must be stressed in relation to some of the countries: relatively low schooling in Guatemala, defeminization and rapid urbanization in Honduras, rapid schooling and feminization in Nicaragua, and universal wage labor and significant tertiary labor in Costa Rica. In effect, the latter country offers the most modern image with regard to its employment structure. Honduras and, to a lesser extent, Guatemala represent the opposite end of the spectrum. The contrasts identified in the former chapter for the year 1950 do not, therefore, appear to have undergone any significant changes during the decades of modernization.

Agricultural Diversification, Industrialization, and Labor

This second section focuses on the two main economic aspects of the modernization process in Central America. As mentioned earlier, the 1950s witnessed a process of significant diversification within the agricultural sector, which centered essentially on the emergence of new exports of rural origin. This phenomenon, along with changes that affected traditional exports (coffee and bananas) and agriculture for internal consumption,[20] is the first to be analyzed. Second, the industrializing process and its impact on the urban world will be discussed. Naturally, in both cases the main objective is to identify the labor relations that arose and how they developed.

In that which concerns the changes that took place in the rural sphere, one must first describe those that affected the region's two main exports, coffee and bananas, for the modernization process also affected both of these areas. Due to the absence of quotas and to partial access to the expanding European market, in the 1950s conditions within the Central American coffee sector favored growth. To this end, it benefited from the support of the financial sector and the state. Nonetheless, this growth had to choose between improvements in output or the expansion of new lands. In Guatemala and especially in El Salvador, this second alternative was not viable because the land that was apt for this crop had already been put to use. Thus, in Guatemala the introduction of technology along with new varieties of crops provoked a whole series of changes in the production process: increase in coffee per unit of land, use of herbicides and fungicides, and pruning by rows of trees (known as *poda por calle*). These in turn had inverse effects on employment: On the one hand, the demand for labor increased due to the fact that the work was now more labor-intensive per area, but on the other hand, the need for permanent workers decreased (PREALC, 1980b: 59–60).[21] Furthermore, this first option, based on improving outputs, implied a stricter control of labor costs on the part of the large properties, which was reflected in strong opposition to all forms of organization carried out by day-laborers (Bulmer-Thomas, 1989: 204). In Honduras, the most obvious case of the second kind of situation occurred due to the existence of an extensive agricultural frontier, which meant the use of wage labor was widespread and included the participation of family workers and the direct supervision of the producer (Baumeister, 1994: 462–465).[22]

In comparison, banana exports could not expand; this was mainly due to two reasons. First, the demand of the North American market began to dwindle during the 1950s, and access to other markets, namely those in Europe, was difficult. Second, the strategy for combating the so-called Panama plague (the *sigatoka* disease) consisted of adopting the policy of cultivating virgin soil. Although, as already mentioned in the previous chapter, this type of strategy was implemented in Central America, in the Pacific zones the great expansion of postwar banana production took place outside the region, in Ecuador. This standstill had serious repercussions for labor resulting in a significant reduction in employment in the three countries in which this enclave proved most important. Thus, in 1950, in the divisions of the main multinational companies operating in the sector (United Fruit, Standard Fruit, and Del Monte) in Costa Rica, Guatemala, and Honduras, there were 58,181 jobs. Ten years later almost half (45.1 percent) of the labor force had been dismissed (Ellis, 1983: table C.9). The immediate causes of this reduction in employment were twofold: the closing of divisions and burdensome plantations in light of Ecuadorian competition, and the introduction of more capital-intensive production techniques, such as fumigation (Bulmer-Thomas, 1989: 202).

Agrarian activities naturally centered on the new export products, among which cotton, sugar, and beef were the most prominent. The importance of these activities was not only the result of the power of the bourgeois fractions associated with the same but the fact that they also "represented a logical response to capitalist modernization on the part of the State; in contrast to bananas, the new products were primarily controlled by nationals; in contrast to coffee, they all required substantial capital investment in processing installations with considerable scope for future integration. In this manner, not only did surplus capitalist labor remain in national hands, but the opportunities for accumulation within the sector were plentiful" (Bulmer-Thomas, 1989: 210).

These new products, especially cotton, provoked an important change in the type of agricultural unit and its relation with the two fundamental production factors: labor and land. Thus, the use of advanced technology, the higher capital to land ratio, and the increased rotation of capital invested in inputs meant the importance of these two factors became relative (PREALC, 1986: 143). This implied that in terms of employment (the topic covered by this analysis), apart from the jobs created during the respective processing phases, these activities' demands for labor were essentially seasonal.[23] Cotton and sugar cane were highly mechanized crops, and only cattle managed to generate permanent wage labor, albeit on a reduced scale.[24] Consequently, these activities emerged as mere complementary sources of employment and incomes for a labor force that was fundamentally involved in agriculture for domestic use. In this sense, the key to understanding how labor markets were structured within the Central American rural sector and what differences arose among the various national contexts is to analyze how the modernizing changes affected the most vulnerable agricultural sector: that of domestic use.

The background to these changes can be found in the relation between export agriculture, be it traditional or new, and this sector. Two factors that determined how this relation functioned have been identified for the 1950s.

On the one hand, there was increasing evidence of the double equation: export agriculture = large *fincas*, and agriculture for domestic use = small *fincas*. The exception was coffee in Costa Rica and Honduras;[25] the peculiarity of rice must also be mentioned as, although it responded to a domestic (and especially urban) demand, it developed on medium- and large-scale units. The difference between these two strata was evident in the link between the number of establishments and the percentage of land controlled: The large *fincas* (over 50 hectares), with hardly 6 percent of the total units, controlled 75 percent of the cultivated land whereas the small *fincas*, with 80 percent of the producers, possessed a mere 10 percent of the area. Although the modernization process resulted in the reduction, to a certain extent, of the average size of the large units, the percentage of land concentration increased slightly, implying a more rapid fragmentation of small properties; thus, the average extension between these two strata increased (PREALC, 1986: 145–153).

On the other hand, the 1950s were marked by a demographic explosion (increase in birth rates in some countries and decrease in mortality rates, especially that of infants, in the entire region). This demographic impact fundamentally affected small farmers, thereby increasing the pressure on land. That is, it further contributed to the fragmentation of the vulnerable sector.

This series of changes affected labor in a variety of ways. First, there was an increase in migration, which was correlated to the spatial mobilization of the labor force. In this sense, Bulmer-Thomas (1989: 212, 248–249) has pointed to the existence of two initial patterns. On the one hand, the dismissal of the labor force in areas taken over by the new export products provoked an increase in the flow of migration to the cities. This was the case in El Salvador and Nicaragua. In the remaining countries, on the other hand, migration was intrarural as it was marked by the seasonal nature of employment, mentioned beforehand. Later on, in the 1960s, the control of new lands for export agriculture meant this second pattern became less relevant and that, instead, migration to urban centers accelerated. Vilas (1994: 65) has pointed out the existence of different flows in this regard: the move toward agricultural frontier areas or cities, human settlements based on government projects, and temporary migration to agroexport areas. Second, the majority of the rural population could be classified as landless workers and *minifundistas* (small farming peasants), although these census categories disguised a wide variety of labor situations. In this respect, Torres-Rivas (1989: 146ff.) in his classical study on Central American social development identified five different situations: the *colonato* system, *aparcería* (share-cropping), day-laboring, the agricultural salary, and the peasant *minifundista* economy.

Third, the impact on agriculture for domestic use implied a significant increase in proletarianization along with subsequent impoverishment. In this sense, the exhaustion of the agricultural frontier led to differences arising between countries. Thus, whereas in Honduras and Nicaragua and, to a lesser extent, in Guatemala the peasantry benefited from the possibility of accessing new lands, this process was not possible either in El Salvador or Costa Rica.[26] Nonetheless, it is important to point out that while cotton seized the most productive lands from the peasantry, cattle farming expropriated marginal lands (Williams, 1986: 158–159). Therefore, the agricultural frontier did not constitute a secure peasant redoubt even in those countries where it had not yet been exhausted.

In relation to this process of proletarianization, it has been said that

> although it is not possible to underestimate the magnitude of permanent wage labor, especially in the cattle farming sector, there is no doubt that the capacity of the impoverished peasantry to find work outside the *finca* itself was linked to the cycle of agricultural tasks, which was highly seasonal. In this way, a process of proletarianization was developed in which the workers did not break their direct ties with the land, although the irregular access to these forced them to perform wage labor during certain periods, determined by the agricultural export sector's peak periods of labor demand.

Consequently, a structure was formed wherein the *minifundio* absorbed unemployment when wage labor services terminated and fixed labor reproduction conditions. (Vilas, 1994: 63)

All these changes induced by the impact modernization had on Central American agriculture and its labor have been clearly set out by PRE-
ALC, the Regional Program for Employees of Latin America and the
Caribbean (PREALC 1986: 166–184). In short, four phenomena should be
emphasized. In the first instance, the jobs created in the agricultural sector during this modernizing period were scarce. Second, the occupational
incorporation structure was maintained, as in the early 1980s, a little over
half of the labor force was working on small plots of land as family workers. Third, the modern sector (*fincas* devoted to export products) generated full employment for limited periods (between three and four
months according to the harvesting season), thereby demanding temporary labor. Surplus labor was returned to the traditional peasant sector,
which given its low productivity was well-known for its high underemployment. It is precisely this combination of temporary full employment
in the modern sector with high underemployment in the traditional sector that the PREALC analysis identifies as Central American agriculture's
major problem. Finally, the payment of permanent workers on the *fincas*
was not associated with the development of productivity but rather with
the conditions of a market influenced by the surplus supply of temporary
workers.[27] For their part, the latters' salaries, together with the diversification toward nonagricultural activities, served to attempt to compensate
for the decline in the peasants' incomes.

The second modernizing process to be discussed is that of industrialization. This followed the familiar model of import substitution. However, a series of characteristics are worth mentioning, albeit briefly.

First, this process took place within a framework of regional integration, which resulted in the creation of the Central American Common
Market. Emphasis must be placed, above all, on the fact that this did not
affect the interests of the agricultural exporting oligarchies because the
export products and the production of basic grains (wage goods in this
model) were not included in this integrating scheme; moreover, the customs tariffs on inputs for the exports were not altered (Bulmer-Thomas,
1989: 226). In other words, the industrialization process was integrated
into the prevailing accumulative model, making way, instead, for a combined redefinition of the same. Second, in addition to the context of regional integration, two other state mechanisms promoted this industrializing process. As in other Latin American countries—but with lower
ceilings—a protectionist framework was established for fostering this
sector. In addition, considerable financial incentives, based on the ex-

TABLE 2.5 Employment in Manufacturing Industry According to Handicraft
and Manufacturing Strata

Country and Year	Total (in thousands of employees)	Handicraft %	Manufacturing %
Guatemala			
1962	128.5	75.6	24.4
1968	152.7	70.9	29.1
1975	219.5	68.4	31.6
El Salvador			
1962	87.3	56.0	44.0
1968	101.8	53.9	46.1
1975	118.8	43.9	56.1
Honduras			
1962	44.9	65.9	34.1
1968	57.3	63.5	36.5
1975	78.7	53.2	46.8
Nicaragua			
1962	50.3	59.4	40.6
1968	65.8	55.0	45.0
1975	90.6	46.0	54.0
Costa Rica			
1962	40.9	46.0	54.0
1968	57.1	49.7	50.0
1975	90.6	45.9	53.9

SOURCE: PREALC (1986, table 21).

emption of imported raw materials and capital goods and on income tax,
were granted (Guerra-Borges, 1993: 38–39). Third, this industrialization
process was, from the outset, largely financed by external sources. This
implied a dominating presence of foreign investment. Moreover, the
geopolitical context, in which the Alliance for Progress had been established and guerrilla focal points had emerged in Guatemala and
Nicaragua, meant support was provided by the United States government for the Central American Common Market and, consequently, for
its industrial component (Bulmer-Thomas, 1989: 251–256).

Table 2.5 illustrates the development of industrial employment, making
a distinction between the handicraft sector and that of the manufacturer.

In the first instance, it must be stressed that in the early 1960s,
Guatemala and El Salvador were the two countries that from the point of
view of generating employment showed the highest level of industrial
development. In this regard, one must bear in mind that the first factories
to be set up in the region were established in Guatemala.[28] A second stage
of industrialization took place in this country, beginning at the time of
the revolution in 1944 and characterized by the installation of small na-

tional firms, brought about by the relative expansion of the domestic market both in urban as well as rural centers, namely on the south coast (Poitevin, 1977). With regard to El Salvador, the level of employment in the late 1940s has been estimated at 11,242 jobs created by 1,017 establishments, of which a mere 32 employed more than 50 individuals (Menjívar, 1982: table 5). Furthermore, in this first observation, the handicraft sector—which, as was to be expected, absorbed most of the labor—must be highlighted, especially in Guatemala's case. The Costa Rican exception should also be pointed out because the predominance of the manufacturing sector was yet another example of this country's greater level of modernity.

The manufacturing industry generated employment throughout the entire period in question, although the pace differed from country to country. In this respect, two interesting cases should be mentioned: that of Guatemala—the Central American country with the broadest industrial base—where despite the fact it was the early 1960s, jobs doubled; and Costa Rica, which showed the least development in terms of employment-generating activity, a phenomenon that was not disassociated from a more capital-intensive use of technology than that of other countries.[29] Finally, it has been noted that in spite of the industrializing process that took place in the 1960s, the handicraft sector does not appear to have been replaced to any significant extent by the manufacturing industry. Even in Guatemala during the mid-1970s, more than two thirds of the industrial labor force was employed in handicraft establishments. As a result, the figures, on the contrary, suggest that these two strata complemented one another. This phenomenon is a response to two factors: On the one hand, modern industry largely substituted imports from outside the region; and, on the other hand, the handicraft sector benefited from the urban development generated by industrialization (Bulmer-Thomas, 1989: 255).

This last observation raises the issue of how employment developed in the region's metropolitan centers, which were the true scenarios of this industrializing process. This phenomenon can be observed in Table 2.6.[30]

Attention must be drawn to the fact that during the two census intervals taken into consideration, all the centers' respective EAPs underwent a significant period of growth. In comparison with the national rates set out in the previous section, these urban areas proved themselves to be important employment-generating zones. Nevertheless, the lowest rate, corresponding to the Costa Rican capital in the 1950s, should be mentioned, as it demonstrated a certain measure of rural inertia on the part of this society; in addition, as mentioned previously, Guatemala City's rate suffered a deceleration in the 1960s. The same table illustrates the fact that in the 1970s, these metropolitan centers absorbed approximately one

TABLE 2.6 Employment in Metropolitan Areas

Indicators	Guatemala City[a]	San Salvador[b]	Tegucigalpa[c]	San Pedro Sula[d]	Managua[e]	San José[f]
EAP in 1950	107,866	70,485	n.a.	n.a.	36,605	56,534
Growth Rate in the 1950s	6.2	7.5	n.a.	n.a.	7.9	4.3
Growth Rate in the 1960s	3.0	6.4	7.9	6.6	6.9	6.9
% of Total EAP in the 1970s	16.5	18.1	13.1	8.5	22.7	25.6
% of Urban EAP in the 1970s	41.7	42.6	39.6	25.8	47.0	40.2

NOTES:

[a] Municipality of Guatemala for 1950 and 1964; capital city for 1973.

[b] San Salvador for 1950; district of San Salvador (urban area) for 1961 and 1971.

[c] Morazan district (urban area) for 1961; central district for 1974.

[d] Cortes district (urban area) for 1961; San Pedro Sula for 1974.

[e] Managua district (urban area) for 1950 and 1971; Managua City for 1983.

[f] Province of San José (urban area) for 1950, 1963, and 1973.

SOURCES: For the first census observation (in the 1950s), DGEC (1952) for Honduras 1950; DGEC (1954) for Nicaragua 1950; DGEC (1953) for Costa Rica 1950; DGEC (1953) for El Salvador 1950; DGEC (1957) for Guatemala 1950. For the second census observation (in the 1960s): DGEC (1963) for Honduras 1961; DGEC (1967) for Nicaragua 1963; DGEC (1966) for Costa Rica 1963; DGEC (1965) for El Salvador 1961; DGEC (1971) for Guatemala 1964. For the third census observation (in the 1970s): DGEC (1975) for Honduras 1974; DGEC (1974) for Nicaragua 1971; DGEC (1974) for Costa Rica 1973; DGEC (1977) for El Salvador 1971; DGEC (1975) for Guatemala 1973.

fifth of the work force of their respective country.[31] Only Guatemala showed a slightly lower percentage, demonstrating, as pointed out earlier, that the process of deruralization was less widespread there. However, in relation to the urban EAP, the Guatemalan capital tended to resemble the other capitals, with the exception of Managua, Nicaragua. This was indicative of the primacy of Guatemala City within its respective urban system, referred to earlier. That is, Guatemala demonstrated the highest concentration, in relative terms, within its metropolitan center of the urban employment generated.

This second stage of modernization, which gave rise to the illusion of a "golden age," as stated earlier, was short-lived. The crossbreed that originated from the fusion of industrialization and the primary-export model was faced with a series of constraints. The first of these concerned the need for a balanced industrial development among the countries in the region that would not affect the weaker of these. The tendency toward structural deficits related to interregional trade illustrated the failure of this attempt, which tragically materialized in the war between Honduras and El Salvador, resulting in the demise of this first effort at regional integration. Another constraint was imposed by the fall in value of exports, due to several causes in the second half of the 1960s, resulting in the familiar problems concerning the financing of imported inputs required by industry. Finally, this hybrid model adversely affected the distribution of incomes, thereby increasing impoverishment, especially in rural areas (Bulmer-Thomas, 1989: 256–258). Thus, the crisis that was to break out in the 1970s and that forms part of the historical context of the next chapter began to make itself felt.

Modernization and the Trade Union Movement

At the end of the previous chapter, reference was made to the fact that only the Honduran trade union movement had consolidated its position for confronting the modernization process. In the remaining Central American countries, the end of the oligarchic crisis had in a variety of ways resulted in a weakening of worker and peasant organizations. In this section four problematic aspects will be covered in order to analyze the development of the trade union movement during these decades.

The first of these deals with the international angle this development acquired as a result of the events that occurred in Guatemala in the first half of the 1950s and the beginning of the Cold War, which turned Central America into a confrontational arena in this regard.

Attention must be paid, above all, to the fact that continental trade unionist tendencies had been present in and had been influencing the region for some time. In this sense, the Latin American Workers Confederation (CLAT) and its historical leader, Vicente Lombardo, must be mentioned along with its influence on Costa Rica and, to a lesser extent, on Nicaragua. Emphasis must also be placed on the attempt to propagate Peronist ideals, which had a certain measure of success, mainly in Guatemala.[32] However, the onset of the Cold War meant the United States government seriously contemplated influencing the trade unionist organizations in the region. This attempt, the scope of which was continental, materialized in the late 1940s with the setting up of the Interamerican Workers Confederation by the American Foundation of Labor and anti-Communist Latin American organizations; however, the confederation was short-lived. In 1951 the Interamerican Regional Organization (ORIT) was formed; this entity, in comparison, had a major impact on Central America as well as other parts of Latin America during the subsequent decades.

The ORIT's first ally in the region was Costa Rica's Rerum Novarum, which as mentioned in the previous chapter was created by the Catholic Church to counteract the Communist influence of Costa Rica's trade union movement.[33] However, the new organization also influenced other Central American countries. Thus, in Guatemala it contributed, with the help of the Guatemalan Trade Union Council (CSG), to the above-mentioned trade union "reorganization" project proposed by the Castillo Armas government. Attempts at organization were also made in El Salvador in the 1950s, culminating in the formation of the General Trade Union Confederation (CGS) (Menjívar, 1985: 103). Even Nicaragua saw the rise of the United Trade Union Council (CUS) in 1962 (Villagra, 1980: 89–90). However, even more significant were the events that took place in Honduras—as already mentioned, this country's trade union movement was the most consolidated. Thus, from the moment the 1954 banana strike was coordinated, the Tela Railroad Workers Trade Union (SITRATERCO)—this country's most important union organization during these decades—was set up. The ORIT took part in its formation, thereby demonstrating that its influence dates back to the very beginning of Honduran trade union development (Meza, 1991: 100–101).[34]

A second aspect to be considered is that related to the development of labor rights, namely the codification of the benefits of modernization for the workers. With regard to this aspect, each national context is unique.

Thus, in the first instance, one must be reminded of the fact that starting from the previous period, with the exception of Honduras, all the countries had been passing labor legislation. However, among these, there were two countries in particular in which this kind of legislation had been developed to a greater extent. On the one hand, although in Costa Rica the outcome of the 1948 conflict meant political setbacks for trade union organizations, as described in the previous chapter, social achievements were valued. On the other hand, a different situation arose in Guatemala as a result of the fall of the Arbenz government. It may be said that during Castillo Armas's government a counterreform process took place in relation to labor. Thus, the business sectors that had participated in overthrowing Arbenz sought to minimize the labor rights that had been set down in the Constitution. However, the most significant aspect of this was the proclamation of two presidential decrees early in 1956 that restricted the right to form a trade union to strictly corporative purposes and limited the right to strike to the private sector; furthermore, public-sector worker organizations were banned. Nonetheless, the "reorganized" trade unions themselves assumed the defense of the labor code, thereby illustrating—early on—the constraints of co-opting the running of trade unions (Witzel, n.d.: 48ff.). This implied that this regression would not lead to a return to the period prior to 1944. In effect, the urban and banana enclave workers were able to maintain some of their acquired rights, and the social security system continued to operate, increasing its coverage, which by the late 1950s included almost 25 percent of the work force, a percentage similar to that of Costa Rica (Bulmer-Thomas, 1989: 218).

With regard to El Salvador, it is important to stress the slow reorganization of the trade union movement throughout the 1940s, in which the Workers Trade Union Reorganization Committee (CROS), later declared illegal, played a key role (Lungo, 1987: 44–45). However, this effort at reorganization meant that a series of social rights for workers were set down in the Salvadoran Constitution. These were included in the Constitution's chapter titled "Labor and Social Security"; moreover, at the same time, other laws were passed such as that of workers' unions, collective contracts, holidays, and so on. (Guido Béjar, 1990: n20). This process culminated in the passing of the labor code in 1963. In respect to Nicaragua, in the early 1960s, the Somoza regime granted some concessions, such as the proportional payment of the seventh working day and holidays or the establishment of minimum wages, which were, by and large, not applied (Gutiérrez Mayorga, 1985: 240). Without a doubt, Nicaragua allowed the most limited social achievements to workers, due, in equal measure, to the strength of the Somoza regime and the limited and weak development of the labor movement.

However, it was in Honduras that the trade union movement obtained major achievements during this new period. First, an immediate effect of the 1954 strike was the creation of a Labor Secretariat in the following year and the passing of a series of decrees with a tendency toward regulating labor relations, among which the Labor Guarantees Constitutive Charter was prominent. This was the immediate background to the labor code that was passed in 1959 and that constituted a second, more far-reaching, effect of the banana strike (Meza, 1991: 103–104). Another important period was that of the military reform of the 1970s. Two important decree laws must be mentioned in this regard: on the one hand, the creation of the Honduran Professional Training Institute; and on the other hand, the obligatory payment of all workers subject to collective contracts, regardless of whether they were trade union members. This second decree satisfied one of the main demands of the Honduran labor movement (Meza, 1991: 148).

The growth of the trade union organizations is a third aspect that should be taken into account. It can be said that on the whole, the modernization process aided the increase in the number of trade unions in all of Central America. This process was not an automatic response to economic changes but was also a result of the formation of correlations of political forces in each country.

In Guatemala between 1954 and 1978, 138 urban associations and organizations were set up (Witzel, n.d.; annex 3). Over one third of these were recognized between 1966 and 1970 by the so-called Third Revolutionary Government presided over by Méndez Montenegro. This expansion was due to factors of both an economic nature (industrialization and its urbanizing effects) and a political one (weakening of the postrevolutionary governments' strategy to co-opt the trade union movement and a certain level of openness on the part of the government). It must be added that Catholic-orientated trade unionism played a fundamental role in this growth. Youth groups constituted the basis of the National Workers Center (CNT), formed in 1968, which with the help of its federations organized the majority of trade unions created in the late 1960s and early 1970s (Levinson-Estrada, 1994: 80ff.).

El Salvador registers an increase from 78 trade unions comprising 25,917 members in 1962 to 127 organizations with 64,186 members thirteen years later (Menjívar, 1985: table 7). This increase was disputed among the two main trade union confederations that emerged during this period. Thus, the above-mentioned government-orientated CGS had 46 trade unions in 1960, a figure that had reached 67 by 1970. On the other hand, the General Workers Confederation of El Salvador (CGTS), founded in 1957 and influenced by the Communists, covered up to 40 trade unions; it later became part of the Salvadoran United Trade Union Federation (FUSS) (Flores Macal, 1980: 18). In the mid-1970s the government-orientated CGS comprised the most trade unions: approximately one third of the total number of organizations (Menjívar, 1985: table 10).[35]

Concerning Honduras, it is important to mention the creation in 1964 of the Workers Confederation of Honduras (CTH), sponsored by the ORIT, which was set up in the first major confederation on a national scale. In addition to being made up of the main workers' organizations, the CTH incorporated the country's most powerful peasant organization in the National Peasants' Association of Honduras (ANACH) (Meza, 1991: 129–130). The founding of the Social-Christian orientated General Workers Confederation (CGT) should also be mentioned. In the early 1970s, and in particular starting from the military reform process of 1972, a significant increase in organizations and memberships took place. Thus, the above-mentioned decree of obligatory payment implied a considerable increase in this respect. Between 1972 and 1975, 55 new trade unions were registered, which meant that by this date 131,377 workers were members; furthermore, it is estimated that the above-mentioned ANACH grouped together 80,000 peasant families (Meza, 1991: 153–154).

In Nicaragua this growth was much more modest. In the 1970s approximately ten trade union confederations were formed, although this term should not, in truth, be applied to all of these because some could hardly lay claim to a single organization. They had a wide variety of tendencies, ranging from Somoza- to Sandinista-orientated, including the ORIT and the socialist and Communist parties (Gutiérrez Mayorga, 1985: table 5).

In Costa Rica the trade union crisis extended to 1965, the year in which the number of organizations began to increase. At the end of that decade the labor movement recovered somewhat, due to a number of factors: failure to meet certain basic needs; disillusionment of expectations provoked by industrialization, rise of other popular movements, and change of attitude on the part of the Ministry of Labor regarding trade unions (Aguilar, 1989: 168–170). Between 1970 and 1976, 239 trade union organizations were created, bringing the number registered in 1976 to 393. This increase took place in all branches of the economy, though it was undoubtedly in the service sector and, in particular, the public sector that this growth was most noticeable. Thus, whereas in 1963 there were 40 organizations in this area with a total of 5,082 members, these figures had risen to 114 and 31, 263 respectively in 1976 (Rojas Bolaños, 1985: 278). Three new trade union confederations emerged during these decades. In the first instance, the Costa Rican Democratic Workers Confederation (CCTD), which defined itself as of a Social-Democrat tendency, was founded in 1966. Second, as of 1962, a trade unionism with a Christian-Democrat bias began its first attempts at organization, which culminated ten years later in the emergence of the Costa Rican Workers Confederation (CTC). In addition, as a result of a split in the CCTD, the Authentic Democratic Workers Confederation (CATD), which also described itself as Social-Democrat, was set up in 1971 (Donato and Rojas, 1987).

Nevertheless, despite this growth, trade unionism's influence on the world of work in Central America was very limited. It has been estimated that in 1973 the highest level of trade union activity corresponded to Costa Rica, with a mere 11 percent of the labor force, followed by Honduras, with a rate of almost 9 percent; however, the social basis of this affiliation differed: It was urban and state-related in the first country and rural in the second. In El Salvador, despite the development of trade unionism in the urban sphere, trade union coverage represented a mere 5 percent of the workers at that time. In Guatemala and Nicaragua the rates of trade union coverage were insignificant, even registering a decrease in Nicaragua that by 1973 had fallen to 2 percent (Bulmer-Thomas, 1989: 259–260). That is, despite the growth it had undergone as a result of modernization, the trade union movement was a long way from representing the interests of the working masses.

The final issue to be taken into account is that of the type of trade union activity developed during the decades of modernization. In this respect, there are various aspects to be considered.

First, it must be stressed that the strike was established as the uppermost instrument of trade union action. In this manner, strike action was very limited in Guatemala between 1954 and 1970; only the major union organizations had the capacity to confront the business sector's reluctance to negotiate. Nonetheless, in the late 1960s, labor conflicts arose in both the public and industrial sector and, above all, in the field of transport. Between 1972 and 1974, major strikes were held as a result of the increase in the cost of living (Witzel, n.d.: 327–359, 378–409).

However, it was following the devastating earthquake of 1976 that, as we shall see further on, trade union action not only increased but also became more radical. In El Salvador, a total of 15 strikes were registered between 1974 and 1977, mobilizing over five thousand workers and obtaining varying results (Menjívar, 1985: table 12). Guido Béjar (1990: 61–66 and table 3), in his more historical perspective, has specified different intervals between 1957 and 1981 in relation to strike action in El Salvador. Thus, little activity was registered for the periods 1957–1966 and 1973–1976, whereas intense disputes occurred between 1967–1972 and, above all, 1977–1981; 208 strikes mobilizing a total of 88,708 workers were recorded for this latter period.[36] The 1965 strike in Honduras is important for two reasons: It represented the recovery of the workers' movement following the suppression it had suffered after the *coup d'état* in 1963, but it resulted in the major transferal of the central zone, which had always been subjected to action undertaken on the northern coast, especially in the banana enclave (Meza, 1991: 131–134).

In Costa Rica the trade union movement is said to have been relatively active between 1950 and 1962; up until 1958, 107 collective conflicts, 15 stoppages, and 16 strikes had been registered, half of which were held in the banana sector (Rojas Bolaños, 1985: 276).[37] It is worth stressing that this is the only sector in which a process of trade union unity, which strengthened the belligerent capacity of these workers, took place and where the right to strike was secured. This union progress in the 1950s occurred in the Pacific zone and represented the high point of trade unionism in Costa Rica's banana sector. However, in the following decade it met with strong resistance from employers supported by the state; this, together with internal problems, led to its decline. In the 1960s, trade union developments in the banana sector were transferred to the Atlantic region, where a rekindling of trade union activity was registered in the area in which, decades before, the first trade union organizations had been established (Aguilar, 1989: 124–129, 154–161). In addition, between 1972 and 1980 a significant increase in labor conflicts meant 173 strikes were reported; some of these were particularly relevant due to the type of institution involved (Costa Rican Social Security Institute, Costa Rican Electricity Institute, etc.), whose demands centered on the recognition of trade union guarantees and wage increases (Rojas Bolaños, 1980: 77–80).[38]

Even in Nicaragua, the country with the slowest trade union development, the years 1973 and 1974 are mentioned as those in which various stoppages occurred, mobilizing up to 30,000 workers; and, above all, emphasis has been placed on the fact that strikes were used systematically in an attempt to make labor demands heard, implying a qualitative change compared to the previous period (Gutiérrez Mayorga, 1985: 237–238).

This phenomenon is not unrelated to the process of radicalization that affected the region's trade union movement on the whole and that represented a second aspect that should be taken into account. In Guatemala the National United Trade Union Committee (CNUS) was formed by the Social Christian headquarters in the heat of the Coca-Cola labor dispute, which was to achieve considerable international renown. This organization was not a result of programmatic unity but was rather a response to specific problems faced by the workers: defense of collective negotiations as a mechanism for preventing wage decreases, and the right to set up legally recognized trade unions (CITGUA, 1989: 60; Witzel, n.d.: 436). The creation of the CNUS demonstrated the unity of independent labor forces in the aftermath of the devastating earthquake of February 1976— a natural disaster that had a major impact on the living conditions of popular sectors and that left no doubt as to the social divide that existed in this country (Balcárcel, 1985: 54–55; Levinson-Estrada, 1994: 124–131). In addition, the rise of the Peasant Unity Committee (CUC) must be mentioned, for it played an important role in the years of violence. This radicalization took place during the Laugerud presidency, which was the least repressive of the military authoritarian governments; Kjell Laugerud implemented a policy involving a certain level of political openness that sought legitimacy in order to compensate for the fraudulent elections by which he had obtained the presidency. In the mid-1970s in El Salvador the confrontations involving the trade unions versus the business sector and the state intensified. In this sense, trade union action became more radical, subjecting union organizations to political ones and relegating reformist tendencies within the Salvadoran trade union movement (Guido Béjar, 1990: 82–83). In Honduras, the influence of the ORIT within the SITRATERCO, the main trade unionist organization in the country, was distanced (Posas, 1980: 45–46). In Nicaragua, Sandinista ideals started to gain popularity among the workers, especially those in rural areas. Moreover, the Costa Rican Communists once again began to exert an influence on their country's trade union movement.

The background to this insistence on the use of strike action includes one of the basic factors in labor relations: wage developments. This is the third aspect to be considered. Table 2.7 illustrates the development of minimum wages in three of the countries in the region, making a distinction between those granted in the agricultural and industrial sectors. Emphasis must first be placed on the fact that due to the extensive openness of its economies, the region was subjected to a high level of imported inflation, which affected prices at the national level; an increase in world prices and the oil crisis, in particular, were the factors that gave rise to this process (Bulmer-Thomas, 1989: 267–268). As Table 2.7 shows, Costa Rica tended to differ from the other national contexts, illustrating the fact that it was the only country with an active minimum wage policy (PREALC, 1986: 84). Therefore, although agricultural wages fluctuated during the first years of the period observed, they tended to rise as of 1973; this tendency was more apparent in the industrial sector. In comparison, El Salvador shows a downward trend, which became more acute as of 1974 with regard to both branches of activity. However, the most obvious case of a decline in wages over the course of time corresponds to Guatemala.[39]

In addition to this study on the development of these types of wages, several characteristics pertaining to the Central American wage structure may be identified. First, an inverted association between the level of schooling and the distribution of wages has been detected. Second, the average wage in the industrial sector tended to coincide with the national average. Third, the same coincidence occurred in regard to the average salary of the national average level of schooling. Fourth, the differences between this average wage and the wages of the skilled work force were greater in countries with lower levels of education. Fifth, there were considerable differences between average urban salaries and average agricultural wages, which were located at the bottom of the wage structure (PREALC, 1986: 88–93).

The last aspect to be considered concerns the relation between the trade union movement and the state, a major problem not only for the region but also for the rest of Latin America.[40] With regard to Central America,

TABLE 2.7   Development of Real Monthly Minimum Wages in Selected
Countries, 1965–1977 (Constant Prices for Each Country)

Year	Guatemala[a]		El Salvador[b]		Costa Rica[c]	
	Agriculture	Industry	Agriculture	Industry	Agriculture	Industry
1965	—	97	72	165	261	—
1966	—	100	73	180	260	494
1967	—	102	72	186	257	531
1968	—	104	70	190	254	575
1969	—	106	70	192	265	585
1970	—	104	68	193	259	607
1971	—	105	66	195	270	673
1972	—	105	67	192	267	653
1973	—	92	68	193	258	638
1974	25.6	80	68	185	261	602
1975	22.7	73	62	143	266	580
1976	20.5	72	67	171	306	657
1977	18.2	68	63	145	332	714

NOTES:
[a] Quetzals
[b] Salvadoran colones
[c] Costa Rican colones
SOURCE: PREALC (1986, table 16).

this relation was set—in the 1970s—within two processes that were noted
in the previous analysis. On the one hand, there was the issue of incon-
clusive proletarianization in the agricultural sector along with increased
impoverishment.[41] On the other hand, there was a growing decrease in
payments. In this respect, Bulmer-Thomas (1989: 290–295) has pointed
out that the state's response was fourfold: support for the creation of cooperatives, a minimum wage policy, social security programs, and agrarian reform. The emphases on these actions varied from country to country.

In almost the entire region, the 1970s witnessed the growth of the cooperative movement, which had already been promoted in the previous
decade within the framework of the Alliance for Progress strategy. In effect, around 1963 there were 327 cooperatives in Central America, with a
total of 32,267 associates; ten years later these figures had increased to
1,361 and 203,906, respectively. Three countries were highlighted in the
1970s: Costa Rica, Guatemala, and Honduras.[42] It must also be stressed
that processes of unification occurred during this decade, which resulted
in the creation of coordinating entities related to this movement. In Costa
Rica, agricultural cooperativism began, as was to be expected, in the coffee sector, but it rapidly overwhelmed it. This type of cooperativism in-

fluenced employment in a more direct manner.[43] In Guatemala the fall of Arbenz implied a regression of the cooperativism that had been generated by agrarian reform, and it was not until the 1970s that this phenomenon made a strong comeback. However, the role played by Acción Católica (Catholic Action) in Guatemala must be emphasized as it undoubtedly constituted the leading force in cooperativist activity, especially in the indigenous *Altiplano* (highlands). This was later to have important political consequences on the period of violence, for it implied the modernization of the communities, and it was precisely the agents who had contributed to this development who were responsible for initiating a process of awareness regarding social inequalities at the national level. It must also be pointed out that in Honduras in the mid-1960s, the practical application of the type of model implicit in its first agrarian reform—that of 1962—began to be modified. The origins of this change included the success of the *Guanchías Limitada* agricultural cooperative set up in 1965 by peasants who had formerly been wage workers on the banana plantations. This experience represented the model responsible for the spread of cooperativist collectivism, which managed to embed itself in the heart of the Honduran Agrarian Reform Cooperatives Federation (FECORAH). This growth was reinforced in the 1970s with the second agrarian reform, enacted by the military reformist government (Posas, 1989: 46–47).

With regard to minimum wage policies, as seen earlier, the only Central American country that may be said to have had an active policy that even took agricultural wages into account was Costa Rica. In the remaining countries, it appears to be rather the developments of respective labor markets that determined wage levels.

In Guatemala and, above all, in Costa Rica, social security coverage was most significant. In the 1970s this coverage became more extensive with regard to the latter country, reaching up to 60 percent of the labor force by the end of the decade. Guatemala also experienced an increase, which boosted its coverage to 30 percent in 1978, although this level began to decrease after this date. It is important to point out that the social security system in Honduras developed considerably, and by the late 1970s it had reached a level of coverage similar to that in Guatemala. In the remaining countries, social security coverage was very low, even in urban areas.

In Central America, the modernization process, supported by the Alliance for Progress, did not succeed in implementing any far-reaching agrarian reform experience. The efforts made in this respect, which had been proposed in the previous decade, had come to a standstill in Nicaragua by the 1970s. In El Salvador an attempt was made in 1976, but this was aborted due to resistance by the landowners. Moreover, agricultural modernization focused more on developing agriculture for internal consumption, namely that of basic grains, based on large *fincas* (Bulmer-Thomas, 1989: 290–295). In Guatemala, the extension of the agricultural frontier on the northern transversal border essentially served to make senior military figures into landowners, thereby even further impeding the possibilities of applying agrarian reforms there. In Costa Rica, the exhausting of this border resulted in a considerable reactivation of the peasant movement in the later 1960s in the form of land encroachment.[44] The outcome was a more collectivist approach to production by means of self-management community firms. However, this model was questioned by the change in state policy in the mid-1970s, which succeeded in lowering peasant mobilization on the basis of three courses of action: increased public investment, redefinition of institutions, and a return to the division of land into plots (Menjívar, Kam, and Portuguéz, 1985: 451–461). It was in Honduras that the most serious attempts at land redistribution were made. One must bear in mind the agricultural reform of the early 1960s, the scope of which was limited by the military government established in 1963—although it must not be forgotten that in practice, as mentioned earlier, the cooperatives experienced a significant process of growth. However, the second military regime of the 1970s, which had reformist tendencies, promoted this development. Thus, the law decree on leasing, which benefited the peasantry because it imposed a system of obligatory leasing, was passed, followed by new traditionalist legislation in 1975. Although this benefited a minority within the peasantry, it shifted the emphasis from the division of land into plots to a collective approach to production (Posas, 1989: 48).

Consequently, from the point of view of labor, the Central American context in the 1970s was a dangerously tense one because the majority of impoverished peasants were unable to access land and because wages tended to decrease as a result of growing inflation. To this must be added the radical approach adopted by trade union leaders. The state's response to this situation was crucial in terms of the political standpoint assumed during the crisis in the 1980s. Thus, both Costa Rica and Honduras had possibilities of institutionalizing the conflicts. In the first case, one must take into account the less polarized socioeconomic structure and, above all, the authentic social policy developed by the state, as seen earlier, in regard to minimum wages and social security. In this sense, one may speak of the development of a true welfare state, although this was not based on a productivity pact such as that of the European social democrat model but rather on a political client-based approach of a populist nature. Reformist developments had been imposed in Honduras, and besides being linked to the force of the labor movement, these were accepted by the military itself, which played a key role in that country's modernization process.[45] In contrast, in the remaining countries, the political system maintained a detached position, making it impossible for social demands to be met. As Bulmer-Thomas(1989: 295) has clearly pointed out,

> The difference between the two groups of countries is, therefore, very surprising. The state did not bother to stimulate the workers movement in any of the republics, although in Costa Rica and Honduras the new working class militants provoked a policy of convenience interrupted by occasional periods of suppression. In the remaining republics, the new militancy met with extreme hostility and suppression, although in Guatemala there was a period of ambiguity during Kjell Laugerud's presidency (1974–1978). The hostility of the state towards the labor movement in El Salvador, Guatemala and Nicaragua drove the worker organizations over to the left and forced some of them to join small revolutionary groups that emerged in the 1970s. . . . This alliance boosted the influence of the revolutionary movements in El Salvador and Guatemala enormously, although in Guatemala this was counteracted by the fierce suppression unleashed by the Lucas García administration (1978–1982)."

Notes

1. In this sense, this author is right to suggest the relevance of the term oligarchy "for conceptualizing these groups that combined traditional values with remarkable economic vision, in that it covers the wide array of dimensions that result in a class identity: the economic field, undoubtedly—and above all the large landowner properties—but also politics, ideology, education, lifestyles, historical continuity. . . . From an oligarchic point of view, we are dealing with a legitimate superiority that is not only economic and political, but above all, historical, cultural and racial; the exercising of political power is a product of this superiority and is legitimized by it" (Vilas, 1994: 89).

2. This implies that the indicators are not identical to those used in the previous chapter even though they refer to the same phenomena. Furthermore, the year 1950 is considered a census observation. This comment is also applicable to the next table.

3. The high growth rate for Nicaragua is due, above all, to the difference in category span between the two census observations, which dropped from age 14 to age 10. This naturally resulted in an increase in the number of students. However, it is assumed this indicator's growth rate was higher (although not to a great extent) than that of the overall EAP.

4. This country's high rate appears to be related to the difference in span between the two census observations already mentioned in regard to the inactive student population. However, a comparison between these two tendencies indicates that a significant number of young women were incorporated in the labor market to the detriment of their schooling.

5. This minus sign refers to the peculiarity of the data in this country's 1950 census mentioned in the previous chapter. Rates of female participation, classified in a similar manner (age 10 and over), indicate that Guatemala and Honduras were the only countries in which there was no increase between 1950 and 1960. Increases were registered for the other countries, in particular El Salvador, where this rate reached the highest level (16.1 percent) in the region for 1960 (PREALC, 1986, table 8).

6. Increasing the EAP in the case of the new female labor force and simultaneously decreasing the inactive population, if this labor already formed part of the population of working age.

7. Furthermore, in these three cases it is possible that the schooling of the potential work force could have had a gender bias, whereby young males were favored to the detriment of the women.

8. Such an abrupt increase for Costa Rica points to the existence of methodological problems regarding the data provided by the 1963 census, which shows an overrepresentation of the inactive population. However, the direction of this tendency is not disputed.

9. Costa Rica showed a growth rate of the inactive population for the period 1950–1973 of 2.0 percent, which was below the 4.0 percent registered for that of the student population.

10. This country presents methodological problems similar to those already mentioned regarding the inactive student population. Nonetheless, the low growth rate of the female EAP in the second interval of the census indeed suggests a deceleration of this tendency.

11. This variable is included in this table and not the following because the spatial factor corresponds to the workers' place of residence and not to their place of work.

12. The occupational category that underwent the greatest change in the first census interval was that of unpaid family workers. This phenomenon has already been mentioned in the previous chapter, in which it was explained in terms of methodological aspects.

13. However, the peculiarities of this country's 1950 census must be remembered along with the importance, in this particular case, of unpaid family work.

14. The data concerning these percentages for the last census observation may be found in Table 2.4 and to the tables corresponding to 1950 in the previous chapter.

15. In effect, this group represented less than 1.0 percent of the total EAP at that time.

16. These correspond to those identified by PREALC, which in my opinion provided the most accurate analysis of the problems of segmentation. It must be pointed out that both the formal (urban) and modern (agricultural) sectors involve the use of wage labor whereas the traditional (agricultural) and informal (urban) sectors represent individual or family units. In accordance with the criteria used by PREALC itself, this implies an underrepresentation of the informal sector because small businesses are not taken into account.

17. It is important to mention that in this country, the process of formalization was due to a large extent to the expansion of public employment, which between 1950 and 1985 increased at an annual rate of 6.7 percent (PREALC, 1986: 80).

18. The first column of this table contains the rate of growth for each country of the variable corresponding to the modernizing trend estimated for the two census intervals dealt with in the previous tables. The second column demonstrates the relative importance of each variable with regard to the inactive population in the case of schooling and in relation to the EAP for the remaining variables. (Aspects such as wage labor, professionalization, and tertiary labor should be calculated in relation to the employed population; however, to be consistent with the other variables and with previous tables, these have been estimated in relation to the EAP). Thus, an attempt is made to combine the direction of each trend with its relative importance for the end of the period in question.

19. The tendency toward rejuvenation has not been considered in this table. However, this tendency demonstrates that labor was not modernized in the sense that the older age groups within the work force could retire from the labor market at an earlier date. Nonetheless, the importance of this age group (65 and over) in the period around the 1970s was marginal in that it varied between 3.3 percent in Honduras and 4.1 percent in El Salvador.

20. This is based on Bulmer-Thomas's (1989) sectorial analysis proposal, which undoubtedly constitutes the most accurate interpretation of current economic development in Central America.

21. It has been said that in El Salvador, the nontechnological segment of the coffee sector that was required was 0.38 persons per hectare per year; this doubled to 0.86 after new technology had been introduced (PREALC, 1977: 321).

22. It should be pointed out that in Honduras this late development should be traced back to the persistence of the *ejidal* (tenant farming) properties that the weak state system made no attempt to suppress in the first decades of the present century, as had occurred in other countries in the region (Williams, 1994: 138ff.).

23. However, with respect to cotton, it has been argued that the payment of low salaries became a competitive factor for Central America (Guerra-Borges, 1993: 28). In Guatemala's case (which could be applied to the other countries), Baumeister (1993: 122) has stressed this crop's high level of seasonal labor, which is above that of coffee. For an analysis of the proletarianization induced by the cotton export sector, see Williams (1986: 60–67).

24. Conservative estimates indicate that cotton generates six times more employment per acre than cattle farming; sugar generates seven times more; and coffee, thirteen times more (Williams, 1986: 117).

25. The historical importance of family property in Costa Rica's coffee sector has already been referred to in the previous chapter. With regard to Honduras, Baumeister (1994: 439–441) has proposed the hypothesis that the displacement of peasants from the lowlands due to the expansion of cattle farming could have led them to grow coffee in the highlands, where this proved a more profitable activity than the production of basic grains.

26. With regard to the latter country, reference has been made to the fact that between 1950 and 1973, agricultural workers underwent a unequivocal process of proletarianization that became more pronounced in the 1960s due to the exhaustion of the agricultural frontier, which represented the main mechanism for *recampesinización* in Costa Rica (Rodríguez, 1993: 53).

27. Hintermeister (1982: 41) argues that in Guatemala, when there was a surplus supply of labor, the salaries of these permanent workers tended to be on a par with the level of income obtained in subsistence agriculture.

28. The Cantel textile factory, close to Quezaltenango, deserves to be highlighted. This factory, established in 1883, was the subject of an interesting study by Nash (1970) in the 1950s concerning its interaction with the local community, comprised mainly of indigenous members.

29. In effect, labor productivity in Costa Rica's manufacturing industry became the highest in the region, surpassing even that of Guatemala (PREALC, 1986: table 21). However, one must not lose sight of the fact that the rate at which jobs were created in El Salvador's manufacturing industry, as mentioned in the previous section, declined. This occurred in its manufacturing sector and, more specifically, in the so-called small business segment (establishments employing between 5 to 19 persons) (PREALC, 1977: 155–157).

30. This table includes the five capitals in the region, to which San Pedro Sula has been added in the case of Honduras. This addition is justified for two reasons: On the one hand, the Honduran urban system has a dual primacy, and on the other hand, it is this city that constitutes the true economic capital where the majority of the industrial sector is based.

31. In Honduras's case, both cities are considered jointly.

32. This phenomenon also occurred in Costa Rica, where it was conceived as a result of a split in the CCTRN, giving rise to the formation of the National Workers Confederation (CNT)—which did not, however, develop beyond its founding organizations and, moreover, was short-lived (Aguilar, 1989: 89–91).

33. In this regard, one must bear in mind that from 1952 to 1955, Luis Alberto Monge, the former leader of the CCTRN, was secretary general of the ORIT.

34. See Posas (1990: 29ff.) for an account of the ORIT's influence on the SITRATERCO.

35. Within this process of organizational growth, reference must be made to events that occurred in the agricultural sector. Since the 1960s, the Catholic Church had been encouraging peasant organizations; this process culminated in the founding of the Christian Federation of Salvadoran Peasants (FECCAS) in 1965. At its third congress, held in 1969, the organization proposed the following as the main points in its policy: integral agrarian reform, trade union freedom, unity of workers, and development of cooperativism. In this manner, its radical orientation was hinted at (Lungo, 1987: 64).

36. Lungo (1987: 93ff.) considers the period 1976–1980 the "fundamental years" for understanding the war and the nature of the popular struggles of the 1980s. These five years not only witnessed a consolidation of trade unionism but also saw the urban workers of San Salvador begin to organize themselves. However, it was essentially the farm workers (poor peasants, subordinate middling peasants, and the agrarian proletariat) who became the protagonists in popular sectors and who later comprised the social basis for revolt.

37. In the early 1950s Costa Rican workers resorted to action aimed at obtaining the signing of collective conventions, a right included in the labor code but that had not been put into effect. However, this mechanism was only applied in

the urban sphere, and moreover, it was ultimately controlled by the entrepreneurs (Aguilar, 1989: 95–99).

38. For a detailed analysis of trade union action (in terms of collective work conventions, conflicts of an economic and social nature, and strikes) in the 1970s see Donato and Rojas (1987: 53ff.).

39. Bulmer-Thomas (1989: table x.7) presents data on real urban and rural salaries corresponding to the 1970s, which confirm the tendencies noted. Moreover, information is also available regarding Honduras and Nicaragua. In the former, urban wages underwent a significant decline as of 1974, although they had recovered by the end of the decade. In Nicaragua, this same type of salary was eroded with the passing of time in contrast to rural salaries, which tended to increase slightly.

40. With regard to Costa Rica, Donato and Rojas (1987: 70ff.) have made an in-depth analysis of the labor policy of the 1970s and, in particular, those of the Figueres and Oduber governments. The authors describe the move from policies of negotiation to government censure and the suppression of the trade union movement.

41. A proletarianization that in regard to cotton implied a transformation of the old client type personalized relations between landowner and peasant due to the rise of the company boss, whose only obligation was the payment of wages (Williams, 1986: 156–157).

42. In the first country the number of cooperatives corresponded to 269 and that of associates to 76,858; in Guatemala and Honduras, the respective figures were as follows: 512 and 55,552, and 258 and 36,681 (ACI, 1991: table 7).

43. The 1970s-in particular, 1972 to 1978—was a period in which technology was introduced to agrarian cooperatives. Later, when the country was submerged in the crisis, the state promoted the creation of self-management cooperatives as a means of mitigating the growing number of disputes in the short term and attempting to reactivate production in the midterm (Mora, 1987: 219, 175).

44. These infringements were carried out by the so-called *precarista* movements, which in some cases were instigated by trade union organizations (Mora, 1992: 28).

45. In effect, this force was recognized by López Arellano as early as in 1963, when he described the moderate trade union movement and the armed forces as the country's "two new powers" for promoting modernization (Meza, 1991: 127).

3

More Than a Lost Decade:
The Crisis and Labor Adjustments

In the second half of the 1970s, Central America was already beginning to feel the effects of a decline in its economic growth, which foreshadowed an important crisis. The latter made itself known in the early 1980s throughout the entire region, although a distinction must be made between three types of situations (Pérez Sáinz, 1994a: 18–21).

The first is exemplified by Honduras and Costa Rica, in which a shift from a period of decline in the first half of the decade to one of relative growth in the second half of the 1980s transpired; this process is more apparent in Costa Rica, which suffered a deep recession in 1982. The opposite occurred in Nicaragua. Evidence of growth in the first half of the decade turned into a period of recession in the latter half. It could be said that among the factors that may explain these two different modes of development, the ones related to politics appear to have been particularly relevant. In this regard, one must bear in mind that neither Costa Rica nor Honduras were directly involved in armed conflict, and that, on the contrary, they benefited from their geopolitical condition. This is clearly evident in the case of Honduras, where economic activity was influenced, during the latter half of the decade, by the massive inflow of external resources, especially U.S. aid. This was the payment it received for aligning with the Reagan and Bush administrations' regional policies. Nicaragua, in contrast, suffered the ravages of a low-intensity war, which meant that following the reconstruction process at the beginning of the decade, the country was forced to develop a war economy. This, along with the economic errors made by the *Sandinista* government, provoked the deep recession in the latter half of the decade.

Guatemala and El Salvador represented an intermediate position in which they succeeded in overcoming the period of inactivity and recession. In this respect, it must be remembered that both countries, just like Nicaragua, had been affected by armed conflict. The recovery that took place in the second half of the decade responded to different causes. In Guatemala's case, it corresponded to the virtues of the Christian Democrat government's first stabilizing plan, although in the midterm this initiative came to nothing. In regard to El Salvador, it may be said that the slight recovery demonstrated that the economy had adapted to the conflict situation in which external aid and remittances played a key role.

With regard to social issues, the 1980s was a period of sharp decline. Thus, in terms of the development of the Gross Domestic Product (GDP) per inhabitant, during the first half of the decade all the countries had negative rates—including Costa Rica, which in the previous period of modernization had experienced considerable social developments. Nonetheless, during the second five-year period, this country recovered; and Honduras, for its part, showed inactivity in regard to this indicator. However, in the other countries, the rates remained negative, and social decline worsened. Nicaragua should be mentioned in this respect, as this nation's economic crisis in the second quinquennium had a dramatic social impact (Pérez Sáinz, 1994a: 23). These tendencies are confirmed by the fact that in all the countries, consumption per inhabitant decreased in the last decade, resulting in a decline comparable only to that provoked by the 1930s crisis (Bulmer-Thomas, 1989: 334).

Consequently, it is not surprising that around the mid-1980s, almost three quarters of the population in Central America were poverty-stricken, and half were living in conditions of extreme poverty. Sectors such as the child, indigenous, and rural populations and those made up of individuals employed in more hazardous working environments—such as subsistence agriculture and the informal urban sector—were the most vulnerable in this respect. However, in terms of impoverishment, the region appeared to be divided. On the one hand, in Costa Rica less than half the population found themselves impoverished; on the other hand, in the remaining countries impoverishment affected over two thirds of the population—and in Honduras, El Salvador, and Guatemala, over three quarters were impoverished (Menjívar and Trejos, 1992). This division responds not only to the intensity of the crisis and the form it assumed in each country but also to the type of modernization that took place beforehand. Thus, Costa Rica is well known for its broad middle sectors and, in particular, for the development of state policies aimed at mitigating social deficiencies. In contrast, in the other countries there was a greater socioeconomic divide during these decades, and social action on the part of the state was very limited (PREALC, 1986).

Nevertheless, the crisis in the 1980s did not only have economic and social repercussions, as was the case in the rest of Latin America. What sets Central America apart is that from a political point of view, the crisis intensified to such an extent that in several countries, it manifested in the form of armed conflicts. This intensity should be understood from the point of view of the accumulation of contradictions whose roots may be found in the inadequately resolved oligarchic crisis of the 1930s. In this sense, the 1980s were marked by the coexistence of two processes: first, the old oligarchic crisis, which had not been overcome by bourgeois renovation; and second, the capitalist crisis itself, which had been unleashed by the popular struggles that were a response to state authoritarianism (Torres-Rivas, 1987: 49).

In terms of labor, the crisis reflected a series of significant phenomena that will be discussed in the present chapter. In the first instance, the labor markets in the region naturally underwent processes of adjustment. This aspect is analyzed in the following section. The second section broaches the issue of informality, a phenomenon that, as seen in the previous chapter, was already of fundamental importance by the 1970s. The latter was reinforced by the crisis for two reasons: On the one hand, the crisis affected urban employment, above all; on the other hand, this type of employment constituted the labor markets' main adjustment mechanism. The chapter ends with an analysis of the economic and political effects the crisis had on the trade union movement.[1]

The Crisis and Labor Market Adjustments

An initial outline of the type of adjustments that have been made to Central American labor markets is presented in Table 3.1. The most evident adjustment mechanism–open unemployment–is shown, as is another less evident and more complex mechanism—underemployment.

In the first instance, as it may be noted from this table, the growth of the EAP was very similar in all the countries; the annual growth rates varied between 4.0 percent in Nicaragua and 3.1 percent in Costa Rica. These figures do not differ from previous tendencies, from the point of view of the region as a whole, as the annual growth rate for the EAP in the 1970s was 3.4 percent (Gallardo and López, 1986: table 3.2). However, El Salvador represents the one exception to this, with a rate of only 1.3 percent. This low rate is associated with the phenomenon of mass emigration that marked this country throughout the 1980s. It has been estimated that between 10 and 15 percent of the population emigrated during that time, and those who did so were predominantly males aged between 20 and 29 from urban areas and with a higher level of education. Moreover, this emigration phenomenon has had multiple effects on the Salvadoran labor market: The sending of remittances has adversely affected the participation of nonemigrants, though it has also been demonstrated that the rate of participation is higher for women belonging to households with emigrants and areas with a higher percentage of emi-

TABLE 3.1   Employment Situation in Central America in 1980 and 1990

Country and Year	EAP (thousands of persons)	Rate of Open Unemployment	Rate of Underemployment
Guatemala			
1980	2,193	3.2	43.0
1990	2,982	2.0	63.0
El Salvador			
1980	1,626	16.1	55.0
1990	1,862	10.0	50.8
Honduras			
1980	1,021	15.2	64.0
1990	1,426	5.0	36.0
Nicaragua			
1980	870	11.2	49.0
1990	1,251	10.0	46.5
Costa Rica			
1980	770	6.0	26.0
1990	1,033	4.0	18.0

SOURCE: PREALC (1992).

gration; salaries have been affected; and it has been suggested that pressure in terms of unemployment has eased (Funkhouser, 1992a).[2]

The other two indicators in the table demonstrate different forms of labor market adjustment, and in this regard, three kinds of situations may be observed. First, improvements may be noted in some cases, such as those of El Salvador, Honduras, and Costa Rica. In these three situations both the level of open unemployment and that of underemployment decreased. However, it is important to consider aspects unique to each national context. Thus, in the case of El Salvador, one must bear in mind the significant flow of emigration of the work force (mentioned above), which appears to have lifted the pressure on the labor market. For its part, the Honduran results, which show the most radical change, are surprising because the economic recovery that took place in the second five-year period was not as outstanding as to be able to justify such a spectacular improvement in the field of employment.[3] The Costa Rican results, in contrast, are more credible, for they illustrate the more solid revival of that country's economy. It is worth taking a brief moment to look at El Salvador and Costa Rica, albeit for different reasons. In the first case, one is faced with the country in which it is presumed that armed conflict had the greatest impact on developments in the field of employment; the second case represents the country in which the structural adjustment strategy was applied both at an earlier date and also in a more far-reaching manner.

With regard to El Salvador, reference may be made to Funkhouser's (1994b) revealing analysis.[4] Funkhouser differentiates between the direct and indirect effects the conflict had on the labor market. In respect to the first, the results are predictable: changes in the spatial distribution of employment and internal migration from the affected areas, especially between 1979 and 1985. In contrast, the task of identifying the indirect effects is rather more complex. In the first instance, no major differences have been detected between areas affected by the conflict and the rest of the country with regard to a number of labor aspects—participation in the labor market, generation of self-employment, salaries, and the international flow of emigration. However, the conflict itself has conditioned macroeconomic policy and the rationale for public spending. This may explain the absence of such differences, as pointed out by the author, and the fact that the armed conflict therefore indirectly affected the entire work force.

Concerning Costa Rica, it has been argued that the structural adjustment strategy has, on the contrary, had a positive effect on the labor market for a number of reasons. First, the decline in wages during Costa Rica's economic recession, which took place between 1980–1982, was greater than that required; as a result, it permitted the subsequent recovery in wages without endangering competition. Second, price stability, external adjustment, and the economic recovery achieved following the period of recession created a more favorable climate for investment. Third, in the same manner, a new financial and economic framework, with clearer rules for firms, was established. Fourth, not only were new exports to third markets promoted but the processes of reconverting firms was also supported. Finally, labor institutions were not affected, and compensatory measures were, moreover, implemented in favor of the minimum wage (García, 1993: 63–64).

The table reflects a second situation within the regional context: In Nicaragua, despite a slight improvement, the magnitude of existing problems related to both open unemployment and underemployment was, in contrast, prolonged. In Guatemala, the adjustment took place by means of a significant increase in underemployment that is, moreover, essentially linked to its invisible variant, which affected all sectors of the economy, including the modern one.[5]

Consequently, this first observation suggests that the mechanism for increasing open unemployment did not constitute a key instrument in the region in terms of labor adjustment mechanisms. The only exception was in Costa Rica, where during the recession in 1982 a significant shift was experienced, although this declined rapidly when the economy recovered. This phenomenon implied that it was only in the region's most modern economy, in terms of labor, that this type of mechanism func-

TABLE 3.2   Development of Wages According to Country (Index 1980 = 100)

	Guatemala		El Salvador		Honduras		Nicaragua		Costa Rica	
Year	M	A	M	A	M	A	M	A	M	A
1980	100.0	100.0	100.0	100.0	100.0	100.0	100.0	100.0	100.0	100.0
1983	115.3	126.0	76.5	—	96.5	—	57.8	83.4	99.3	78.5
1986	68.6	81.0	57.5	67.0	85.3	89.0	19.6	19.8	118.7	97.8
1990	48.2	78.5	34.8	64.6	87.1	93.0	8.4	14.8	120.5	87.2

NOTES:
M = Minimum
A = Average
SOURCE: Weller (1994b, table 5).

tioned, albeit for a limited period of time. In the other countries it was the increase in underemployment or other responses, such as emigration in the case of El Salvador, that affected the labor market, thereby indicating that the structures related to the same maintained important traditionalist features, as seen in the previous chapter.

Table 3.2 illustrates, in a much more limited manner and solely in reference to wage labor, the development of wages, which has in almost all the countries constituted another labor adjustment mechanism for this group of workers, although its origin—inflation—is not to be found in the labor market.

The figures clearly reflect how a considerable decline in wages occurred in the region—with the exception of minimum wages in Costa Rica, where the gradualist handling of structural adjustment (a result of the tradition of state intervention) did not permit a decline in basic wages. In effect, this would be the only case in Central America in which wage decreases did not play a part in labor adjustment to the detriment of the workers, apart from the aforementioned recession at the beginning of the decade. For the remaining countries, three situations may be identified. The first corresponds to Guatemala and El Salvador, where the differences in the decline of minimum and average wages are considerable. These differences could be attributed to the fact that given the wide range of salaries, the eroding effects of the crisis were not consistent.[6] In this respect, agricultural salaries must be mentioned: Guatemala's average was equivalent to a mere 40 percent of the average nonagricultural wage; in El Salvador, 41 percent of the rural work force—excluding unpaid family workers—earned incomes that were lower than the minimum wage for unskilled farm laborers (Weller, 1994b: 24). This was not the case in Honduras, where the decrease in wages, which was less acute than in the two previous cases, is thought to have had a less varying impact. Finally, Nicaragua stands out due to the harsh decrease in wages, which is an eloquent indicator of the global crisis that broke out in there at the end of the decade, for reasons already known. (The labor policy implemented by the *Sandinista* regime, in particular that related to wages, will be analyzed in the third section of this chapter.)

A more detailed analysis of these processes of labor market adjustment may be made by taking into account a greater number of aspects during the course of this decade and making a more in-depth study of factors that intervene in both the supply and demand of the labor force. However, this exercise is only possible in two cases, that of Guatemala and Costa Rica, because they are the only countries for which data is available. This exercise is of interest in that it contrasts two types of work structures that to some extent represent the array of situations within the region and that—as demonstrated earlier—were affected by different adjustment mechanisms during the years of crisis. Table 3.3 allows one to, in effect, study these mechanisms more closely and analyze them on the basis of the type of work force involved.[7]

In the case of Guatemala, overall developments indicate that it was, by and large, in the first five-year period that an increase in the rate of occupation was registered. In this sense, it has been suggested that during the recession, the crisis must have forced households to incorporate more of their members in the labor market in order to obtain more incomes; subsequently, despite the economic recovery at the end of the decade, there did not appear to be a return to the levels of participation that had been recorded at the onset of the crisis. The rate of unemployment, for its part, increased in the first period and later decreased. However, the most important aspect of this dimension is its low level. In other words, as seen at the beginning of this section, unemployment did not constitute an adjustment mechanism in Guatemala's labor market. Consequently, the increase in employment must have taken place in precarious working environments.

The figures for Costa Rica show a different process. First, the greater level of labor participation, also manifest in Guatemala, must be emphasized, especially with regard to women and young people. This implies that the labor market was more accessible to vulnerable groups. In contrast, the rate of employment for the older age group is lower, reflecting the development of a Costa Rican welfare state. For its part, the rate of employment developed in the opposite direction to that of Guatemala. The first period showed no movement, whereas the second five-year period witnessed an increase; in this sense, employment activity simply followed that of macroeconomic cycles, as may be the case in modern labor markets: limited amount of jobs created during the recession, and developments when the economy is reactivated. That is, this difference in development processes is linked to the level of modernity of the two labor structures under consideration, as argued in the previous chapters.[8]

TABLE 3.3 Rates of Employment and Unemployment According to Country and Sex and Age Group

| | Guatemala | | | | | | Costa Rica | | | | | |
| | *Rate of Employment* | | | *Rate of Unemployment* | | | *Rate of Employment* | | | *Rate of Unemployment* | | |
Sex and Age groups	*1981*	*1986–87*	*1989*	*1981*	*1986–87*	*1989*	*1981*	*1985*	*1989*	*1981*	*1985*	*1989*
Men	70.4	75.3	75.7	1.7	2.8	1.6	71.9	70.7	74.3	5.3	6.5	3.8
Women	11.7	22.6	23.7	1.7	5.7	3.2	18.9	23.5	28.3	7.8	7.9	5.3
Under 20s	22.4	30.6	30.6	2.8	5.2	2.8	27.8	26.7	29.8	15.0	13.8	9.3
Age 20–49	51.6	62.1	60.9	1.6	3.5	2.1	59.9	59.4	63.9	4.3	6.2	2.1
Age 50 and over	46.1	55.6	51.6	0.9	0.7	0.7	37.8	33.8	36.8	2.3	2.7	0.4
Total	40.7	48.3	48.7	1.7	3.5	2.0	46.8	46.6	51.0	5.9	6.8	3.8

SOURCES: For Guatemala, INE (1985; 1987, 1990); for Costa Rica; DGCE, *Encuesta nacional de hogares empleo y desempleo,* (1980, 1985, 1989).

Finally, unemployment developed in a similar manner to that of Guatemala, though an important variation must be stressed. The rate is higher for Costa Rica, and in 1982, the year in which the crisis was most acute, it reached 11.3 percent; in effect, 1985, the year considered in this table, corresponds to the period in which unemployment declined and gradually continued to do so until the end of the decade (Tardanico, 1991–1992: table 5).

These tendencies may be compared by taking into account the two basic sociodemographic aspects of the labor force. In Guatemala, all the categories considered increased their labor participation in the first period, although two in particular are highlighted: women and those of mature age. In the first case, it has been suggested that as in other Latin American societies, the incorporation of the female labor force has been one of the households' main responses to the impact of the crisis; this, in turn, implies women have taken on an even more important role in terms of the subsistence of the respective households.[9] In terms of unemployment, there are no surprises, for it is the most vulnerable groups—women and young people—who were most affected by this phenomenon. (One must bear in mind that in Guatemala this problem bore little relevance.)

Two phenomena must be emphasized in terms of the rate of employment in Costa Rica. On the one hand, during the course of the decade an increased feminization of employment may be observed, regardless of the economic period. In this sense, the process is not dissimilar to that of Guatemala, and the same arguments may therefore be employed.[10] However, the tendency related to the labor incorporation of the older age group seems to have been the most affected by macroeconomic developments.

Table 3.4, for its part, illustrates the changes that took place in terms of the labor force's two main facets of incorporation in the production structure.

It may be observed that in Guatemala at the beginning of the 1980s the two main job categories (wage labor in private establishments and self-employment) were very much on a par. At the beginning of the second half of the decade, the first of these had increased slightly while the relative importance of self-employment had decreased. Nevertheless, these changes did not mean that the crisis induced a higher level of wage labor. In effect, if public employees, which comprise the other category corresponding to wage labor, are added, this type of labor force represented half of the EAP both at the start of the decade and in the mid-1980s. What occurred was that the decrease in self-employment was more than compensated by the increase in unpaid family work, the relative importance of which doubled.[11] These tendencies were maintained until the end of the decade.

TABLE 3.4 Employed Population per Country According to Job Category and Branch of Activity

Job Category and Branch of Activity	Guatemala			Costa Rica		
	1981	1986–1987	1989	1980	1985	1989
Owners	1.6	2.5	1.5	4.3	2.9	3.9
Public Employees	8.2	6.6	7.4	18.5	17.8	16.3
Private Wage Workers	39.0	42.3	41.3	56.8	56.5	54.5
Self-Employed	40.1	31.9	33.4	15.2	17.4	20.1
Unpaid Family Workers	6.8	16.6	16.5	3.9	4.2	4.4
Agriculture	54.0	51.9	49.9	26.9	26.8	25.9
Manufacturing						
Industry	10.5	12.7	13.7	16.2	16.0	18.6
Trade	8.7	13.7	13.2	18.1	18.6	15.7
Services	12.8	14.4	14.7	22.9	25.1	23.5
Remaining activities	10.5	7.3	8.6	14.6	12.2	15.6
Total	100.0	100.0	100.0	100.0	100.0	100.0
	(1,683,828)[a]	(2,644,288)	(2,840,358)	(770,972)[b]	(887,456)[c]	(1,025,548)[d]

NOTES:

[a] Includes 58,614 cases unaccounted for.

[b] Includes 10,214 persons seeking employment for the first time.

[c] Includes 11,526 persons seeking employment for the first time.

[d] Includes 7,469 persons seeking employment for the first time.

SOURCES: For Guatemala, INE (1985; 1987, 1990); for Costa Rica, DGCE, *Encuesta nacional de hogares empleo y desempleo* (1980, 1985, 1989).

Thus, it is suggested that the households responded to the crisis by developing labor activities centered on the family. This implies that the higher level of incorporation in the labor market, identified in the previous table, was not necessarily always based on obtaining additional incomes, although it may be assumed that a greater percentage of the work force involved in these type of activities would mean an increase in total incomes.

Taking into account the importance of the presence of women in the employment structure, the latter showed an increase in all the categories during the course of the decade and especially during the recession. The most significant increase was that related to self-employment and unpaid family labor.[12] In this sense, different processes were identified in terms of gender. Thus, the men experienced a process of increased wage labor during the crisis, in which wage workers in private establishments went from representing 36.5 percent of the male EAP in 1981 to 43.5 percent in 1989; at the same time, self-employment decreased from 44.1 percent to 33 percent. The opposite occurred regarding women. On the one hand, wage labor declined to the extent that while in 1981 over half (53.6 percent) the female EAP corresponded to the category of company wage workers, in 1989 this figure had dropped to less than half (43.5 percent). On the other hand, self-employment reached one third (32.6 percent) by the end of the decade, in comparison to a little over a fifth (22.2 percent) at the beginning. In other words, the increase represented by the new female labor force, as seen in the previous table, appears to have centered—by and large—on self-employment. In this respect, one must bear in mind that this favors the incorporation of women in the labor force as it facilitates the combination of domestic tasks and employment by means of a more flexible handling of time and spatial factors.

In Costa Rica, the first aspect to be considered is that the employment structure is clearly dominated by wage labor; this is in contrast to Guatemala's more diverse employment structure. This predominance persisted throughout the decade, implying little change to this structure. Furthermore, contrary to expectations, in Costa Rica the early application of structural adjustment programs did not provoke a decrease in public employment but, rather, quite the opposite. The interrelation between the Social-Democratic state structure, the clientele-based electoral policy, the context of war, and the important flow of North American aid helps to explain this peculiarity (Tardanico and Lungo, 1995: 226). Nonetheless, evidence of a relative decline in wage labor in favor of that which did not involve wages was perceived. Within the latter, it is, without doubt, the category of self-employment that has shown the highest growth. In effect, this phenomenon is the most notable of the minor changes that occurred in Costa Rica. This implies that in contrast to the Guatemalan experience, the households' reactions were based more on individual initiatives than on the development of family-orientated activities.

The Costa Rican figures do not, unfortunately, permit a gender analysis of the job categories such as that carried out for Guatemala. This can only be undertaken with regard to wage workers, who, it must be remembered, constituted the most important category. Both in the private and public sector there was an increase in female participation. Thus, by 1981, women made up 23.9 percent and 35.7 percent of these employment sectors, respectively. These percentages reached 29 percent and 38.6 percent by the end of the decade.

The lower half of Table 3.4 shows the other basic facet of the labor force's incorporation in the productive structure. No significant changes were identified for Guatemala. Agriculture maintained its prominent position, absorbing approximately half of the EAP, although its importance in the employment structure fell slightly. Within the latter, it was the production of basic grains and certain nontraditional exports that increased the demand for labor; in contrast, traditional exports, in particular cotton, reduced their level of employment (Weller, 1994a: 9–10). In a similar manner, it may be observed that the three branches of activity that follow, in order of importance—manufacturing industry, commerce, and services—became more significant; the most important change taking place was with respect to commerce during the recession. That is, there was an increase in more urban-related activities to the detriment of the rural sector *par excellence*.

However, it does not appear that any radical changes occurred that may imply that the crisis accelerated the process of urbanization with its subsequent flow of migration from the country to the city and, in particular, the capital.[13] Nonetheless, two phenomena occurred during this decade that affected Guatemalan agriculture and, in particular, the western region. First, one must remember the drastic reduction, mentioned above, of the cotton production sector, which implied a decrease of 70 percent in the demand for labor. Second, one should not lose sight of the violence that affected indigenous areas, resulting in important migrations of the population (Baumeister, 1993: 122).[14] Moreover, it has been suggested that significant changes were taking place in the region. In this respect, it has been argued that the dualist model (large agricultural exporting *fincas* on the south coast, subsistence *minifundios* in the *Altiplano*) was being redefined. On the one hand, in the traditional agricultural exporting areas, a more proletarianized work force was being created due to the different factors (population growth in the region, processes of *minifundización*, and the introduction of technology to crop production) that reduced the need to employ seasonal labor from other regions (Negreros, 1989b).[15] On the other hand, in the *Altiplano*, a certain degree of "independence" from permanent or temporary wage labor was taking place due to the incidence of several processes: improvements in agricultural production capacity (both regarding the production of subsistence crops and new crops for export), diversification in the form of nonagricultural activities (handicrafts and commerce), and migration to the north accompanied by the sending of remittances (Baumeister, 1991).

In a more specific interpretation in terms of gender, it must be pointed out that in the first period considered, the relative presence of women increased in all the economy's main branches of activity. However, this increase is undoubtedly all the more significant with regard to commerce, in which women went from representing a third (33.5 percent) of the employment in this branch of activity to over half (56.9 percent) midway through the decade. Despite the fact that at the end of decade the relative importance of the female labor force fell (as was also the case concerning services), commercial activity is the only sector in which women outnumber men in absolute terms. Thus, this was a predominantly female activity. Nonetheless, it is also important to draw attention to the fact that by the last four-year period, the most significant increase of the relative presence of women was registered in the manufacturing sector. Thus, by 1989, 42.9 percent of this activity's labor force were women. This phenomenon is linked to the rise of the new *maquila* industry, which tends to have a preference for female labor.

For its part, the activities structure in Costa Rica differed somewhat from that of Guatemala, and these differences persisted throughout the decade. Thus, on the one hand, agriculture became less important. With regard to this activity, it has been pointed out that the modern sector increased its relative significance but could not make up for the increase in employment of the peasant sector; in other words, the development of modern agriculture served mainly to absorb part of the underemployed work force (Weller, 1994a: 8–9). On the other hand, a greater sectorial diversification than in Guatemala is observed and manifested itself in the form of a more pronounced importance of the residual category. There is no evidence of tendencies sustained during the course of the decade that may have implied clear processes of sectorial redefinition. Nonetheless, the greater relative importance of industrial activity must be emphasized. This phenomenon, as in the case of Guatemala, is linked to the development of the *maquila* and Free Trade Zones.

As in the case of occupational categories, a more detailed analysis—in terms of gender—of branches of activity should also be limited to wage workers. In terms of commerce, it may be said that the relative importance of the female work force has continued to represent approximately one third of the total employment in this regard. The same could be said of services (the only activity in which women represent the majority), in which women have remained a little over half the total employment. Only in the manufacturing industry did the relative importance of women increase, as was the case in Guatemala. In addition, as mentioned earlier, this phenomenon is related to the redefinition of the industrial model, in which employment tended to become more female-orientated, although this tendency was more prominent in Guatemala than in Costa Rica.

This section will conclude by referring back to the conclusions made in the previous chapter regarding the labor market's modernizing tendencies and investigating what changes they underwent during the crisis in the 1980s. In this regard, Table 3.5 contains the same aspects of modernity, defined in the same manner, and compares the importance each one of these had in the corresponding 1970 census observation with data provided by household surveys carried out in the 1980s.[16]

In the respective conclusions set out in the previous chapter, all the aspects considered had shown some level of modernization, though the pace and scope varied. Thus, in the first instance, feminization was the least dynamic tendency, the rate of growth of the female EAP being even lower than that of the total EAP. Therefore, as it may be seen from the table in question, this type of trend changed in all the countries, and it may be confirmed that the crisis induced the feminization of labor, as already observed in the case of Guatemala and Costa Rica during the 1980s. Nevertheless, as the evidence for Guatemala demonstrated, this greater incorporation must have taken place in precarious employment, given the logic of gender discrimination that prevails in Central American labor markets, as in other parts of Latin America.[17] It should be added that Tardanico and Lungo (1995: 240–244) have carried out a more detailed analysis of this tendency in relation to Costa Rica, limiting it to the urban environment and shedding light on the following aspects: Formal employment was feminized to the same extent as informal employment; in sectorial terms, it was the manufacturing industry that boosted the presence of women most; and in regard to incomes, there was a tendency of these to, on the one hand, decrease in intergeneric terms, but on the other hand, the opposite occurs within each generic group.

Schooling and professionalization were seen to be the two most dynamic tendencies. It may be said that this trend remained the same in the latter case but tended to decline in the former. Nonetheless, with regard to schooling, two phenomena should be highlighted. On the one hand, the increases that occurred in Guatemala and Honduras implied that, as in the rest of the region, approximately one third of the inactive population was devoted exclusively to study. On the other hand, the case of Costa Rica is worth mentioning, as it was here that this tendency was reversed, a fact that was reflected, by the end of the decade, in an EAP higher than the inactive population. This phenomenon may conceal de-

TABLE 3.5 Employment and Modernizing Tendencies According to Country

Modernizing Tendencies	Guatemala		El Salvador		Honduras		Nicaragua		Costa Rica	
	1973	1989	1971	1985	1974	1988	1971	1985	1973	1989
Schooling	22.8	31.0	35.9	39.7	29.1	36.8	31.5	n.a.	32.6	27.7
Inactive population	1,929,718	2,931,914	1,209,265	1,691,842	983,912	1,437,214	682,821	1,069,975	624,680	908,957
Feminization	14.0	25.5	21.6	37.8	15.7	21.4	21.9	33.2	n.a.	28.5
Urbanization	39.0	n.a.	42.5	54.8	33.2	43.8	48.4	56.3	n.a.	45.3
Wage labor	48.0	47.7	52.8	48.4	44.2	44.3	58.1	54.4	73.5	70.9
Professionalization	3.7	5.1	3.5	5.3	4.1	6.9	5.0	6.3	8.0	9.5
Tertiarization	12.5	14.4	17.8	17.5	11.5	17.0	19.8	24.1	20.3	23.5
EAP	1,545,658	2,898,316	1,766,479	1,653,409	762,795	1,393,065	505,445	1,063,610	585,313	1,025,548

SOURCES: For the first observation (in the 1970s), DGEC (1975) for Honduras 1974; DGEC (1974) for Nicaragua 1971; DGEC (1974) for Costa Rica 1973; DGEC (1977) for El Salvador 1971; DGEC (1975) for Guatemala 1973. For the last observation (in the 1980s), DGEC (1988); *Encuesta permanente de hogares de propósitos múltiples* for Honduras 1988; DGEC (1989), *Encuesta nacional de hogares empleo y desempleo* for Costa Rica; INEC (1985) for Nicaragua 1985; MIPLADES (1985) for Guatemala 1989; INE (1990) for Guatemala 1989; INEC (1985) for Nicaragua 1985; MIPLADES (1985) for El Salvador 1985.

mographic changes, with an older population than in the rest of Central America.[18]

Tertiary labor also represented a dynamic tendency, although it had not succeeded in making any significant impact. In the period under consideration, with the exception of El Salvador, this tendency persists, although with less force. However, with respect to this sectorial dimension, it is worth mentioning the considerable decrease in the importance of agricultural employment, as this is not reflected in the table under consideration, in regard to which the following countries represent the opposite ends of the spectrum: El Salvador, from 54.2 percent in 1971 to 28.3 percent in 1985; and Guatemala, from 57.2 percent in 1973 to 48.9 percent in 1989. In effect, in the last observation under consideration, agriculture no longer absorbed more than half the work force in any of the countries. However, this phenomenon is not synonymous with deruralization but, rather, reflects how nonagricultural rural employment assumed ever-increasing importance.[19]

These comments on agricultural activities serve to raise the issue of the changes provoked, during this period, due to the implementation of agrarian reforms in three countries: Honduras (1975); El Salvador (1980); and, Nicaragua (1981). In the first two cases, the impact of the same on the employment structure has been analyzed. Thus, for Honduras, a distinction must be made between two subsectors: first, the so-called concentrated rural development devoted to agroindustrialization and/or exports, and second, "consolidation," which produces basic grains. Some commodities from the first subsector (sugarcane, African palm, and bananas) generate a considerable demand for wage labor, albeit temporary in the first two cases; for its part, the consolidation subsector, which groups together two thirds of the reformed peasants, suffers from underemployment (Posas, 1989: 52–56). A similar differentiation may be found in the case of El Salvador. The so-called cooperatives in the first phase are devoted to agricultural export crops that require seasonal labor, whereas the units created during phase three produce basic grains and generate self-employment (Aquino, 1989: 34–37).

Finally, wage labor and urbanization appear as tendencies that were not very dynamic but made a substantial impact. In regard to urbanization, based on the data available, it may be said that this type of tendency was maintained, and in effect, El Salvador and Nicaragua appear—from the point of view of labor—predominantly urban in the 1980s. In contrast, in the period under consideration, certain changes may be observed in relation to the first of these tendencies. On the one hand, Guatemala and Honduras showed no change; on the other hand, a process of relative decline took place regarding wage labor in the three remaining countries.

Consequently, it appears the majority of modernizing tendencies maintained the same level of development, although this seemed to have been less forceful than in past decades. Nonetheless, two aspects must be stressed: the evidence of a relative decline in wage labor, implying that the heterogeneity of the labor markets was reinforced; and the dynamic tendency illustrated by the feminization of employment. In effect, it may be suggested that the latter, ironically, represented the crisis's contribution to the modernization of labor in the 1980s.

The Crisis and Urban Informality

The previous chapter showed that in all the countries in the region, informal employment was seen to constitute the urban occupational environment most capable of absorbing the work force in the 1970s. That is, the development of the modernization process had given rise to informal urban employment, which was an important tendency for the structuring of city-based labor markets.

The first regional estimates showed that less than one third of the labor force in metropolitan areas was involved in the informal sector at the beginning of the 1980s.[20] These percentages decreased in urban areas that had more modern economies, such as that of San José. At that time, Central American informality was presented as a sector in which more women were involved than in the formal sector; the opposite poles of the range of age groups were present due to a higher proportion of both young people and older individuals; and in contrast to other Latin American contexts, the figures available showed a predominance of migrants due to the formal sector's limited ability to absorb this labor force. Concerning job characteristics, self-employment is seen to have prevailed in the informal sector; there was a strong tendency toward tertiary labor, especially in regard to commerce, due to easier access to the same in the case of retailers; and where information was available, incomes were seen to be lower in the informal than in the formal sector, resulting in the former being associated with poverty (Haan, 1985; PREALC, 1986: 101–136).

Problems of a methodological nature (defining informality, geographic coverage of surveys, etc.) make it very difficult to compare regional estimates on the development of informal employment in the EAP of metropolitan areas during the course of the past decade. Roughly speaking, it may be said that this type of employment represented a little under 30 percent of the said EAP in the early 1980s and that by the end of this decade, the average corresponded to approximately one third or a little over. Naturally, there are notable differences that demonstrate the diversity within the region. Thus, at the beginning of the decade, this percentage represented slightly over a fifth of the EAP in San José and remained at this level during the course of the same. In contrast, with respect to

Managua, informal employment represented a little over one third of the EAP in the early 1980s, and by the end of the decade, it had increased to approximately half. Given the crisis and social decline Nicaragua is currently undergoing, the percentage has now, most probably, surpassed this figure (Haan, 1985; PREALC, 1986; Pérez Sáinz and Menjívar Larín, 1991).

Data provided by household surveys carried out at the end of the past decade or beginning of the present indicate the following levels of informal employment in urban areas: Guatemala represented 53 percent in 1989; El Salvador 55.3 percent in 1990; Honduras 48.9 percent in 1989; Nicaragua 63.8 percent in 1993; and Costa Rica 34.4 percent in 1991.[21] Thus, the tendency referred to in the previous paragraph is confirmed. Occupational diversity prevailed, and two cases were highlighted: Costa Rica, where informal employment was not as significant as the regional average, and Nicaragua, which was probably one of the Latin American countries in which the importance of informality was most noteworthy and where it is presumed that this employment sector was becoming saturated.

As noted in the previous section, the empirical evidence suggests that informal employment constituted the main mechanism for labor market adjustment in metropolitan areas throughout Central America during the crisis that affected the region in the past decade. Nevertheless, it is important to differentiate between two kinds of situations. On the one hand, this global view was representative of the majority of these areas (Guatemala City, San Salvador, Tegucigalpa, San Pedro Sula, and Managua), and in this regard, two aspects must be taken into account. First, another adjustment mechanism—open unemployment—represents an unacceptable cost for contexts in which urban poverty, a characteristic of the cities mentioned above, is widespread. Second, in these metropolitan areas there is a tradition of informal labor, which means that in this regard, one may speak of a work culture in which it is not that difficult to become involved in these activities if one generates one's own employment. However, on the other hand, this image becomes relative with regard to San José because since open unemployment has succeeded in constituting an option due to the fact that the levels of poverty are lower.

Table 3.6 presents the situation of the informal phenomenon in the main metropolitan areas in the region in the late 1980s, taking into account both sociodemographic factors related to the labor force and the type of position occupied.[22]

With reference to the sociodemographic factors, it may be noted that the female work force was as significant as male labor in the Central American informal sector, and the presence of women workers is therefore more evident. Age groups had polarized, indicating that informality constituted both a port of entry to the labor market for the new work force and a sector in which working lives could be prolonged. In addi-

TABLE 3.6 Basic Characteristics of Informality in Metropolitan Areas

Characteristics	Guatemala City	San Salvador	Tegucigalpa	San Pedro Sula	Managua	San José
% of women	41.7	53.4	50.7	48.0	46.8	32.5
% of under 20s	8.4	9.8	13.1	9.7	15.4	9.7
% Age 60 and over	12.8	11.5	6.0	8.3	6.9	10.1
% without schooling	11.9	15.3	15.2	15.7	13.1	2.8
% of self-employed laborers	51.1	50.8	62.7	63.9	57.1	67.3
% trade	39.6	48.9	46.3	49.5	44.4	35.9
% 45 working hours and over per week	59.4	61.6	54.2	54.3	19.5[b]	54.3
Incomes[a]	1.4	—	1.9	2.1	1.2	1.88[c]

[a] Division between average income in formal sector and average income in informal sector.

[b] Percentage corresponding to 50 hours and over.

[c] Independent professionals are not included in the data regarding the formal sector.

SOURCE: Pérez Sáinz and Menjívar Larín (1991, tables 1, 2, and 3).

tion, the level of schooling was low, and well below that of the population employed in formal activities, thereby confirming the sectorial segregation of this kind of labor market. Moreover, in terms of the intraregional differences pointed out above, San José has differed from the other cities with respect to two tendencies. On the one hand, the presence of women was lower. This, as argued earlier, is a result of the higher level of schooling of Costa Rican women, which has allowed them entry into the formal sector, in particular that related to public activities (PREALC, 1986). On the other hand, the existence of a widespread coverage of education, reflecting the existence of a welfare state during the previous decades, explains the differences in terms of levels of instruction.[23]

It should be pointed out that two of these factors—gender and education—had a considerable impact on the pattern of choice of employment. In effect, Funkhouser (1994c: 16–17) has, on the basis of a multivariable analysis, estimated that the higher the level of education, the less likelihood there is of involvement in the informal sector; and women are more likely to become involved in informal activities even when other variables are controlled.[24]

With regard to job characteristics, the first noteworthy aspect is the predominance of self-employed workers—a phenomenon that has pointed to the diversity of this world of labor in which subsistence logics prevail over those of accumulation. Commerce emerged as the most important branch of activity, thereby confirming that it was an easily accessible activity. In addition, there is evidence that informality was a precarious form of labor in the sense that it was known for its long working days, and the physical exhaustion of the work force constituted a mechanism for compensating for this type of activity's low productivity. This precariousness was all the more apparent due to the fact that incomes were lower than those earned in the formal sector.[25] Nevertheless, this last observation should be modified because in some cases certain informal categories, namely that of microenterprises, have been able to obtain incomes higher than those paid to wage workers in the formal sector. This fact reminds us that the association between poverty and informality is not absolute and that not all poor people are informal laborers, nor are all informal laborers poor.[26]

As noted from the previous table's occupational perspective, Central American informality has, like that of the rest of Latin America, demonstrated it possesses a heterogeneous nature, which has been influenced by different types of logics.

Two conclusions resulting from the case study on establishments—both those of microenterprises and of the self-employed within the metropolitan areas mentioned—are worth noting.[27] On the one hand, there were no widespread processes of accumulation. In reference to Guatemala City, San Salvador, and San José, less than a third of the establishments studied had made any form of investment during the previous year (or three years in the case of machinery or equipment); this percentage was even lower for establishments in Managua. Thus, it was the logics of simple reproduction or subsistence that tended to prevail, thereby contradicting the idea of widespread business potential in the informal sector. On the other hand, differences have been identified between the various occupational categories in this respect. In Guatemala City, San Salvador, Managua, and to a lesser extent San José, microenterprises showed a greater investment capacity than self-employed workers. This difference was also evident in Tegucigalpa and, on a smaller scale, in San Pedro Sula, where the density of capital (value of assets per person employed) was higher with regard to those running microenterprises than for self-employed workers. Consequently, although subsistence logics prevailed, evidence of accumulative processes was also detected, thereby demonstrating the diversity of the situation. Moreover, in this sense, microenterprises have tended to focus more on accumulation logics while self-employment has been characterized by subsistence and simple reproduction (Pérez Sáinz and Menjívar Larín, 1991).

Table 3.7 allows for a more in-depth study of this phenomenon of the heterogeneity of the world of informal employment in Central America.[28] Two results taken from the upper half of this table should be pointed out. On the one hand, in all the areas under consideration, as was to be expected, investment in machinery and/or equipment was higher than that of means of transport. On the other hand, the most notable differences were those related to formal accounting, which reflected the variety of situations identified in the previous regional study regarding the informal sector. Therefore, in San José—the area with the least impoverishment—there was a higher incidence of formal-type rationalities, whereas in the more precarious areas (Guatemala City, San Salvador, Tegucigalpa, and Managua), rationalities of a substantive nature appeared to prevail.

The combination of these criteria has led to the elaboration of a typology, as seen in the upper half of this same table, which combines accumulative dynamics and management rationality.[29] The results illustrate two phenomena. First, the diversity of the nature of informal establishments in all the areas under consideration was reinforced. Second, two basic situations, apart from that of El Salvador, proved unusual.[30] On the one hand, the Guatemalan, Honduran, and Nicaraguan contexts' subsistence informality prevailed whereas this predominance became relative in San José. In this sense, the differences within the region, mentioned earlier, were consolidated. Thus, in Central American contexts affected by

TABLE 3.7 Investment, Accounting, and Type of Establishment According to City

	Guatemala City	San Salvador	Tegucigalpa	Managua	San José
% that invest in machinery and equipment	37.2	64.4	24.3	38.5	48.4
% that invest in means of transport	13.6	8.0	10.3	20.1	13.6
% using formal accounting	8.4	6.8	6.9	15.4	31.3
Type of establishment					
Dynamic	7.3	6.4	5.3	15.4	23.1
Intermediary	35.6	61.2	26.2	29.0	35.3
Subsistence	57.1	32.4	68.4	55.6	41.6
TOTAL	100.0	100.0	100.0	100.0	100.0
	(191)	(250)	(263)	(169)	(221)

SOURCE: Menjívar Larín and Pérez Sáinz (1993, table 2).

poverty and instability, subsistence informality prevailed; in less impoverished urban areas, dynamic informality was gaining ground.

Along these same lines, Table 3.8 demonstrates which of the informal
establishments' labor dimensions were most closely related to this typology, as this is the aspect that is relevant to the present text. One may note
that the "number of workers" variable is significant in all the cities under
consideration and, furthermore, in a manner that was to be expected: The
higher the dynamism, the higher the number of workers employed, and
vice versa.[31] With regard to the type of labor force employed, the results
propose two conclusions in this respect. First, the most differentiating aspect appears to be that of the paid work force, of which the dynamic stratum made the most use. Second, the most significant differences were
seen to occur in the three cities where subsistence informality prevailed:
Guatemala City, Tegucigalpa, and Managua. Thus, it was in areas of
widespread poverty that a higher incidence of socio-labor differences
manifest itself.

In effect, this last observation is reaffirmed on taking into account the
gender dimension.[32] In this respect, it has been demonstrated that in
Guatemala City, Tegucigalpa, and in particular, Managua, men tended to
center on the dynamic informal sector while women focused on subsistence activities. In the two remaining cases this distinction did not apply.
With the relative exception of El Salvador, it may be argued—once
more—that the determining factor could have been the context of an urban economy. Thus, when poverty prevails, imposing subsistence informality, as in the cases of Guatemala City, Tegucigalpa, and Managua, the
lack of resources implies differentiated access to these in terms of gender
discrimination against women. In contrast, when urban poverty is more
limited, as in the case of San José, sufficient resources are available, and
gender discrimination does not occur on a significant scale.

Furthermore, these generic differences can be studied in greater detail
from two points of view. In terms of logics of mobilization toward informality, male mobilization has been seen to be directed toward commodity-orientated logics while female mobilization centers on the domestic
environment. This differentiation is most clearly expressed by Costa
Rica, whereas in El Salvador the differences were manifest rather in
terms of the fact that commodity-orientated logics have had more impact
on men than on women. However, in all the cities in question, the participation of women in domestic tasks was much higher than that of men,
and the latter are still the wrongful heads of households. That is, incorporation in informal occupations does not appear to question the assigna-
tion of traditional roles within the domestic sphere.

Consequently, the diversity of informality is seen to be reflected not
only in establishments, but also in the home.[33] The subordination of

TABLE 3.8 Establishment According to Characteristics of the Labor Force, City, and Type of Informality

Characteristics of the Labor Force	No. of Workers	% Majority Women	% Majority Family Members	% Majority Paid Workers	Total
Guatemala City					
Dynamic	3.4	25.0	25.0	75.0	100.0 (14)
Intermediary	1.2	33.3	51.8	64.4	100.0 (68)
Subsistence	0.8	52.8	69.4	36.2	100.0 (109)
p<[a]	.000	.019	.052	.001	
San Salvador					
Dynamic	2.1	60.0	46.7	80.0	100.0 (16)
Intermediary	1.1	66.0	46.7	70.2	100.0 (153)
Subsistence	0.8	71.1	52.6	65.8	100.0 (81)
p<[a]	.000	.722	.554	.595	
Tegucigalpa					
Dynamic	2.0	7.7	7.7	77.1	100.0 (14)
Intermediary	1.5	10.2	36.7	61.2	100.0 (19)
Subsistence	1.1	7.0	64.0	34.0	100.0 (180)
p<[a]	.000	.296	.001	.000	
Managua					
Dyanmic	4.9	23.0	30.7	82.1	100.0 (26)
Intermediary	2.0	24.4	46.5	56.1	100.0 (49)
Subsistence	0.9	54.0	68.0	34.0	100.0 (94)
p<[a]	.000	.296	.001	.000	
San José					
Dynamic	2.1	37.5	45.0	90.0	100.0 (51)
Intermediary	0.7	40.5	52.4	61.9	100.0 (78)
Subsistence	0.4	22.2	55.6	66.7	100.0 (92)
p<[a]	.000	.607	.634	.000	

NOTE: [a] Hypothesis test for number of workers, analysis of variance. Remaining variables, chi-square.
SOURCE: Menjívar Larín and Pérez Sáinz (1993, table 6).

women in the domestic environment has in material terms implied constraints in terms of time availability within the occupational sphere, which, given low productivity, demands long working days in order for it to be economically viable. Moreover, women's job orientation has been conditioned by their strong identification with their respective domestic units. This has implied different logics of incorporation in the informal sector, where men work to support the home while women work in the home itself.

In short, besides valuing the importance of informal employment and identifying its morphology, the studies developed in the region on this phenomenon have brought to light the diverse nature of this work environment. In this sense, the main conclusion is that in order to comprehend the logics that make up this diversity, one should ultimately refer to the socio-urban context in regard to which differences between cities repeat themselves. These differences do not contradict those already identified at the national level.

The Crisis, Armed Conflicts, and Trade Unionism

The crisis in the 1980s presented the trade union movement with two major challenges: on the one hand, its reaction to the recession and the adjustment policies that were beginning to be applied in each of the countries; and on the other hand, its relation with the state and the political system within the context of intensified conflict, which in several countries manifested in the form of war. These two challenges, along with their impact on the trade union movement (in terms of organization and direction), are the aspects to be discussed in this section. In this regard, it is necessary to distinguish at least three situations. The first of these corresponds to Guatemala, El Salvador, and Nicaragua, each marked by armed conflicts. Nicaragua may even be set apart from the other two cases because the *Sandinista* regime created a favorable climate for the development of trade unions, in contrast to the other two countries, where suppression was the most common tonic. However, in all three cases the political aspect was the most crucial. The second situation is represented by Costa Rica, where armed conflicts had less of an impact, which meant that the economic effects of the crisis and the application of structural adjustment programs (which were, moreover, the first to be implemented in the region) were among that country's key issues. Honduras, in contrast, was in an intermediary position: Although its territory was free of armed conflicts, the influence of these was more deeply felt there than in Costa Rica.[34]

With respect to the first of these aspects, namely, how the trade unions reacted to the economic effects of the crisis and the adjustment policies that followed, it was in Costa Rica that, as mentioned earlier, this reached greater proportions. Three stages, in terms of trade union action, have been identified for this period. The first (1979–1982) is marked by a worsening of the conflict, especially in the banana sector. The differences that arose at the heart of the labor movement due to a variety of reasons (diverging strategic proposals, involvement of political parties, etc.) and the demobilization induced by the forthcoming elections implied a decline in union activity, both in terms of strikes and collective conventions. Thus, a second stage (1982–1985) began, marked by the regression of trade union action and splits at the heart of the labor movement. In addition, from 1986 until the end of the decade a third stage was initiated with a recovery, to a certain extent, of the presence and action of the unions, the most notable example of which was the setting up of the Permanent Workers Council (CPT); this gave the trade union movement greater pressuring and negotiating power (Donato and Castro, 1990: 30–33).

However, perhaps the key factor with regard to the crisis was the way in which the Costa Rican state responded to the same by applying a structural adjustment strategy, which was the first to be implemented in the region in a coherent manner, aided by that country's political situation. In this respect, the fundamental characteristic of this process was its gradual implementation. That is, measures were applied without using shock therapy and without seeking to break with the past, which in this country meant that social policies with a universal scope were not questioned. This implied that in contrast to other Latin American countries where the imposition of orthodox stabilizing measure packages resulted in violent popular reactions, in Costa Rica a consensus, which was a fundamental element in this society's politics, prevailed and subsequently neutralized the trade unions' fighting spirit. In this sense, two phenomena emerged in the 1980s that changed the relation between the trade unions and the state. On the one hand, in terms of wage policy—which as already mentioned in the previous chapter had been enforced in this country—a new mechanism for fixing wages was introduced that sought to readjust salaries prior to inflation; thus, the possibility of union demands was limited, and the debate assumed clearly technical overtones. On the other hand, collective negotiations within the public sector were restricted in the 1980s due to the changes made to legislation regarding public administration in 1979 (Donato and Castro, 1990: 17–20).

Nonetheless, these years saw the rise of two conflicts that were of historical significance for Costa Rica. In 1984 the longest strike (72 days) in the entire history of the banana sector was held, which ended in a major trade union defeat. The union organizations, therefore, were to lose their influence in the sector in which they had made the most progress. Also, the previous year witnessed the most significant mass movement in

Costa Rica since 1948 as a result of the increase in electricity rates (Rojas Bolaños, 1988: 12). As in other Latin American countries, this type of mobilization was undertaken by urban resident organizations, and the trade unions remained largely relegated; in other words, the focus was seen to be on the reproductive sphere and that of the neighborhood rather than on the realms of production and enterprise.

Toward the end of 1986, official statistics indicated the existence of 387 trade unions comprising 141,785 workers. Although half of these organizations belonged to the private sector, the number of members was scarcely above a third of the total trade unionized labor force. However, as Rojas Bolaños (1988: 17–18) has been right to point out, the state of the union organizations in the private sector was of much more concern than these figures demonstrate.[35] In fact, during the course of the 1980s, trade unionism had been replaced by *solidarismo*, which represented the most important phenomenon, in terms of labor organizations, to occur in Costa Rica during the past decade.

This movement, which was promoted by employers, began to develop in Costa Rica in 1948 and sought harmony and cooperation between workers and employers by means of a pact whereby the work force obtained certain social benefits in exchange for relinquishing trade union inclinations. In short, *solidarista* associations administered funds from membership fees as well as those provided by the firm itself, which formed part of the severance pay fund. This fund offered a loan program to the workers that was, without doubt, the main lure of the *solidarista* movement; moreover, at the end of the year the fund shared out its profits and offered a series of programs related to the working environment (canteens, medical services, recreational areas, etc.). Probably the most important aspect is that the solidarity associations aimed—in an informal manner—to support the direct agreement mechanism to the detriment of the collective convention, which was the trade unions' principal instrument of negotiation. In this sense, Trejos (1992) has argued that the solidarity movement represented the method by which consensus was secured within Costa Rican firms.[36]

Within the context of the crisis and adjustment, this movement underwent spectacular progress. In effect, the number of *solidarista* associations in Costa Rica in 1981 was a mere 216, with a total of 31,000 members; seven years later these figures had risen to 1,065 and 115,000 respectively.[37] At the same time, with regard to labor negotiations, whereas in 1980, 93 percent of these were represented by collective negotiations, in 1987, 47 percent already corresponded to direct agreements (Rodríguez García, 1990: 46–47). In this sense, it has been argued that the adjustment situation favored those in entrepreneurial positions, implying a subsequent weakening of trade union action that manifested in the questioning of collective conventions, both in the public and private sector. In this manner, the *solidarista* movement was economically guaranteed, and, at the same time, legitimized from a political point of view. In other words, this consolidation was in line with the prevailing neoliberal ideology and with the combination of national and international factors that have favored its development (Rodríguez, 1989: 23–24).

This *solidarismo* boom in Costa Rica led to its expansion to the rest of Central America, although it had far less success there. Thus, by the end of the decade, Guatemala had 215 associations, almost half of which were registered in the agricultural sector. In El Salvador these were known as Worker-Employer Commissions, and they totaled a mere 18. In Honduras they were called Development Councils and began to appear in the region of San Pedro Sula (Rodríguez García, 1990: 54–58). However, Posas (1990: 164) has put forward the argument that the *solidarista* movement in Honduras was a challenge the trade union movement could have overcome. There were two aspects on which to base this assumption. On the one hand, the belligerent potential of Honduran trade unionism succeeded in accumulating important social benefits, which exceeded those offered by the *solidarista* movement. On the other hand, a policy of open government support of the *solidarista* project unleashed strong trade union opposition, which placed the precarious political system in the balance. In other words, the governing capacity of the democratic process being implemented at the time was, according to Posas, brought into question.

From a regional point of view, it may be assumed that the higher level of development of the *solidarista* movement in Costa Rica was also a result of the culture of consensus that predominated in this society in contrast to the logic of confrontation that prevailed in the rest of Central America. Moreover, along these same lines, it is important to recall, as Aguilar (1989: 133) has effectively done, that

> This consensus was reconstructed by means of the social pact that the middle sectors and ruling class established after 1948. The working class, on the other hand, did not endorse this pact with direct action; it did not play a prominent role in this historical event, although it was subsequently the main recipient of the consequences derived from this union. . . . One of the most negative consequences resulting from the social pact between the middle sectors and the ruling class were the restrictions on trade union liberties themselves.

Honduras, as mentioned above, represented an intermediate case in which both the effects of the economic crisis and the *sui géneris* political situation that country experienced in the 1980s due to the armed conflicts taking place in all its neighboring countries—especially El Salvador and Nicaragua—made their mark. It must be remembered that toward the end of the 1970s, the suppression of the trade union movement was on the increase once more (Meza, 1991: 161ff.). For its part, the economic crisis placed the wage demands of the workers at center stage. It was in regard to these demands that the confederations already in existence since the previous period—the CTH and CGT, as well as the newly created (in 1981) left-wing United Workers Federation of Honduras (FUTH)—obtained greater unity. Two of the main strikes held during these years were based on wage demands. This was the case in the conflict that broke out in 1984 at the National Electricity Institute, which was politicized due to the kidnapping and disappearance of that institution's main leader. In addition, in 1987 the powerful SITRATERCO also began strike action for wage reasons.

During the first years of democratic openness, between 1982 and 1985, 64 strikes were reported in Honduras. Almost three quarters of these were held within the public sector. The application of the first stabilizing measures has been discussed alongside the fact that within the framework of the "national security" strategy implemented by the Honduran government, funds were transferred to army institutions to the detriment of social spending. This situation meant that the hostility of state workers became more acute (Meza Pineda, 1990: 199–200).

The clearest and also most conflictive examples of the relation between trade unions and the political system were presented by the countries experiencing armed conflicts. The previous chapter described Guatemala, in 1954, as the scene of the dismantling of organizations that had emerged, especially during the Arbenz era, and how, as of the 1960s, the trade union movement gradually recovered, mainly due to Catholic forces. During the Laugerud era, a decline in the level of suppression and a certain measure of political openness meant the trade union movement reached new heights, which hastened the consequences of the 1976 earthquake and the setting up of the CNUS. An event crucial to this, due to the mass support it generated, was the Ixtahuacán miners' march in November 1977 from the province of Huehuetenango—on the border with Mexico—to the capital. Along the same lines, the strike involving 85,000 public employees demanding better pay must be mentioned, as must the popular revolt that took place in October 1978, when Lucas García was already in power, which was the result of increases in the cost of basic necessities and public transport. This revolt overwhelmed the CNUS itself. However, alongside this peak period of labor and popular struggles, the insurgency policy began a fierce suppression of popular organizations, including trade unions. With regard to the latter, the assassination in 1977 of well-known labor lawyer Mario López Larrave must be mentioned. A year later, after the October events, forty people were assassinated and 800 arrested, among them numerous trade union leaders. During the two more violent years that followed, 27 CNT leaders were assassinated in June 1980, and a further 18 were murdered in August. This meant the trade union movement was forced to return underground (Jonas, 1991: 125).[38] Furthermore, in addition to this brutal suppression, the effects of union-related problems were also being felt: lack of internal democracy; subjection to political projects (including those related to insurgency); and the dilemma, resulting from the achievements regarding unity, between "pluralism v. hegemonism" (Witzel, n.d.: 638). Thus, the new boom of trade union activity ended in much the same way as it had done in 1930 under Ubico and in 1954 following Arbenz's downfall.

However, in Guatemala's case, there is another key organizational phenomenon, which was already referred to in the previous chapter: the rise of the Peasant Unity Committee (CUC). This movement had clear ethnic inclinations, especially at the outset, although it also had leanings toward labor issues, which were manifest in its most significant collective actions. Its origins were set within the indigenous revival that took place in Guatemala in the 1970s, where modernization did not necessarily imply ladinization. This revival had various dimensions,[39] though of interest to this work is that corresponding to the heart of the communities in the central zone of the western *Altiplano*, which gave rise to the CUC. It has been pointed out that this movement originated in the less impoverished sectors of communities that had experienced a certain level of modernization: handicraft workers, tradespeople, and peasants who, thanks to the impact of the so-called "green revolution," succeeded in breaking the vicious circle of subsistence agriculture and the need to undertake seasonal migrations to the *fincas* on the south coast. Subsequently, it spread to other types of communities where peasants' subsistence had to be supplemented by temporary wage labor. This dual area of action reflected the ambiguity of this movement with respect to the community: On the one hand, it was more deeply rooted in the communities than any other organization had been; but on the other hand, it had a class-based approach, by which it attempted to make the class struggle within the community converge with social conflicts at the national level (Le Bot, 1992: 164–167). Thus, the search for an alliance between indigenous peoples and poor ladino peasants was proposed. According to Le Bot (1992: 168–170) this alliance was not formed because the CUC did not succeed in integrating itself either in the ladino areas of colonization or in the eastern region of the country. Le Bot believes the decisive element in the rise of this movement corresponded to links with the community rather than class.

This initial development was from an organizational point of view essentially informal, as demonstrated by the multiple community actions that had begun to be implemented on the south coast and, above all, in the central western *Altiplano*. The key event, which implied a qualitative change in this regard, was represented by the above-mentioned Ixtahuacán miners' march. This event highlighted the need for a greater level of coordination of the numerous local initiatives. Therefore, in mid-April of 1978, the congress that institutionalized and named the CUC was held, and it made its first public presentation at a May 1 demonstration. Incorporation in CNUS leadership circles followed. In this respect, it is no coincidence that the killing of *kekchí* indigenous people in Panzós, which represented the onset of the ethnocide that was to take place during the ensuing years, occurred shortly afterward. Another fundamental event was the assassination of 21 leaders and militants of the CUC during the attack on the Spanish embassy carried out by police forces at the end of January 1980. This bloody incident led to the meeting at Iximché, which houses the ruins of what was once the capital of the *kaqchikeles*, where indigenous organizations denounced the event and practically proposed declaring war on the military regime; this meeting was not explicitly supported by the CUC (Arias, 1985: 102–103).

At the same time, a wage demand movement had begun, in late 1979, in the cotton and sugar *fincas* on the south coast. Around mid-February the CUC launched a strike by taking over the Pantaleón mill. From that moment on, an increasing number of workers joined the stoppage, and it has been estimated that a total of 75,000 people participated in this action; this was the most significant mobilization that had taken place in Guatemala's agricultural sector since 1954 (Jiménez, 1985: 338–339). The extent of this event led to the start of negotiations; however, the government imposed a unilateral wage increase.[40] The repression and dismissals carried out by the owners of the *fincas* meant this increase was not implemented. In September 1980, the CUC made an unsuccessful attempt to renew strike action, this time in the coffee *fincas* in the Costa Cuca region. In this area the importance of tenant farmers, who were more dependent on the landowners, was greater, and the group members were, by and large, from the Huehuetenango area where the incorporation of the CUC in the communities was less evident. As of that moment, the CUC found itself involved in the logic of armed confrontation that led to its downfall as a social movement (Le Bot, 1992: 173).[41]

In El Salvador, three periods have been identified in reference to trade union action (Lazo and Herrera, 1985: 7ff.). The first extends from 1979 to August of the following year. This was a period of much union activity, with strikes and mobilizations that materialized, initially, in the form of the Revolutionary Mass Coordinator (CRM) and, later on, with the Democratic Revolutionary Front (FDR). This demonstrated that from the late 1970s, trade union activity could not be divorced from the action carried out by the popular movement in general (Lungo, 1990: 102). A second stage covers the period from September 1980 to September 1983 and, in contrast to the previous stage, is characterized by the setbacks the unions experienced due to an increase in state repression. However, a strike held by the workers of the Urban Housing Institute in September 1983 marked the reappearance of trade union action. This revival was composed of several dimensions. First, public employees were involved in formulating demands. Second, the type of organization favored was interunion unity, overcoming ideological differences. Third, the demands were initially of a corporate nature (defense of wages and posts), although they began to include political demands in an unequivocal manner due to the intensification of the armed conflict (Guido Béjar, 1990: 83–84).

The two historical tendencies of Salvadoran trade unionism reappear during this period with a new look. On the one hand, the reformist tendency emerged in the form of Democratic Popular Unity (UPD) sponsored by the American Institute for the Development of Free Trade Unionism (IADSL). On the other hand, the radical tendency took on the form of the United Trade Union and Guild Movement of El Salvador (MUSYGES), which maintained a nonorganic relation with the guerrilla forces (Lazo and Herrera, 1985: 29). Most important was the convergence of both tendencies, which coincided not only in their corporate but also their political demands, whereby human rights and a dialogue in favor of peace emerged as the claims made by the trade union movement in that country (Rojas Bolaños, 1988: 20). This convergence resulted in the setting up of the National Salvadoran Workers Unity (UNTS) in 1986, which was undoubtedly the most important unifying organism in the history of Salvadoran unionism. It gathered together not only labor but also peasant organizations as well as cooperatives, in addition to elaborating a platform for the masses with proposals for national policies (Guido Béjar, 1990: 86–87).

With regard to Nicaragua, it must be remembered that of all the countries in the region, this was the one in which trade unionism was the least developed. The defeat of the Somoza dictatorship and the installation of the *Sandinista* regime meant an unprecedented rise of trade union organizations. In this respect, it has been pointed out that during the four decades of Somoza's rule, only 138 trade unions were legalized, whereas by the end of 1979, 188 new union organizations had been registered (López, Brenes, and Jiménez, 1990: 209). This growth continued, and by the end of 1986 it is said that the 260,000 trade union members represented 56 percent of the total number of wage workers (Vilas, 1989: 136–137). Those who benefited most from this boom were the confederations with *Sandinista* leanings: the *Sandinista* Workers Confederation (CST) and the Rural Workers Association (ATC). Although the *Sandinista* regime maintained a monopoly on rural organizations due to the fact that rural trade unions had not existed during the Somoza era, this was not the case in the urban environment. Despite its limited development and very marginal participation in the revolutionary process, during the *Sandinista* era, there was a trade union movement that proposed action related to corporate demands. In contrast, *Sandinista* organizations found themselves stifled by their support of the revolutionary project.[42] That is, they emerged as politically co-opted entities, which led to their progressive decline. However, within the *Sandinista* trade union movement itself it is possible to identify a split, to a certain extent, between its leaders at the national level, who were guided by the revolutionary process, and its grass-roots organizations that had to face day-to-day hardships. These differences, which were largely determined by the labor policy implemented by the *Sandinista* regime, as described below, became more acute with the passing of time.

In the initial stages, qualitative improvements manifested not only in the above-mentioned organizational boom but also in the widespread use of collective contracts, extended coverage of social security, and greater efficiency in the social services offered by the state (Vilas, 1989: 137). However, the development of obstacles aimed at obstructing the revolutionary process, which originated largely but not exclusively as a result of external harassment on the part of the United States government, began to give rise to contradictions, especially in terms of the wage policy.[43] The latter's cornerstone was the implementation of the so-called National Labor and Wage Organization System (SNOTS). This was a complex system inspired by the Cuban experience, which was based on the principle that the worker should be paid the same salary for the same level of occupational complexity. The system included a variety of components such as a basic wage, the difficulties the work entailed, education and experience needed to carry out the work, and responsibility of the post. Nevertheless, as mentioned above, aspects particular to the Nicaraguan context were not taken into account (marked differences in production within the same activity, absence of adequate supply of skilled labor, existence of "multiemployment," etc.) (Vilas, 1989: 145–147). Furthermore, it must be noted that its application was not complete, for it began in 1984 with only the basic wage, and the other elements were to be implemented in a gradual manner. However, the soaring inflation that began to affect the country around the middle of that decade made the system inoperative from the outset. The result was that the SNOTS became one of the most conflicting issues between the *Sandinista* government and the workers.

The state's initial reaction was to increase the so-called social salary—in other words, it extended social state services. However, the decline of these meant payment in kind was imposed, which in some sectors represented almost half of the salaries.[44] This phenomenon affected labor actions in a number of ways. First, it questioned the minimum wage as a benchmark, thereby impairing this relationship. Second, it induced a lack of labor discipline, which undermined one of the most important banners of *Sandinismo* and the CST's ideology that was increased productivity and, consequently, production. In addition, it meant the incorporation of the wage workers in informal economic circles, due to the fact that this was where the majority of this salary in kind ended up (Vilas, 1989: 148–149).[45] Thus, this type of remuneration distorted the condition of the worker as such, resulting in the informalization of wage workers exposed to different identity logics.

Finally, it must be pointed out that the decline in the economic situation forced the *Sandinista* government to take drastic stabilizing measures in 1987. These affected public employment because some institutions that were considered redundant were merged. The policy of cutting back on government spending meant that as early as 1988, 3,000 central government posts were eliminated as a result of the merging of ministries. However, it was not until the following year that the government, faced with growing economic difficulties, applied the above-mentioned merging policy, which affected 9,000 people working in the central government and a further 8,000 who lost their jobs in autonomous entities and state firms. Although the government proposed that this surplus labor incorporate itself in the agricultural sector by joining cooperatives or forming new units, it is believed the majority remained unemployed or were forced to enter the informal sector (Evans, 1995: 223).

Toward the late 1980s, in 1987, Costa Rica registered 356 trade unions with 138,145 members, which indicated a rate of trade unionization, with respect to the total EAP, of 14.1 percent. These had joined together in the form of seven confederations, in addition to a considerable number of independent trade unions. At that time, they comprised just over a quarter of all members. Worth mentioning are the CATD, whose origins have already been described in the previous chapter, and the left-wing United Workers Confederation (CUT), which was founded in 1980; these comprised 19.9 percent and 17.1 percent of trade union members respectively (Donato and Castro, 1990: tables 2 and 4). In qualitative terms, it has been argued that the 1980s was a period in which trade unions joined together and made the Costa Rican labor movement a valid means of interaction for the state. However, this unity was made possible by the weakness of all the trade union forces that made it impossible to establish any form of leadership. This weakness was manifest in two ways. On the one hand, aggressiveness dwindled; on the other hand, trade unionism died out in the private sector due to the solidarity boom mentioned above. This meant the presence of trade unions was limited to the public sector, thereby implying that actions took on a middle-class quality (Donato and Castro, 1990: 34–35).

With reference to Honduras, in 1986, 204 trade unions with 208,109 members were registered, the majority of which centered on the northern part of the country, as had been the case in the past (Rojas Bolaños, 1988: 26). Posas (1990: 165) claims that the greatest challenge faced by trade unionism in Honduras in the late 1980s was that of unity. Along the same lines, Meza Pineda (1990: 201) stresses the setting up of the FUTH, which implied the elimination of the traditional control mechanisms exercised by foreign entities; moreover, this organization succeeded in bringing together strategic public sector trade unions that, as seen earlier, had a more aggressive approach during these years.

It has been argued that the fierce suppression the Guatemalan trade union movement was subjected to, resulting in its relegation to clandestine activity in the late 1970s, has had a negative impact on the same that was twofold: It prevented it from being consolidated as an institution, and it impeded the passing down of experiences from one generation to the next. In addition, the democratic openness in Guatemala as of 1986 gave rise to contradictory tendencies in terms of its relation with the state: The level of suppression decreased on the whole, but new and more selective forms of violence aimed at trade union circles appeared (Enríquez, 1990: 122, 131). Democratic openness meant the union organizations began to publicly reorganize themselves. Thus, Catholic-based trade unionism reappeared in the form of the Guatemalan General Workers Confederation (CGTG), which was present in agricultural areas and tertiary activities. The emergence of a class-based trade unionism, the Guatemalan Workers United Trade Unions (UNSITRAGUA), which centered on the industrial sector, must also be mentioned. However, perhaps the most significant, due to its unifying character, was the founding of the Trade Union and Popular Action Unit (UASP). This entity joined together not only the majority of trade unions but also other kinds of organizations, in particular indigenous ones, which proved to be the most active; to these should be added the revival of the CUC.[46]

The Salvadoran movement experienced a similar repressive situation. However, the armed conflict developed differently in both countries; whereas in Guatemala, as of 1982 the balance began to shift in favor of the army, in El Salvador it remained even. From a circumstantial but, above all, subjective point of view, this implied that the popular organizations were not on the defensive. After overcoming the setbacks at the beginning of the decade, the most important trade union alliance in Salvadoran history was formed. In addition to this, it must be stressed that due to the context of the war itself, the workers' organizations made demands related to respect for human rights and peace in the country.

In Nicaragua, the main organizational problem faced by the trade union movement during the *Sandinista* period was the lack of coordination between far-reaching and short-term demands. Thus, the former were dealt with by the government-oriented sector that focused on war and production, whereas the remaining trade union groups concentrated on demands related to living conditions and labor (López, Brenes, and Jiménez, 1990: 226).

As a result, it may be concluded that at the regional level, the crisis weakened the region's trade union movement, just as it had done in other parts of Latin America. Moreover, two additional factors left their mark on Central America. On the one hand, this movement's developments were insignificant during the decades of modernization, as may be seen in the previous chapter. On the other hand, the existence of armed conflicts in the region created a hostile and suppressive environment for popular organizations in general and labor organizations in particular.

Alongside this regional consideration, it is also important to highlight specific national characteristics. Thus, with regard to Costa Rica, one must mention the splits within trade unionism, its marginal presence in the private sector due to the spectacular growth of the *solidarista* movement, and consequently, its confinement in the public sector. In Honduras, the crisis and suppression constituted severe blows to the trade unions, but by the end of the 1980s that country's labor movement was still the least fragile in the region. It was in Guatemala that the suppression had the most devastating effects, and the year 1981, in which trade unions were forced to survive as an underground movement, represented a situation similar to that of Ubico in 1930 or the overthrow of Arbenz in 1954—that is, the dismantling of the labor movement following a period of expansion. In regard to El Salvador, suppression also left its mark, though the fact that neither side came out of the armed conflict a winner meant that trade unionism was able to benefit from the popular movement. In effect, the most significant moment of trade union unification in the history of El Salvador occurred when the war and the crisis were in full swing. Finally, in Nicaragua, the faltering *Sandinista* regime directly affected its labor organizations, which were the most significant among the considerable trade union developments that country had undergone during the *Sandinista* revolution.

Consequently, the trade union movement in Central America faces the challenges of productive restructuring that began to be implemented in the 1990s, in a weakened state, both from a corporate and political point of view, as a result of the 1980s crisis. The rise of new activities such as the *maquila* industry, with its new labor force that has little trade union experience and strong management opposition to union organization, or state reforms with their subsequent reduction in public employment, have left the labor movement embedded in a defensive position.

Notes

1. It should be pointed out that a considerable number of studies on labor issues were produced in the region in the 1980s. For an assessment of these, see Funkhouser (1994a) and Pérez Sáinz (1994b).

2. Funkhouser (1992b) has also analyzed the effects of emigration in Nicaragua. As in the case of El Salvador, the population that emigrated were, by and large, of working age, had a higher level of schooling, and were not occupied in manual jobs. In the same manner, the remittances have had a negative impact on labor participation, though they have also, to a limited extent, had positive effects on generating self-employment.

3. This points to the existence of problems of a methodological nature regarding the information available.

4. The analysis is based on a comparison between three milestones (1978, 1985, and 1991/1992), which allows a distinction to be made between two periods during the war.

5. In effect, this rate corresponded to 52.5 percent. However, as in the case of Honduras, such an abrupt variation may respond to problems related to the data.

6. In a study on the incomes of the labor force in the district of Guatemala, Funkhouser (1993) has demonstrated that the incidence of factors related to human capital (education and work experience) is higher in the modern sector. Nonetheless, this incidence has a tendency to decline toward the late 1980s.

7. Two comments must be made on this and the following table. First, the 1981 observation for Guatemala refers to a national census; this implies certain methodological differences with regard to the other two observations, based on surveys, which will be explained in due course. Second, the three observations for Costa Rica correspond to the same month, July. Until 1988, three surveys were carried out in this country per year; this was later reduced to one, which is carried out in July.

8. Tardanico (1991–1992: 94), limiting himself to San José, has argued that the main characteristic of the development of employment between 1979 and 1987 has been the gradual nature of the changes it has undergone. This is explained by institutional factors, within the context of the wars being waged in the region, whereby this country's sociopolitical regime gave it geopolitical advantages.

9. Naturally, in terms of female employment the problem of underrepresentation is ever-present. In this sense, it may be concluded that part of the increase is due to more care being taken in the gathering of information, which is a result of growing awareness of this problem. Moreover, it must be stressed that a survey appears to be more adequate for correcting this underrepresentation than a census. In regard to the latter, the rate of female participation estimated on the basis of the National Family Incomes and Expenditures Survey carried out between

1979 and 1981 is 19 percent higher than that of the census (García and Gomáriz, 1989: 197).

10. Tardanico (1990–1991: 102) has observed that with reference to San José, this higher level of incorporation in the labor market corresponds to middle-aged and older women.

11. This job category may involve problems of underrepresentation similar to those of female employment mentioned earlier.

12. This phenomenon has also been emphasized by Negreros (1989a).

13. In fact, the level of urban predominance in this country—one of the highest in Latin America—began to decline in the late 1970s (Pérez Sáinz, 1992).

14. In this respect, it has been estimated that 440 towns were destroyed, over 100,000 people died or "went missing," and over one million had to abandon their place of residence (a considerable percentage were forced to go into exile, to Mexico in particular) (Jonas, 1991: 49).

15. With regard to the three main agricultural export goods, the estimates for temporary workers who reside in the districts where these crops are grown are the following: 60 percent for coffee and sugar cane, and 14 percent for cotton (Baumeister, 1993: 131).

16. Naturally, certain methodological problems arise when comparing census data with that of a survey (especially in terms of the EAP in El Salvador), although for this type of analysis—involving a comparison between two time intervals—these do not have serious consequences. The observation made in reference to Table 2.4 must also be taken into account: The percentages of some of the tendencies (wage labor, professionalization, and tertiary labor) should be calculated in relation to the employed population, but in order to be consistent with the previous analysis, these have been estimated in relation to the EAP.

17. Within the region, three countries have been analyzed in the well-known World Bank study on differences in income according to gender. Yang (1992) has estimated the difference for Costa Rica at 19.2 percent, which drops to 9.2 percent in the public sector, where wages are higher and labor relations are regulated. This same phenomenon is identified by Gindling (1992), who, furthermore, argues that discrimination against women in the workplace is no less in this country than in the rest of Latin America. Gindling detects the same discrimination in Honduras, which becomes more pronounced in the formal sector (Winter and Gindling, 1992). With regard to Guatemala, Arends (1992) concludes that overall, the differences in incomes are not marked, although women are underrepresented regarding self-employment, as are men in regard to wage labor. Differences appear to be greater in the formal sector. Naturally, the differences in incomes in the three countries cannot, for the most part, be explained in terms of human capital.

18. In effect, estimates for 1993 indicate that a little over a third (36.6 percent) of the population of Costa Rica was aged under 15; in the rest of the region, this age group tended to correspond to almost half the population (FLACSO, 1995, table 6).

19. Martínez (1993: 47) has estimated that this type of employment has reached levels that vary between 28 percent of the rural EAP in Guatemala to 59 percent in Costa Rica.

20. In the 1980s, the first studies were carried out—in the majority of the countries—on the informal phenomenon with differing emphases. Worth mentioning

are those undertaken by PREALC (1977), Briones (1987) and Cruz (1984) in El Salvador. In Guatemala, the FADES (1987) study should be highlighted. For Nicaragua see, among others, Aburto (1988), CETRA (1987) and Redondo and Juárez (1987). With regard to Costa Rica, those of Haan (1984), Moller (1985) and Murillo, Martínez, Ramírez, and Villalobos (1984) should be mentioned. Moreover, in Costa Rica there are a number of studies that analyze the informal sector within the context of the crisis and the adjustment of the labor market, such as Uthoff and Pollack (1985), García-Huidobro (1987), Gindling (1986, 1989), and Tardanico (1991–1992).

21. These estimates have been facilitated by Edward Funkhouser. The informal sector covers the same categories as those used by PREALC (self-employed workers, unpaid family workers, owners of and wage laborers working in establishments employing under five persons). Professionals and technicians have been excluded; domestic workers are included.

22. These data have been obtained from household surveys, which were reprocessed within the context of a regional investigation carried out by FLACSO focusing on six metropolitan centers in the region: the five capitals and San Pedro Sula (Pérez Sáinz and Menjívar Larín, 1991). Among the national studies, those on El Salvador (Briones, 1991) and Honduras (Del-Cid, 1991) must be highlighted.

23. This profile is very similar to that identified by Funkhouser (1994c: 12–13) based on the analysis of the data from the last household surveys for the five countries in the region.

24. In regard to this problem of urban labor market segmentation, it must be pointed out that—in relation to Costa Rica—studies have been undertaken to verify, in an empirical manner, the hypothesis on segmentation. Thus, Uthoff and Pollack (1985) have established that the expected income was higher in the public than the private sector and higher in the formal than the informal sector for individuals with the same qualifications. Gindling (1986), in comparison, has demonstrated that there were considerable differences, in terms of income, between the public and private sector, but this was not the case between the formal and informal sectors. Nonetheless, that author has subsequently questioned this second observation on the basis of a more methodologically reliable exercise using wage equations instead of incomes. The outcome resulted in the confirmation of formal/informal segmentation (Gindling, 1989).

25. Funkhouser (1994c: 21) has demonstrated that the difference between incomes earned by men and those earned by women is higher in informal than formal activities.

26. Edward Funkhouser, in a personal note, has pointed out that at the national urban level, the data show sociodemographic and job profiles very similar to those reflected by metropolitan areas.

27. These cases have also been included in the aforementioned first regional investigation carried out by FLACSO.

28. These figures correspond to a second regional research project undertaken by FLACSO, which also takes into account Panama City (Menjívar Larín and Pérez Sáinz, 1993). On this occasion, among the national studies worth highlighting are those of Guatemala (Bastos and Camus, 1993a) and Costa Rica (Goldenberg, 1993).

29. Two criteria are used in this typology. On the one hand, investment in machinery and/or equipment and in means of transport reflects the presence of processes of accumulation. On the other hand, the second criterion is related to the type of accountancy that characterizes the establishment's management. Accumulation combined with the use of formal accountancy defines the dynamic mode; the absence of both defines subsistence; and the presence of one or the other points to the intermediary mode. Moreover, it must be stressed that the concept of informality employed refers to the definition of this phenomenon as "economic urban activities that, in a context of peripheral capitalist modernization, are characterized by a simple division of employment whereby the owner of the means of production is directly involved in the process of producing goods and services" (Pérez Sáinz, 1994a: 48).

30. The predominance of the intermediary type responds to the high percentage of cases (the highest for all the areas) in which investments are made in machinery and/or equipment as seen in the top half of the table. Nevertheless, it must be pointed out that it was the Salvadoran case that presented the lowest percentage in terms of formal accounting. Therefore, a paradoxical context emerges in that there was accumulative development but little business rationality, implying that this development could have been purely circumstantial and that subsistence informality would eventually prevail.

31. These results reinforce the definition of informality based on the labor process because it may be assumed that an increase in workers tended to make the division of labor more complex, thereby implying that the owner of the establishment would no longer be directly involved in the material production of goods and services and that his/her condition could therefore no longer be described as informal in accordance with the definition of this phenomenon used herein.

32. In this regard, it must be pointed out that in FLACSO's second regional study this sociodemographic dimension is privileged from an analytical point of view. In this sense, the present text has aimed to go beyond simply analyzing the presence of women in the informal sector by comparing it with the male presence. In contrast, the regional study carried out by the Fundación Arias(1992) limits itself to focusing on the presence of women in informality. We take this opportunity to mention the existence of two works, also of regional scope, in which the issue of female employment is discussed in global terms: that of García-Huidobro (1989) and that of Dierckxsens (1990).

33. In this manner, a fundamental methodological premise of the FLACSO studies on labor markets in Central America is reaffirmed: the process of the reproduction of the work force as an interpretative reference, and the home as a unit of unavoidable analysis. This emphasis is evident in the studies developed by this institution on Guatemala City and, namely, those regarding the incorporation of women in the labor force (Pérez Sáinz and Castellanos de Ponciano, 1991) as well as that of indigenous persons (Bastos and Camus, 1989; Pérez Sáinz, Camus, and Bastos, 1992). In addition and from an analytical perspective, Achío's study (1987) on industrial workers in Costa Rica and their subsistence logics must be mentioned.

34. In this regard, Rojas Bolaños (1988) has carried out a comparative analysis of the trade union movement in three countries in the region that presented dif-

ferent political reactions to the regional crisis at the beginning of the decade: Costa Rica, where little change was reported; El Salvador, which was torn by civil war; and Honduras, which was affected, in an unusual manner, by the presence of three armies on national soil.

35. In effect, while the rate of trade unionization in the public sector reached 58.4 percent in 1987, this corresponded to a mere 6 percent in the private sector (Donato and Castro, 1990: 21).

36. See Vega (1989) for information on *solidarista* ideology.

37. These types of organizations were given legal recognition in this country in 1984.

38. One of the very rare exceptions of a trade union that stood its ground was that of Coca-Cola, which led a long and bloody conflict and survived. In this regard, the international support it generated was fundamental for its permanence. See Levinson-Estrada (1994: 176ff.) for further information.

39. For an analysis on these, see Bastos and Camus (1993b: 23–27).

40. The pay was one quetzal per day (at that time this was equivalent to one dollar), and the workers demanded five. The increase offered by the government was 3.20 quetzals.

41. Carmack (1988) provides a vivid account of how one of the first communities in which the CUC developed (La Estancia in the province of El Quiché) found itself dragged into armed confrontation.

42. A summary of the positions of different trade union confederations regarding the *Sandinista* economic plan may be found in Brenes (1987).

43. PREALC (1980a) carried out a study between 1979 and 1980 that illustrates the wage structure that existed at the time and the challenges it posed for the *Sandinista* regime.

44. Along the same lines, changes in the distribution of basic goods, which were heavily subsidized by the state, must be mentioned. The number of these was increased, but they were limited to trade union workers only. Nonetheless, the supplying difficulties weakened this wage compensation system.

45. In this regard, it is interesting to recall how during 1983 and 1987, Sandinism described informality in general as a parasitic and speculating sector that was responsible for inflation (Chamorro, Chávez, and Membreño, 1991: 220–222).

46. Bastos and Camus (1993b: 59ff.) describe these indigenous organizations as "popular" as opposed to "ethnic."

4

An Uncertain Future: Globalization, Productive Restructuring, and Labor

This chapter attempts to examine the post-crisis period—in other words, the processes that are currently taking place in Central America. All the countries in the region, as in the rest of Latin America, are undergoing structural adjustment programs that imply a radical redefinition of the economy. In this manner, it has been assumed that a significant productive restructuring process is being put into effect, involving the setting up of an emerging tradables sector as the new axis of accumulation incorporated within the dynamics of globalization that characterizes the world economy. This entails considerable changes with regard to the labor market, especially that of urban areas.

With regard to defining the urban employment structure in the phase prior to modernization, there is consensus on two key aspects: first, that it was a heterogeneous structure, and second, that this heterogeneity was seen in terms of the difference between formal and informal employment. However, the failure to reach an agreement on the definition of this difference has given rise to widespread debate on the phenomenon of informality in Latin America. Nonetheless, this image, regardless of how this sectorial difference is interpreted, no longer seems to reflect the new emerging reality. In this sense, three hypotheses have been proposed regarding the changes being experienced in terms of occupational diversity.[1]

The first of these deals with the emergence of a new tradables sector, as mentioned above, which has manifested in Central America in the form of phenomena such as nontraditional agricultural exports,[2] the *maquila* industry, and tourism. It is worth stressing the fact that this emerging sector may reflect two types of accumulative processes, which are not mutually exclusive, within the same national context. Thus, new local and foreign investment is developed; with regard to the latter, the growing importance of Asian capital in Central America must be mentioned.

A second accumulative process is represented by the reconversion of firms that were formerly operating within the context of previous development (in particular, industrial firms focusing on the regional market) but that have succeeded in redirecting their activities toward exports in the so-called third markets.[3]

The second hypothesis focuses on the decline of the formal sector. It is a well-known fact that this area of employment was the hardest hit by the crisis. In other words, the unemployment in the 1980s was a result of the elimination of posts in that sector and, more specifically, in private firms. The current outlook is far from promising. Thus, the opening up of economies, a key element in the structural adjustment programs, represents a crucial dilemma for formal firms: their transformation into firms dealing in tradable goods and services, be they export-based or competing with imports, or their relegation and possible disappearance. The public sector perspective is equally as pessimistic. The structural adjustment programs themselves involve state reforms that cut back on jobs in this sector. This process began to be enforced in the region in the 1990s with Nicaragua, given its particular political circumstances, registering the most dramatic decrease in public employment.[4]

The third hypothesis deals with the changes that took place within the informal sector. In this regard, it has been suggested that although activities described as informal still existed, their creation, development, and materialization with respect to the national (and even international) economy have varied. That is, the increasing decline in importance of the formal sector meant that the development of informal employment depended on other processes such as that of globalization and its complement, exclusion. This led to the redefinition of the diversity of this occupational sector and the proposal that the term "neoinformality" be used to describe it (Pérez Sáinz, 1994a: 111–114). In this respect, three contexts have been identified: an economy of poverty, subordination to the tradables sector, and agglomeration of small dynamic firms.

The present chapter aims to explore some of the changes that are taking place. In short, two issues are considered: In the first section the *maquila* industry, which has undergone dramatic developments in the region during the past few years, is discussed; in the second section, the new forms being adopted by informality are examined.[5] Needless to say, both settings are analyzed from the point of view of labor relations.

The *Maquila,* Free Trade Zones, and Labor

The current industrializing tendency in Central America is undoubtedly induced by production aimed at exports and is no longer based on the import substitution model associated with national and subregional markets. The basic structure of the new industrialization differs from the former in regard to, among others, three main elements. First, it operates within new special regulation frameworks that involve a whole series of benefits (customs and tax exemptions, exchange benefits, etc.). Second, its production is based largely on assembling imported goods. Finally, it centers on exports, thereby incorporating itself in the new globalizing tendency that is currently influencing the world economy. However, this emerging industrializing model may take on different forms depending on the area covered by the specific series of regulations that defines it. Thus, it may focus on the development of a certain region; it may also delimit a group of firms or type of activity or center on very specific areas, as in the case of the industrial parks. In Central America the models that have been developed correspond to the second (by means of the *maquila* industry) and third (the so-called Free Trade Zones) of these.

It must be pointed out that in Costa Rica, privileged tax treatment was being granted to *maquila* industries devoted to the assembly of nontraditional exports as early as 1972; those measures did not impose a particular location for these types of firms, but the majority were situated in the metropolitan area of San José. The Free Trade Zone for Industry and Commerce (ZOLIC) was set up in Santo Tomás de Castilla on Guatemala's Atlantic coast in the following year, though it did not become operational until 1978. In 1974 El Salvador passed legislation in favor of the setting up of Free Trade Zones that materialized in the form of the San Bartolo Free Trade Zone in the Ilopango municipality, close to the capital. In addition, 1976 saw the setting up of the Las Mercedes Free Trade Zone next to Managua airport and that of Puerto Cortés in Honduras, which began to operate two years later.

However, this new industrializing experience was not consolidated in any of these countries. The ZOLIC faced problems related to infrastructure and labor, and moreover, it highlighted the Guatemalan state's inability to confront such responsibilities (CITGUA, 1991; Petersen, 1992). San Bartolo, following a promising start, lost its dynamism due to the impact of the armed conflict on El Salvador. The triumph of the *Sandinista* revolution meant that the firms in the Las Mercedes Free Trade Zone became part of the so-called Area of the Property of the People. Only in the case of Puerto Cortés were initial developments maintained, although this did not imply that it presented an alternative to industrialization. Consequently, this first attempt could be interpreted as just another phase, characterized by the growth of nontraditional exports, in the evolution of the agricultural export model being implemented in the region since the end of the last century (Bulmer-Thomas, 1989).

The current situation in Central America appears different from that of the 1970s. The new industrializing tendency is more sustainable, has a greater area of influence, and is, above all, emerging as one of the axes of the new model of accumulation that aims to favor the production of tradable goods and services. This classification as a new model is based on the changes introduced by globalization that imply an international economy operating differently from that of the world market in which the agricultural export model incorporated itself. Perhaps the most important change is that of the questioning of the national market's relation to development; this explains how unfeasible industrializing strategies such as that of import substitution were at the time. Furthermore, a fundamental aspect is that this new industrializing tendency is set within the structural adjustment strategy being applied by all the governments in the region. This strategy aims to redefine the basis of production in addition to achieving a basic macroeconomic balance. In this sense, it may be said that states are currently making a clear attempt to stimulate this new form of industrial development.

This redefinition of more beneficial regulation frameworks has resulted in a substantial increase in the number of firms taking advantage of these. Three legal frameworks may be mentioned in relation to Costa Rica. There is a considerable number of firms under the so-called export contract system, although given the nature of this system, because there are no restrictions on sales to the local or Central American market, there is no processed information available that reflects how many of these export the majority of their goods outside the region. With regard to the temporary admissions regulations, whereas in the early 1980s only 23 firms benefited from this, by 1990 this figure had increased to 227 (Nowalski, Morales, and Berliavsky, 1993: 16). In effect, these regulations, promoted in 1972, only managed to attract 32 firms between that date and 1983 (Pavez, 1987: 29). In reference to the Free Trade Zone model, private sector information indicates that in 1986 a mere 11 firms were registered whereas in 1991 there were 96.[6] In Guatemala, data provided by the private sector, namely the Non-Traditional Exports Guild (GEXPRONT), indicate an increase of 41 firms benefiting from the legislation regarding *maquilas* in 1986 to 400 six years later. Along these same lines, the growth of foreign firms, among which those of Korean origin occupy a key position, has been dramatic: From only one in 1986, this figure increased to 82 in 1992. The seven Free Trade Zones in Honduras, including that of Puerto Cortés, reported 60 firms in April 1993, while the five Industrial Processing Zones registered 26 (BCH, 1993, table 1). However, Pérez and Varela (1995: 17–18) point to the existence in 1994 of 175 firms, to which 70 must be added, out of the 328 benefiting from the temporary import regulations that may be considered as *maquilas*. For its part, the San Bartolo Free Trade Zone in El Salvador had a mere 14 plants in 1992 (Arriola, 1993: 57); nonetheless, one must mention the current dynamism resulting from the peace process, which has led to operations starting up in other Free Trade Zones. In effect, by 1994, 29 firms were already installed in the five existing Free Trade Zones (San Bartolo, El Pedregal, San Marcos, El Progreso, and Exportasalva) and 152 establishments were declared fiscal grounds (González, 1995: 18).

However, as mentioned in the introduction to this chapter, my aim here is to analyze this phenomenon from the point of view of labor relations.[7] This means various aspects must be taken into consideration: the jobs created, the labor force involved, the type of labor relations system being enforced, the labor process' methods of organization, and the effects of the presence of trade unions.

It must first be pointed out that it is difficult to give an overall view of the jobs created by this new industrializing process. Schoepfle and Pérez-López (1992: table 5) have estimated the number of posts in Free Trade Zones in Central America in 1990 at approximately 25,000.[8] Costa Rica and Guatemala appear as the countries with the highest level of employment—6,000 jobs each—while Nicaragua had a mere 1,500. The importance of this kind of employment, despite the fact it increased during the course of the 1980s, was very marginal, even within industrial employment. Thus, its incidence varied between 5.9 percent of the industrial labor force in El Salvador and 3.3 percent in Costa Rica and Nicaragua. Nonetheless, there is evidence that this phenomenon was more significant than these figures—which only take into account industrial parks—indicate.

Data provided by business organizations show that by 1992, the number of jobs in Free Trade Zones in Costa Rica had reached 13,000; to this must be added those corresponding to the other two export models. In this regard, Nowalski, Morales, and Berliavsky (1993: 18) have pointed out that the number of jobs within the *maquiladora* (assembly plant) sector had already increased to 46,100 in 1990.[9] As for Guatemala, the above-mentioned GEXPRONT indicates that the jobs created in the *maquila* plants increased from 5,000 posts in 1986 to 70,000 six years later; for its part, AVANCSO (1994: table 8) estimated that the jobs created in the *maquila* industry in 1991 totaled 54,274. In Honduras, 17,134 jobs in Free Trade Zones, including Puerto Cortés, were estimated for 1993; and there were an estimated 10,083 jobs in the five Industrial Processing Zones (BCH, 1993: table 1). However, the estimates provided by Pérez and Varela (1995: 17) for 1994 were higher: 48,477 in addition to those of the 70 firms that complied with the temporary import regulations. In El Salvador toward the middle of 1992, the number of jobs in San Bartolo was estimated at 6,500 workers (Arriola, 1993: 58); to this was added the 18,300 posts estimated for El Pedregal and the 1,900 for El Progreso (FUSADES: 1991: 7–8). However, as early as 1994, the five existing Free Trade Zones had created 19,700 jobs in addition to the 40,300 corresponding to establishments declared fiscal entities (González, 1995: table 5).[10]

TABLE 4.1   Socio-Demographic and Household Profiles of the Work Force

Variables	Costa Rica	Guatemala	Honduras
Sex	Women (62.2%)	Women (78.0%)	Women (74.8%)
Age (average)	24.0	21.0	23.0
Marital status	Single women (56.8%)	Single women (56.8%)	Single women (69.7%)
Level of schooling	Up to primary (40.5%)	Up to primary (36.2%)	Up to primary (48.6%)
Portion of wage contributed to household	Less than half (31.1%)	Half (41.3%)	Half (38.8%)
Rate of domestic labor	3.0	4.0	4.0
Head of household	Interviewee (24.3%)	Father (39.0%)	Father (24.8%)

SOURCE: Pérez Sáinz (1994c, table 2).

However, perhaps the most important point to note is that the manufacturing industry was creating jobs and was, moreover, gaining relative importance in terms of the occupied population, as mentioned in the previous chapter. In this respect, it would be reasonable to assume that this dynamism corresponded to the new type of industrialization and not to the import substitution model that tended, rather, to expel labor.

A second aspect that must be taken into account is related to the characteristics of the labor force incorporated in this new industrializing model. Table 4.1 illustrates profiles, based on the results of the regional study carried out by FLACSO,[11] of the sociodemographic characteristics of the labor force, along with those related to some basic aspects of the workers' homes, in order to obtain a better understanding of the nature of this labor force.

As may be noted from the upper half of this table, there is evidence of a profile common to all three areas. This is a predominantly female labor force made up of young, single women, as is usually the case in this type of industry. Furthermore, most have completed primary education, which tends to be one of the firms' hiring requirements.[12] Nonetheless, with respect to this aspect there are certain differences between the areas under consideration, which are not reflected in this table. Thus, in Costa Rica the work force is more educated (almost one fifth of the same have completed secondary school) than in the other two cases, especially that of Guatemala (where one third of the workers have not completed primary education). This difference has already been observed, in global terms, in the previous chapters.

The lower half of this same table refers to homes where a common profile is not as clearly evident. On the one hand, Costa Rica appears to differ from the other two cases in that the head of household category corresponds to the interviewees themselves, there is less participation in domestic tasks,[13] and fewer monetary contributions are made to the home. Nevertheless, this last variable has a bi-modal distribution, and almost a third of the cases contribute their entire income. This phenomenon is in line with the comment made above on heads of households. On the other hand, the differences between the Guatemalan and Honduran contexts with respect to contributions, which are not illustrated in this table, must be highlighted. Whereas in the former, in just over a quarter of cases the contribution consists of the entire salary, in Honduras, in a similar percentage of situations, less than half is contributed.[14] Therefore, it may be assumed that in the former context the households find themselves in a more precarious situation than the latter.

Consequently, there are some dimensions that to a certain extent indicate the existence of a sociodemographic regional profile. In effect, this is made up of a young and therefore single female labor force that does not have a high level of schooling. To a lesser extent, it may be said that this type of worker is not normally the head of her household and does not contribute the majority of her labor income to her family unit, though she does make a substantial contribution to tasks of a domestic nature (Pérez Sáinz, 1994c: 243–247).[15]

Before discussing the third aspect related to labor conditions, it is worth making a few brief observations regarding the mechanisms used to hire labor. This process tended to be carried out by the firms themselves, but in the Free Trade Zones (in Honduras in particular, and also in Costa Rica), it was the managerial level of the industrial parks that recruited the work force. Naturally, the contact networks of the workers themselves play an important part in this process. Firms favor work experience and also age (persons under 25, especially in Honduras) when recruiting, although the complaints concerning the difficulties in obtaining labor are recurrent. In this sense, it is interesting to highlight the fact that cases have been identified in which firms have implemented relocation strategies with the aim of securing local labor markets. One Costa Rican firm set up its second plant in a rural area in the Central Valley, claiming that in its original location, a Free Trade Zone, the hiring of labor is competitive and sometimes disloyally so. This new plant constitutes the only industrial activity in the area, and it benefits from an adequate labor force supply, which is only affected during harvests, especially the coffee bean harvest. This is not an isolated case in Costa

Rica. For its part, in Guatemala the Interamerican Highway, some fifty kilometers from the capital stretching toward the western *Altiplano*, is becoming a popular area for *maquila* plants, especially those of Korean origin. The reason, it is argued, is to avoid the capital city, where there is fierce competition for labor as well as risks associated with trade unions. Consequently, there have been cases in which these types of firms have established captive labor markets in rural areas (Pérez Sáinz, 1994c: 240).

Recruitment naturally always entails an initial period of training in the tasks to be undertaken, which varies in length according to each case. However, apart from this training, there appears to be no general company policy in this respect in any of the three areas under consideration. In this regard, it is important to point out that subsequent training is usually related to two phenomena. On the one hand, it is associated with promotion to higher positions, and on the other hand, it is linked to learning different tasks. According to those who provided information on the firms, this second context does not appear to imply the formation of a polyvalent work force with the aim of incorporating it in line with new principles of flexible specialization. It appears, rather, that this learning process reflects a worker replacement strategy in order to confront problems of rotation and absenteeism. Moreover, in terms of internal mobility, it must be stressed, above all, that these are not internal markets as such because mobility is largely limited to being promoted from the production line to a supervisory position (Pérez Sáinz, 1994c: 249–250).

Considering work conditions, three phenomena must be emphasized. The first deals with the lack of work stability that characterizes this world of labor; this aspect constitutes one of the firms' most common complaints.[16] In the regional study on which this section is based, the average period a post was held for was identified as 16 months in Costa Rica, 12 in Guatemala, and 14 in Honduras (Pérez Sáinz, 1994c: 247). It is interesting to note that this labor force has, on the whole, previous work experience and that this tends to take place within the *maquila* industry itself. That is, the work force is often rotated, but this does not mean it leaves its working environment. It may be argued that the origin of this frequent rotation phenomenon is twofold. On the one hand, this is a young work force, as already pointed out, whose work orientations have not yet been adequately defined. However, these jobs are, on the other hand, largely precarious and do not induce a great sense of job identification, as will be seen below.

The second aspect to be considered in terms of labor relations is related to salaries. This may be discussed from two angles: comparing the wage levels of the countries in the region (or even those of other countries that have also developed this type of industrialization), and contrasting the wages paid in these types of firms with other sectors of the national economy itself.

With respect to the first angle, it has been estimated that wages in this type of industry varied in 1987 between US$.95 per hour in Costa Rica and US$.53 in Honduras, while Guatemala held an intermediary position (US$.88). These levels, however, were higher than those paid in less developed Asian countries where this type of industrialization was underway.[17] Thus, in Costa Rica the wage was 3.6 times higher than the Asian average, and even the Honduran wage was double that typically found in Asia (Schoepfle and Pérez López, 1993: table 2). More up-to-date figures for 1991 related to the garment assembly industry point to hourly costs excluding social benefits, of $US.88 dollars for Costa Rica and US$.45 and US$.48 for Guatemala and Honduras (OIT, 1995: table 1). In regard to Costa Rica it is interesting to note that the main motivation for foreign investment in that country is not based on strictly economic reasons. Political factors (stability or legitimacy of the democratic system) as well as the labor force's level of qualification constitute priorities for foreign firms (Altenburg, 1993: 6–8).

With respect to the second angle, comparisons vary between countries. Thus, it could be said that in Guatemala the salaries paid in the *maquila* industry are no worse than those offered in other labor environments in which this type of industry's predominant labor force—that is, young women without a high level of schooling—could be incorporated. In this regard, an interesting comparison may be found in the work of Pérez Sáinz and Castellanos (1991: table 5.3) on female employment in Guatemala City, which contrasts three occupational settings related to this work force: one within the informal sector (tortilla-making); another focusing on domestic employment, the environment where female labor is most common; and that of the *maquila* industry. The wages earned in the latter were 2.5 times higher than the second and 1.3 times higher than the first.[18] Consequently, in a context such as that of the Guatemalan capital, where work opportunities for women of humble origin are limited to precarious labor environments, the *maquila* industry does not necessarily constitute the worst option.[19]

For its part, the data available for Costa Rica shows a situation in which there are no significant differences between sectors. Thus, Nowalski, Morales, and Berliavsky (1993: 82–84) point out that the average wage in the textile *maquilas* in mid-June 1993 was only 8.1 percent less than the average wage paid by non-*maquila* firms in the same branch of activity. These authors argue that instead, differences appear in relation to the form of payment: a lower basic wage in the *maquila* firms but higher incentive payments, and the opposite in the other type of firms.

TABLE 4.2   Profiles of Valuation of Labor Situation

Variables	Costa Rica	Guatemala	Honduras
Treatment	Good (46.3%)	Good (51.4%)	Good (67.6%)
Overtime	Sufficient (35.8%)	Sufficient (37.2%)	None (70.5%)
Remain in Firm	No (48.6%)	No (76.6%)	No (52.9%)
Disadvantages of Firm	None (55.1%)	None (36.2%)	None (55.0%)

SOURCE: Pérez Sáinz (1994c, table 4).

The Honduran situation showed disadvantages regarding this type of industrialization.[20] Thus, in 1992, average monthly salaries in the industrial parks (Free Trade Zones and Industrial Processing Zones) corresponded to 58.6 percent of those paid in the rest of the manufacturing industry. Moreover, they were slightly lower than the wages paid in the shrimp farming sector and almost half of those paid in the banana sector (BCH, 1993: table 9).[21]

The third phenomenon to be highlighted in relation to work conditions is that of the working day. This tends to be prolonged due to widespread overtime. The volatile nature of the market, with abrupt changes in demand, and constraints in terms of production capacity are the two factors that explain this aspect. Due to the fact that the pace of work, set by the predominance of payment by the piece, is intense, this is a production process that rapidly exhausts the work force. It is therefore not unusual that the labor force is frequently rotated and that a young and, thus, more energetic work force is employed.

The previous paragraphs illustrate labor relations and the working environment from a structural point of view. As a complement to this, it may prove useful to examine the views of the workers and managers involved in this environment. FLACSO's regional study offers just such a contribution (Pérez Sáinz, 1994c: 251ff.).[22]

Table 4.2 brings together value profiles of the workers, which relate—in the first instance—to two controversial issues within this type of labor environment: treatment and overtime. The assessment of treatment, as may be observed in the table, is positive in the three countries, especially in Honduras. The most critical views in this respect are to be found in relation to Guatemalan firms, for almost half of the workers considered this aspect average or even bad. In this and the Costa Rican contexts there are no significant complaints against working overtime, which is considered necessary to complement incomes. Therefore, the reproductive needs of the workers legitimize this capital valuation strategy.

The desire to remain in the firm and the disadvantages this entails allow for a more global evaluation of the labor sphere. In this sense, the Guatemalan context clearly differs from the other two, showing a labor force that by and large is dissatisfied with its current job and is prepared to look for alternative employment as soon as the opportunity arises. In effect, as was to be expected, links can be observed, to a certain extent, between these two variables in all three areas in the sense that those who perceive some kind of disadvantage in their current job demonstrate a greater willingness to leave the firm. However, at the same time, it must be pointed out that approximately two thirds (and in Guatemala, three quarters) of the workers who claimed they had no complaints regarding their current work said they wished to change jobs. In other words, a lack of outward signs of discontent with the firm does not appear to imply that there is any sense of identification with the same, which would encourage the labor force to remain in their current employment.

From the point of view of the employers, it is important to demonstrate the evaluation of three basic aspects of the work forces' conduct: discipline, performance, and cooperation. The assessments were positive, thereby illustrating the fact that the management was satisfied with the work force employed; in effect, the cases in which the assessment was negative (such as bad or very bad) were minimal. It is with regard to discipline that the evaluations are most positive, above all in Costa Rica, where almost three quarters of the cases were described as good. The performance aspect is that in which positive evaluation is less common, though reference must be made to the Honduran context, in which almost two thirds of the firms considered the performance of their workers to be very good. In that which concerns cooperation, Guatemala is the area in which this type of conduct was assessed in the most positive manner, reflected by the fact that it was described as good in two thirds of cases.

The following aspect to be discussed is that which concerns the current logics that structure labor processes in the *maquila* industry. To this end, the FLACSO study must again be consulted because it constitutes the only analytical effort in Central America that focuses on this aspect.

It has been suggested that in Costa Rica the phenomenon of so-called labor involvement was most significant.[23] Nonetheless, it is necessary to differentiate between levels or degrees of participation, which may range from the intensification of informal communication with the workers to the institutionalization of mechanisms such as quality circles or the just-in-time system. In this sense and in relation to Costa Rica, it appears that involvement was consolidated and formalized in only three firms: In one of these there was participation in identifying and solving production problems, and in the other two, quality circles existed (Cordero, 1994: table 2). This was also true of three firms in Guatemala: In one of these, quality circles were established, and the other two employed just-in-time systems, which in an attempt to minimize inventories, sought to substitute the individual production of packages or parcels for the *mano a mano* (equal terms) system that involves greater quality control on the part of the workers as well as team work (Camus, 1994: table 2). In Honduras there were two cases in which participation appeared to be institutionalized: In one plant the machine operators were trained in the maintenance of the equipment and machinery as well as carrying out daily meetings on quality, and in the other firm there was a quality control team made up of the workers themselves (Walker and Gómez Zúñiga, 1994: table 2). In other words, in only these eight firms (out of a total of 67 plants) could it be said there were elements that hinted at the presence of labor relations models based on the principles of flexible specialization.

It must be pointed out that this regional study has illustrated the greater incidence of informal participation mechanisms and that a type of hybrid situation has therefore been identified where different kinds of labor process arrangement principles are combined. Moreover, there is no sign of a clear-cut profile of a labor force more inclined toward involvement (Pérez Sáinz, 1994c: 256–266).

This analysis on labor participation leads to a series of considerations regarding the organization of the work process. The information obtained points to the existence of three kinds of situations in this respect. The first of these concerns firms that implement a primitive form of Taylorism (division of labor based on the routine performance of simple tasks), and no trace of any possible involvement process was therefore detected in these. This is the least common situation, although some of the cases studied confirm the existence of the same. It may be assumed that this type of situation includes certain kinds of reconverted and local capital firms using short-term strategies. Also included in this type of situation would be cases involving subcontractors. The only study in this respect carried out in the region—that of the indigenous community of San Pedro Sacatepéquez in Guatemala—shows a clear case of primitive Taylorism (Pérez Sáinz and Leal, 1992).[24]

The second type of situation, in terms of the organization of the labor process, is the opposite of the first, that is, those cases in which labor participation mechanisms have been formalized. As mentioned earlier, in the study on factories, a total of eight had succeeded in institutionalizing these mechanisms. It appears that in this kind of situation there is no formal model that has a regional scope; rather, participation takes place on the basis of empirical practices that are specific to each firm and national context.

The third and most common situation holds an intermediary position between the previous two. It is characterized by the effective implementation, with regard to the labor process and not society's regulations, of organizational principles based on Fordist principles. In this respect, one must bear in mind that the previous model of industrialization, based on import substitution, was known to be a Fordist imitation; this explains the relevance of it being described as sub-Fordism, which may be understood in two different ways. On the one hand, this is due to the fact that it did not imply the materialization of a form of society's mode of regulation. Only in certain Latin American countries where industrialization was introduced at an earlier stage and during short periods of populist governments could one speak of a certain form of regulation, and at any rate, this was not widespread, for the urban employment structure remained heterogeneous. Nonetheless, in Central America this situation did not arise—with the exception of Costa Rica, where society's regulation is explained by other factors.[25] On the other hand, one may speak of sub-Fordism, or rather sub-Taylorism, as the need did not arise within the production process itself to impose effective control measures on the labor force. It is a well-known fact that this industrial model was characterized by a high level of idle capacity as a result of the limited nature of the internal market, which in turn was due to the persistence of not particularly equitable income distribution structures. The outcome of this idle capacity phenomenon was the lack of a need to fully implement the Taylorist-type principles of organization. The current tendency toward exports implies the disappearance of this idle capacity and, on the contrary, reveals constraints in production for confronting growing demand; this explains why overtime, as mentioned above, is so commonplace and why subcontractors are so frequently sought after. As a result of this new situation, it may be said that Taylorist labor organization principles are now being applied in an effective and integral manner. Naturally, this Taylorist revival does not exclude the non-systemic incorporation of elements related to the flexible specialization model. This constituted the most common type of labor process organization within the new industrializing process taking place in Central America (Pérez Sáinz, 1994c: 267–276).

The last aspect to be discussed here is the presence of trade unions in this sector. It may be said that there is very widespread hostility on the part of the employers regarding trade unions and other forms of labor organizations. The exception to this is the solidarity association, which in Costa Rica tends to be viewed as a suitable form of internal relations for firms within this new context of globalization. This hostility toward trade unionism is reflected in the control of labor relations within this work environment, and the existing labor legislation is denounced as obsolete and inadequate.

Without taking into account Nicaragua, for which data is not available, there are a mere 43 trade unions operating in this sector within the region, which are distributed as follows: seven in Guatemala, ten in both Costa Rica and El Salvador,[26] and 16 in Honduras.[27] It is in the latter country that 12 collective agreements have been made, whereas only one other was made in the rest, in Guatemala (OIT, 1995: table 4). In this sense, it is necessary to mention the existence of a commission, located in San Pedro Sula, in which *maquila* factory managers participate along with owners of industrial parks and trade unions (Ciudad, 1995: 25–29). Consequently, it is not surprising that this country has managed to establish a greater number of trade union organizations and is almost the only one in which it has been possible to hold collective conventions. However, despite this partial exception, the difficulties associated with the presence of trade unions in this sector are more evident. This phenomenon appears to be confirmed by Nicaragua, where employers also strongly reject trade union organizations (Gutiérrez López, 1994: 15–16).

With regard to current labor legislation it must be pointed out that in Guatemala, 32 articles of the labor code have recently been modified in an attempt to standardize specific problems related to this type of industrialization.[28] This reform was made possible due to the consensus of trade unions, employers, and the government at the request of pressure groups from the United States who have denounced the precarious working conditions within the Guatemalan *maquila* industry. However, the powerful CACIF (an entity made up of business chambers) has managed to suspend the two most controversial issues: reincorporation in the case of unfair dismissal, and annual collective bargaining.[29] In this respect, it is necessary to bear in mind that these are the two types of social rights that are most disputed by employers: collective rights (the right to join a trade union, the right to collective bargaining, and the right to strike) and those related to protection against unfair dismissal.[30] In relation to this last aspect, it must be pointed out that two types of situations exist in Central America regarding the protection of employment. On the one hand, Honduras and Nicaragua have provisions that guarantee a certain measure of labor stability; on the other hand, in El Salvador and Costa Rica the termination of labor relations is discretional (Gutiérrez Quintero, n.d.).

Nonetheless, in terms of labor legislation, the key aspect is that of the spatial environment in which it is fulfilled. Throughout the entire Central American region, current labor codes are applicable to the country as a whole, including the *maquila* industry and Free Trade Zones. Naturally, the problem is not so much the adaptation of this legislation to the situation created by the new industrializing process but rather the will, especially that of employers, to apply it.

Neoinformality and Labor:
Three Case Studies

As mentioned in the introduction to this chapter, informality is present in three new settings. In this respect, it is worthwhile to make a few brief and more theoretical observations before discussing the specific examples that have been identified.[31]

The first of these settings concerns the creation of an economy of poverty set within the exclusion process. Although this environment is not new, since it implies the historical extension of the previous subsistence informality, it involves unfamiliar elements with respect to the previous period. On the one hand, the creation of the structural surplus labor force does not relate to the same mechanisms used in the previous modernization process because the new accumulative process, based on the production of tradable goods, does not always imply a capital-intensive technological bias. On the other hand, the so-called *nouveax pauvres* are entering this informal environment; they are, in particular, former wage workers from the previous model's formal sector who found themselves forced to enter this mode of neoinformality.

The second setting identified is that of subordinate informality, which may be divided into two types. The first refers to delocalization production processes induced by the demand for lean production, which means that some of the product's components had to be elaborated outside the firm. In addition, changes taking place in the market as a result of globalization processes mean that the production of tradable goods faces demands that exceed current production capacities, as argued in the previous section. This implies the need to subcontract, which constitutes a second mode within this same setting. It is believed that the latter was the most common factor in Central America.

Finally, the existence of agglomerations of small dynamic firms was detected. This setting implied the presence, to a certain extent, of socioterritorial factors. In other words, these are productive units that are not only physically close but are also and above all in social proximity. This means their development is considerably influenced by the mobilization of social capital. This setting tends to occur in communities that due to specific historical reasons have succeeded in forming an economic agglomeration and that, at the same time have managed to incorporate themselves in the globalization process.[32]

Each of the examples of the three neoinformal settings in the region will be discussed based on these brief analytical considerations. These are represented by ex-public employees currently involved in informal activities in Managua; household workers in the Puente Alto community in Honduras, subcontracted by a *maquila* firm; and Sarchí, the main handicraft center in Costa Rica. Table 4.3 shows the characteristics of each area studied with respect to the analytical factors given priority.[33]

Before tackling the first of these aspects, it is important to point out some basic characteristics of these areas in order to contextualize them.

In Managua's case, the example involves a group of former state employees and workers who were ousted from the public sector in the last years of the *Sandinista* regime and, above all, during Amalia Chamorro's government. In this respect, it is necessary to mention that as part of the first attempt at structural adjustment in this country, a so-called occupational reconversion program was carried out, which, although very successful in quantitative terms,[34] created a series of institutional imbalances in terms of human resources management due to the fact it was applied indiscriminately. The majority of the cases studied in this area welcomed this program or were simply dismissed by Chamorro's government. This labor force is predominantly female, of mature age, and with a relatively high level of schooling. The large majority of the cases studied are currently involved in commercial activities, namely in the retail trade.

Puente Alto is a rural community in the district of Cortés, in northern Honduras, situated between San Pedro Sula and Puerto Cortés. It is one of the ten communities in which a U.S.-Honduran baseball-producing firm subcontracts women who work in their own homes. These women carry out only one phase of the production process (stitching the baseballs)[35] and are paid by the piece based on a scale of proportional increases. This delocalization of the production process was this firm's reaction to the organization of a trade union some years back and has entailed the mediation of contractors and supervisors selected from the communities themselves. This delocalizing process means this firm controls a very specific labor force (women belonging to families in their phase of reproduction) that cannot be incorporated in the labor market outside their homes.

The Sarchí community is located in the western portion of the Costa Rican Central Valley. In contrast to its neighboring cantons, land ownership in and around Sarchí has historically been very concentrated, thereby preventing the creation of an independent peasantry such as that which has predominated in this part of the Central Valley. This resulted in seasonal proletarianization, limited to coffee and sugarcane harvests, and subsequent impoverishment. The population's reaction to this precarious situation was twofold. On the one hand, many migrated to the United States; this is a very common solution throughout Central America but not in Costa Rica. On the other hand, wooden handicraft activities began in two cart-making workshops in existence since the beginning of the century. This second process gradually gave rise to an agglomeration of small establishments that currently total approximately 130. This per-

TABLE 4.3 Examples of Neoinformality in Central America

Setting	Context	Type of Informality	Resources	Challenges	Identities
Former public employees in Managua, Nicaragua	Exclusion	Absence of business rationality. No separation of expenses from those related to the household.	Lack of capital and low-income clients	Low productivity and insufficient demand	Individualization. Activities are mean for subsistence
Household workers in Puente Alto, Honduras	Globalization	Subcontracting by an export firm	Very precarious labor	Vertical external subcontracting	Consolidation of traditional gender identity
Handicraft community of Sarchí, Costa Rica	Globalization	Heterogeneity of dynamic establishments	Social capital (handicraft tradition, networks and bounded solidarity)	Specialization and improvement on competition through imitation	Handicraft and local

severance was recognized midway through the 1980s, when Sarchí was declared "the cradle of national handicrafts." The international tourist boom that has characterized Costa Rica in the last few years has had a dynamic effect.

In the same way, it is important to stress the fact that the three areas under consideration are marked by the presence of informality. Based on the criteria of the division of labor, which has been used to delimit this phenomenon (as explained in the previous chapter) the area studied in Managua is made up—in no uncertain terms—of activities of an informal nature. In effect, in all the cases analyzed, the owners directly participate in the respective labor process that supports its activity. The same may be said of the household workers in Puente Alto, Honduras. However, this group of women may also be described as disguised or indirect wage workers for the firm that subcontracts them. This dual description does not in any way reflect any analytical contradiction but rather expresses the fact that this group of workers is subjected to a dual job category. Moreover, the only area in which informal employment is not as manifest is in the Sarchí agglomeration in Costa Rica. The majority of establishments operate on the basis of a process combining certain business principles and informal logics. Nonetheless, there is a stratum made up of the most humble workshops belonging to small-scale handicraft workers that may be unmistakably described as informal. Furthermore, both this and the second setting tend to be characterized by their heterogeneity— in other words, by the presence of various types of informal establishments such as small- and even medium-sized firms.

In terms of context, the first aspect to be analyzed in Table 4.3, it appears that the area studied in Managua is undoubtedly set within a context of exclusion. This labor force was dismissed from the public sector and has been forced to enter the realms of neoinformality. In this sense, it is important to stress that this involuntary mobility was a result of the structural adjustment measures applied in Nicaragua, particularly those related to the reduction of public spending and the state reform that seeks to minimize the same. Consequently, the incorporation of this group of former public employees in the neoinformal sector is clearly set within the excluding effects structural adjustment programs tend to provoke.

In contrast, it may be said that the Honduran context is set within the globalization process. This group of women work for an export firm that is an example of the expansion of Free Trade Zones that have sprung up in Valle del Sula in Honduras, as mentioned in the previous section. However, it must be remembered that subcontracting implies that this incorporation into the globalization process is mediated and, therefore, fragile. This frailty is manifest in the precariousness of the type of labor process as well as that of living conditions, which characterize the Puente

Alto area and that relate, to a greater extent, to the exclusion phenomenon. In fact, this is a clear example of how these two processes, globalization and exclusion, are not incompatible but are, indeed, two sides of the same coin.

In terms of globalization, there is one characteristic of this aspect that is worth highlighting: the contradiction that is currently affecting production within this environment. On the one hand, the payment of work by the piece, with wages increasing as the volume of work increases, clearly reveals a mass production logic. On the other hand, the recent emphasis placed on quality questions this type of logic. Indeed, one of the basic contradictions of the globalization process in Central America, which was explained in the previous section, is identified: It is the revival of the Taylorist system combined with tendencies toward innovative organization. In this regard, the female workers themselves have provided a response to this contradiction: they have moved from maximizing production to minimizing rejects.

The globalization process also affects the Costa Rican case. This agglomeration has succeeded in marketing its handicraft activities for tourism. Thus, the economic environment created by this series of woodworking activities has not been limited to local or regional spheres but has achieved national, and even international, scope. With regard to the first of these aspects, as mentioned, Sarchí was named "the cradle of national handicrafts," which meant it had a privileged position within the country's socioeconomic structure. Moreover, in the second sense, the current international tourist boom places this community within the globalization context.

Subsistence informality is the predominant mode in the context of the former public employees in Managua. Although accumulation has to a certain extent been detected, this cannot be comprehended without taking into account the fact that the establishments are relatively new; that is, all businesses require a certain level of investment in order to set themselves up. Nonetheless, the absence of a business rationality is notorious in this sector. Furthermore, in the large majority of cases, business costs are not kept separate from those of the household, thereby indicating the close links between economic logics pertaining to the establishment and those of subsistence, which correspond to the domestic unit. Consequently, with the exception of only three cases, the rest show a predominance of straightforward reproduction logics that point to the existence of an environment marked by subsistence informality.

In Honduras, the subordinate nature of the subcontracting mechanism is manifest in the strategy used by the firm in this respect. Three main aspects should be emphasized in this regard. First, a delocalization strategy was identified, which focused on one particular part of the production process. As was to be expected, the most labor-intensive tasks were those which were delocalized. Second, the adoption of the extreme form represented by work carried out in the home appears to be a response to the general hostility created by the setting up of a trade union organization on the part of the workers. In this respect, it must be pointed out that this delocalization process was initially organized in the form of a workshop within the community itself, where the workers went about their tasks in a collective manner. However, the firm disbanded this work center when the trade union organization was introduced. In other words, this strategy involves controlling the labor force by means of its division and relative dispersion. Third, within this same control logic, the firm has consciously attempted to co-opt a very specific segment of the work force: women, of mature age, who due to the fact they belong to families in their reproduction phase, have difficulty entering the labor market outside their respective domestic units.

Sarchí has proved itself to be a dynamic case. Nevertheless, despite this dynamism, it is worth highlighting several aspects related to this economic agglomeration, for they affect this dynamism. First, there is no division of labor within this agglomeration of establishments that would allow specialization economies and complementary aspects to be made the best use of. Second, the current technological level is quite traditional. Third, labor processes are organized in a manner that corresponds to handicrafts, which means these are used to transmit the skills of the trade: This is why it is not unusual that these should function as authentic learning schools that allow the workers to become independent and set up their own business. Fourth, the marketing process is based essentially on direct contact with the final consumers who visit Sarchí, although ties exist with shops in the capital. Finally, this fabric is not invariable but presents a certain level of heterogeneity in terms of establishments. In this sense, the most significant dividing line would be that which confronts small informal producers with owners who have succeeded in combining production with marketing. Two complementary remarks are offered with regard to this last point. On the one hand, there is a relevant example of joint marketing carried out by a cooperative, which constitutes an unavoidable point of reference in this community's development. It is in the integrated groups of establishments, on the other hand, that the most patent examples of business rationality are to found.

As was to be expected, resource availability in a context such as that studied in Managua is very meager. In this respect, there are two phenomena to be highlighted from the study undertaken. First come the problems identified by the informal workers themselves. Among those worth noting are the lack of capital and difficulties associated with demand. The latter is related to a second key phenomenon for understanding the constraints of this type of environment. The consumers of these types of establishments include, by and large, individuals from popular sectors. These are presumably not known for their high purchasing power or for the possibility of constituting a factor that could influence these economic units' dynamism. Consequently, they have a very limited growth potential. It is for this reason that the environment in question has been described as an "economy of poverty," which does not necessarily imply that these informal workers find themselves in an impoverished situation.[36]

In addition, resources also appear to be scarce in the second context under consideration. This constraint is essentially associated with the precariousness of current labor relations, despite the fact that this has been curbed by the achievements of former trade union action, which succeeded in institutionalizing these, to a certain extent, by securing additional pay (paid holidays, Christmas bonus, etc.) for those paid by the piece. However, the workers themselves clearly do not envision many prospects in this type of activity or being able to make progress given the current situation.

The Costa Rican context differs from the previous situations in that the key element is the existence of social capital, manifest in some of its examples.[37] In this respect, it is necessary to—first of all—point out that it is indeed possible to speak of certain values shared by the community. These are linked to labor ethics with strong emphasis on economic initiatives that—above all—seek independent labor. The interesting aspect of this social capital, which appears to be the most forceful in the case under consideration, is that it is based on primary socialization processes. Thus, various interviewees explained how the location of the handicraft activity within the community itself means it forms part of the daily life and outlook of its children. Likewise, it is important to point out that the handicraft activity constitutes a fundamental element within the local identity. In other words, it is this skill that confers an essential and distinctive feature on the inhabitants of Sarchí, that sets them apart from the neighboring cantons.

Second, networks based on reciprocity have also been detected. There are two elements to highlight in this respect. On the one hand, these are particularly valid when the establishments are being set up; in other words, this support plays a fundamental role in the founding of the workshops. On the other hand, these are family-based networks, which lend a domestic feel to these type of activities. Furthermore, within one group of establishments—the informal producers—reciprocity is maintained and therefore transcends the limits of family circles, thereby demonstrating the cooperation mechanisms that exist among this group of handicraft workers.

No signs of the existence of enforceable trust as a form of social capital have been detected. On the contrary, there were elements that suggested the existence of bounded solidarity. Different types of threats, especially the presence in the community of businesses not related to Sarchí and the outside imitation of the handicrafts, that sustained this factor. Nonetheless, it is important to point out that these types of observations are not widely felt, and consequently the incidence of confined solidarity is limited. New threats, however, (rumors of a handicraft market to be established in the neighboring canton and the possible isolation of the flow of tourists that would result from the building of the new road to the Pacific coast) could perhaps mean that this could, in the future, emerge as one of the main sources of this form of social capital in Sarchí.

Closely linked to the aspect related to resources is that associated with the challenges faced by each context. With regard to the case studied in Managua, the typical stagnant situation that characterizes subsistence informality, both past and present, was observed. On the one hand, these establishments have very low levels of production. It must be remembered that the main activity in this environment is that of retail trade; moreover, in order to make these establishments economically viable, long and exhausting working days are required. On the other hand, as mentioned above in regard to resources, there is a lack of dynamism due to the general consumer demand of low-income sectors.

With regard to the case studied in Honduras, it must be made clear that work carried out in the home implies the fragmentation of production, as mentioned earlier. Despite the fact that family production units are set up, these are very primitive in terms of the type of work methods used and labor process organization. The strategy of separating the workers by confining them to their own homes does not allow them to have any kind of notion of developing their production units, either from an organizational or technological point of view. In other words, this type of informality's possibilities of acquiring a dynamic approach are limited by the vertical and hierarchical structure established and sustained by the subcontractors. In this sense, these constitute subsistence activities for the workers with no prospects for growth and accumulation potential.

Despite its dynamic nature, Sarchí faces important challenges if it wishes to maintain itself in a sustainable manner within the globalization process it has become part of. It could be said that the greatest challenge Sarchí faces has to do with specialization. As mentioned in previous paragraphs, the level of specialization is practically nonexistent. Promoting specialization would allow this agglomeration to develop the division of tasks, to a certain extent, in different areas: supply of raw materials (wood), design activities, technological services, and marketing activities aimed outside the community and abroad.

Although this need for specialization may appear obvious, it is important to stress that the producers in this community do not appear to see it that way. The causes of this may be traced back to two fundamental factors that influence current developments in Sarchí. First, competition tends to prevail over cooperation; this predominance is only inverted in the case of the group of small-scale producers and that of specialized establishments. Second, this is due to the fact that the type of competition imposed is based on prices and not quality. That is, the economic success that characterizes this sphere is resulting in the proliferation of establishments (local but also outside Sarchí) whose development is based on imitation and not innovation, which means market niches are rapidly saturated. From this point of view, it appears the Sarchí economy has not managed to achieve that virtuous combination of cooperation and competition that has been the key element in the successful development of the so-called industrial districts of the north.

Consequently, Sarchí's greatest challenge is not a material one. On the contrary, its problem is one of social capital and, more specifically, of introjecting values. In other words, the current dynamism in this community could reinforce a perverse economic culture. The major challenge for Sarchí is to avoid the imposition of imitations over innovation.

The final aspect to be discussed is related to the formation of labor identities in each context. In the case of the former public employees in Managua, there are two divided elements in terms of identity formation, which were already detected in other studies. On the one hand, self-labor identification is based on employment and not so much on the business. Thus, those working in the informal sector consider themselves more as workers than owners of means of production. On the other hand, there is very little tendency toward organization-based action, which creates serious restrictions for the formation of identities of a collective nature. From a diachronic point of view, the frailty of the identities formed is clearly evident. Three types of situations may be observed in this respect. The first and most recurrent is set within the sphere of reproduction, in which the present activity is a mere means of subsistence. The second has been marked by the nostalgia of public employment and the desire to return to professional circles. However, given the reduction of the state system in Nicaragua, which has not yet been completed, it will be difficult for these aspirations to materialize. In contrast, in the third situation, the condition of informality is assumed and projected toward the future in search of the growth of the establishment. In other words, a business orientation exists. It is only in these few cases that the emergence of a subject with a clear direction, albeit of an individual nature, has been observed.

In regard to Puente Alto, two observations may be made. On the one hand, it is evident that the precariousness that distinguishes this labor impedes any notion of forming strong labor identities. Only in that which relates to the relative control of time do certain cases asserting work independence in opposition to wage work in factories, especially in Free Trade Zones, appear. In the same manner, it may be argued, with regard to incomes, in situations where the women themselves or their husbands or partners are heads of the household, family responsibilities are not fulfilled. However, in both cases these types of observations reflect the rejection of the factory and the man as provider of the domestic unit rather than an assertion as self-employed worker or head of household.

In contrast, the reconfirmation and consolidation of traditional gender identities were detected. Family-based reasons have been decisive in terms of labor mobility and in the acceptance and search for this employment; and, equally, these factors considerably influence the value associated with the current occupation. It is necessary to bear in mind that the most important feature of this work force is its age, given it is in the peak period of its life and family cycles. In this sense, the fact that work in the home may be combined with domestic tasks, especially the raising of children, is the key to understanding the logic of the phenomenon in question. This perception is reinforced by the appraisal developed at the heart of the family itself in this respect, on the part of husbands or partners, and the community in terms of the social control of mature women.

As mentioned earlier, this predominant representation proves very useful to the strategy of labor force control that the subcontractors implement. That is, one could speak of a harmonious triangle between the women themselves, their respective spouses (and, by extension, the rest of the community), and the firm where it is not labor but gender identities of a traditional nature that are reinforced. Nonetheless, this harmonious image is relative. The women's work aspirations indicate that although a certain level of resignation exists, in the majority of cases this type of employment in no way leads to the development of the women's working life. The only factor that forces them to continue working at home is the precariousness of their existence.

Finally, as with other aspects, Sarchí offers a more optimistic image. Some forms of existing social capital show signs of identity construction. The existence of shared values with regard to handicraft activities has, without doubt, created a strong sense of identity. This identity benefits from the distinct advantage of having been created within processes of primary socialization, which in turn reinforces it. Furthermore, this process has a collective scope, which focuses on the community. That is, labor and local identities are interconnected: Sarchí and handicrafts are interchangeable terms. Along these same lines, the existence of social capital in the form of bounded solidarity tends to reinforce this identity process. However, this solid identity is also being subjected to eroding and hardly noticeable developments. These are emerging as a result of the prevailing form of competition based on imitation. This type of development tends to favor a distancing and may even create conflicts between communities. In this sense, Sarchí's great challenge to secure a sustainable position within the globalization process also constitutes a challenge for the continuation and strengthening of its identity.

Notes

1. For a more detailed analysis of these hypotheses and the labor contexts they entail, see Pérez Sáinz and Cordero (1994).

2. We have been given to understand that with the exception of the comparative study carried out by Weller (1992: 116–125) on Costa Rica, Honduras, and Panama, there are no studies specifically related to the issue of labor relations in this new activity within the region. In this respect, the main conclusions put forward by this author are as follows: In Costa Rica, these types of activities have served to mitigate the job losses resulting from adjustments to the agricultural sector, whereas in Honduras the outcome was more positive; indirect employment was created, which varied from one indirect post creating five direct posts in Costa Rica to fourteen direct posts in Honduras; these types of crops have reinforced the wage labor tendency with regard to the rural work force, thereby consolidating the predominance of permanent employment in Costa Rica and temporary employment in Honduras; there are opportunities for women who earn better pay than in other traditional agrarian activities; and, in addition, there is substantial evidence of peasant production in some areas. With respect to this type of production, focalized studies (Dary Fuentes, 1991; Rojas and Román, 1993) have shown that these units also have to recur to hiring wage workers and that female participation is a key element.

3. The study undertaken by Bodson, Cordero, and Pérez Sáinz (1995) focuses on urban areas in Costa Rica and demonstrates the importance of making a distinction—in terms of occupations—with regard to this tradables sector.

4. This phenomenon regarding cutbacks in public employment has not been adequately analyzed in the region. The most comprehensive study is that of Valverde, Trejos, and Mora (1993), which examines the consequences of the labor mobilization plan implemented during Calderon's government in Costa Rica.

5. It should be pointed out that the first section is a reworking of a former text (Pérez Sáinz, 1995b), and the second is an attempt to summarize a recent work (Pérez Sáinz, 1996).

6. On the basis of listings supplied by the National Export Promotion Centre (CENPRO), in November 1994, 89 firms benefited from the temporary admission regulations, and 105 from that of the Free Trade Zones (Cuevas, 1994: 19).

7. There is an abundant bibliography on this subject. The first to be mentioned should be the initial studies that aimed to identify the type of labor force and labor relations. Among these, the following are worth highlighting: Pávez (1987); Duarte and Quintanilla (1991); Nowalski, Morales, and Berliavsky (1993); and Altenburg (1993) regarding Costa Rica; Price Waterhouse (1992; 1993) and Caballero

and Sánchez Lam (1992) regarding Honduras; Arriola (1993) on El Salvador; Gutiérrez López (1994) on Nicaragua; and González (1991), Pérez Sáinz and Castellanos (1991), Monzón (1992), Petersen (1992), and AVANCSO (1994) on Guatemala. Other subsequent works have examined the type of organization used within the labor process that is beginning to take shape within this new setting. In this respect, Trejos (1992) has examined the consensus mechanisms that have been set up within Costa Rica's export firms, thereby illustrating the role of *solidarismo* in these. In addition, FLACSO has, based on a regional study in Central America, attempted to analyze how logics based on Fordist principles interacted with developments based on flexible specialization in industrial exporting plants in Costa Rica, Honduras, and Guatemala (Pérez Sáinz, 1994c).

8. With respect to Guatemala, the level of potential employment has been estimated.

9. In the text produced by these authors, the term *maquiladora* covers both the firms adhering to the temporary admission model and those situated in the Free Trade Zones.

10. The 13 firms in Las Mercedes in Nicaragua created 4,100 jobs (Gutiérrez López, 1994: table 1).

11. Because extensive information provided by this study will be used herein, it is important to explain the scope of the same. Two phases have been studied. The first consists of interviews with plant managers and human resources in 67 firms: 24 in Costa Rica, 22 in Honduras, and 21 in Guatemala. The second is related to a survey on workers in a limited number of plants: four in Costa Rica, five in Honduras and three in Guatemala.

12. In effect, from the point of view of schooling, taking into account the national levels of education, this labor force employed in the *maquiladora* industry cannot be described as poorly qualified (CEPAL, 1994: 41).

13. This participation refers to an index of domestic work that has been constructed on the basis of four activities (cooking, laundry, cleaning the house, and shopping) with a value of 1 or 0 being assigned according to whether the corresponding activity is carried out or not.

14. In a study on the Honduran Industrial Processing Zones, Price Waterhouse (1993: 6) found a mere 17 percent of those interviewed to be the sole contributors of income to their households.

15. This type of profile, in that concerning both sociodemographic and household-related factors, is fairly similar to that found by Pérez Sáinz and Castellanos (1991: 67–98) in the survey on *maquila* workers they carried out in four firms in the Guatemalan capital. There are also similarities with the information obtained by Monzón (1992: 46–69) based on 50 case studies on workers from various *maquila* factories also in Guatemala City. Likewise, the Price Waterhouse (1993) study on the Honduran Industrial Processing Zones offers similar results. With regard to Costa Rica, the profile identified is very similar to that of Altenburg (1993) and the sample of 466 employees from diverse plants in three Free Trade Zones.

16. Altenburg (1993: 15) mentions the fact that in Costa Rica some managers encourage the creation of *solidarista* organizations as a means of keeping a hold on the work force.

17. The comparison was made with respect to the average wage in four Asian countries: Thailand, Sri Lanka, the Philippines, and the People's Republic of China.

18. This same study also indicates that in tortilla-making activities the workers put in 46.9 hours per week compared to 54.2 in the *maquila* sector (Pérez Sáinz and Castellanos, 1991: table 5.3). In this sense, it may be argued that when comparing incomes per hour, the differences are reduced. Nevertheless, it must be pointed out that the incomes of tortilla factory owners are overestimated due to the difficulties encountered in deducting all the costs of this activity.

19. Evidence to support this was found—in the mid-1970s—by Pavez (1987: 75–77), who demonstrated that the average wage in the Salvadoran San Bartolo Free Trade Zone was higher than that of the metropolitan area. Nevertheless, this difference has decreased over the course of time.

20. The Price Waterhouse study (1993: 5) on the Industrial Processing Zones allows for a comparison of average wages according to sex. The income obtained by women is scarcely 97 percent of that obtained by men.

21. It must be pointed out that the wage estimate for the industrial parks includes the salaries of 3,400 employees hired for subcontracts, most probably reducing the average.

22. A more in-depth study of this aspect of labor, focusing on Costa Rica in comparison to the Dominican Republic, can be found in Pérez Sáinz (1995a).

23. In effect, in 10 of the 24 plants examined, some form of participation was detected, whereas in Guatemala and Honduras this corresponded to 7 out of 21 and 6 out of 22, respectively.

24. The study (discussed in the following section) on subcontracts as an example of subordinate informality in the Puente Alto community in Honduras confirms this precariousness.

25. Among these, it is necessary to recall factors that have already been mentioned in previous chapters, such as the not very concentrated agricultural property structure, the social reforms of the 1940s, and the sociopolitical pact made following the 1948 conflict, which gave rise to a particular mode of regulation for society that was one of a kind in the region and explains why the political history of this country differed from the tragic outcome of that of the rest of Central America.

26. There is a very well-documented work on the difficulties encountered by trade unions in this country within the *maquila* industry (Arévalo and Arriola, 1995).

27. For an identification of the type of trade union organization present in the *maquila* industry, see Membreño and Guerrero (1994: 87ff.).

28. It is worthwhile mentioning the fact that it is within this context of globalization that the labor codes of all the countries in the region, with the exception of Honduras, have been reformed. However, these reforms do not appear to have been implemented in practice (Frundt, 1995).

29. Chapter V of the Trade and Tariff Act of 1984 states that five labor rights must be respected in order to be able to benefit from the tax exemptions in the United States, which are vital for this industrializing model. These rights are the general right to freedom of association, the specific right to join a trade union, the

banning of forced labor, the banning of child labor, and the right to acceptable working conditions. Since as far back as 1985, Guatemala, along with Nicaragua, has been threatened with exclusion from the General Preferences System. Nicaragua was excluded in 1987, but the petition against Guatemala was postponed due to the installation of a civil government. In the early 1990s this petition was reactivated, resulting in changes being made to the labor code. In 1990, petitions such as these were made against El Salvador, and Costa Rica had to face a similar situation in 1993, which it succeeded in overcoming by introducing reforms regarding trade union benefits.

30. In this regard, it is necessary to mention that the 87 and 98 OIT agreements on the freedom to join a trade union and protecting the right to become a trade union member and to undertake collective bargaining respectively have been ratified by all the countries under consideration, with the exception of El Salvador. For a summary of the ratification of the relevant agreements for this type of industry, see OIT (1995: table 3).

31. These observations are explained more extensively in Pérez Sáinz (1996, 1998).

32. This third setting has been analyzed in the region by Pérez Sáinz and Cordero (1994) with regard to Sarchí in Costa Rica. There is also a study on San Pedro Sacatepéquez in Guatemala, mentioned above, which corresponds to an area that may also be analyzed in terms of the subordinate neoinformal environment because this agglomeration is immersed in subcontracting relations with the capital's *maquila* industry. In this regard, see Pérez Sáinz and Leal (1992).

33. The analysis, due to its exploratory nature, is based on the empirical evidence obtained from the in-depth study of cases in each one of these areas: 20 in Managua and Sarchí, and 17 in Puente Alto.

34. This program involved the reduction of 10,000 jobs, and 25,000 people welcomed the same.

35. The inputs are prepared in one plant whereas the softballs, once they have been stitched by the household workers, are completed in a second factory and then exported to the United States.

36. In effect, out of the twenty cases examined, only four were found to have incomes below the poverty line.

37. This term is understood as meaning how sociocultural factors affect the economic behavior of the members of a community. Four types of social capital may be noted. The first is that described as the introjection of values that relate to a certain code of ethics and economic culture that may be shared as resources among the members of the community itself. The second form is called reciprocity and refers to actions in which personal objectives are sought but which do not involve monetary transactions; in other words, these constitute networks of noncommodity exchange, which in Latin America have been studied in relation to urban marginality. The third is bounded solidarity, which expresses the community's reaction to external threats or harassment. The fourth type of social capital is enforceable trust, understood as the subordination and adaptation of individual aspirations to collective expectations.

5

Conclusions

In the previous chapters numerous processes that have occurred during past decades have been analyzed, and an attempt has been made to examine some of the main examples of the current work environment in Central America. It is deemed necessary, in order to conclude this text, to endeavor to make associations between the main processes while identifying the historical logics that have shaped them. As the aim is not merely to summarize each chapter, analytical guidelines must be sought. In this respect, three key points are thought to exist. The first refers to the process that shapes labor markets, which may be used to set the labor issue within a framework of general economic processes. The second analytical point of reference to be considered concerns work conditions themselves, highlighting the specific nature of the labor issue. The last point deals with the shaping of actors and labor identities that allows the analysis to be directed toward the state and the political system.

Each of these points is to be dealt with separately and diachronically. This implies that for each historic moment in time, emphasis will be placed on the most significant aspects that have been discussed in previous chapters. Table 5.1 summarizes the series of aspects to be examined.

Employment: Some, Although
Insufficient, Job Creation

It is a well-known fact, and one that has been repeated exhaustively, that the majority of the Central American economy was until the middle of the present century structured around coffee production and all that this activity encompassed. There was also another very significant—although to a lesser extent—crop: bananas. However, whereas the latter revolved around the enclave and in agricultural border areas, the coffee sector's influence reached all corners of society. This distinction is important in terms of the type of labor market generated by both crops and their development.

TABLE 5.1 Labor Issues in Central America During the Capitalist Modernization Era

Analytical Dimensions	Background		Previous Modernization			Current Modernization
	Coffee	Bananas	New Agroexports	Industrialization	Crisis	Productive Restructuring
Employment dynamics	Three systems: coercive, wage work, and family work	Captive proletarianization in enclaves	Temporary nature of employment / finca-minifundio binomial	Formal employment	Informalization	New wage labor in tradable goods sector / reduction of formal employment / neoinformality.
Labor relations	Labor in exchange for payment of debts / influence of agricultural frontier on wages	Racial handling of labor force	Loss of importance of wages	Limited regulation of public sector	Decline in wages	Widespread to the precariousness / revival of Taylorism with some organizational innovations.
Actors and identities	Weak identities in coffee sector and banana enclaves / mutualismo in urban handicraft sector / onset of trade unionism		Limited influence of trade unions / trade union action becomes increasingly radical		Economic and political effects on trade union movement / rise of solidarismo	Trade unionism weakened / new labor identities.

The coffee sector's direct integration into society meant that different types of situations arose according to the sociolabor contexts in which production materialized. In this respect, three situations must be mentioned. The first was that of certain regions in Nicaragua and, above all, vast areas of Guatemala in which extraeconomic coercive methods (in which the state played a key role) were used to incorporate the work force in coffee production. It is important to point out that in this regard the sociolabor relations formed within this scenario were profoundly influenced by ethnic factors. As a result, this forced integration had direct and violent repercussions on the indigenous reproductive sphere—the community. The latter found itself subjected to processes of redefinition and socioethnic differentiation, and in Guatemala's case, ladino-indigenous opposition did not escape the perverse effects of this aspect of coffee production. In terms of labor, it is important to stress that within this first type of situation, it is not, strictly speaking, possible to discuss the existence of labor markets in which the purchase and sale of labor is, in extraeconomic terms, carried out freely. In Guatemala these kinds of coercive mechanisms did not begin to be questioned until the 1930s, and it was not until the fall of the Ubico dictatorship and the 1944 revolution that labor force exchange could be carried out without having to resort to direct coercion.

In contrast, the second situation is linked to the formation of labor markets in the traditional mode, which corresponded to processes of classic proletarianization. This context was true of areas of Costa Rica situated east of Cartago and, in particular, in El Salvador. Nonetheless, with regard to this second situation, reference must be made to the *colonato* phenomenon, which sought to reinforce the link between wages and land use by granting plots for the workers' own subsistence.

The family labor system, based on peasant productive units, constituted the third type of situation. This took place in certain areas of northern Nicaragua and, above all, in the western part of the Costa Rican Central Valley and the north of this same country. Strictly speaking, a labor market as such did not exist because although the hiring of labor took place to a certain extent, the majority of the activity centered on the family work force. However, from a more open and less orthodox analytical point of view, the goods market (that of the coffee sector itself) gave this work social recognition. Furthermore, in Costa Rica, where the accumulative process materialized mainly, although not exclusively, in the realms of processing (profits of the bean) and trade, family work has been interpreted as disguised wage labor. Moreover, it must be remembered that the small coffee farmer often had to temporarily join the proletariat in order to complement his meager peasant income with the wages obtained.

The banana plantations formed more homogenous labor dynamics. In this regard, several phenomena must be highlighted. First, one must bear in mind that this type of activity was established in Atlantic virgin lands, which meant the virtual absence of indigenous labor. In this sense, the bananas enclave—in its efforts to attract the labor force from other activities and regions—represented a first, although largely unsuccessful, attempt to nationalize labor markets. The reaction of the banana companies was twofold. On the one hand, they resorted to labor within Central America: Salvadorans moving into Honduras, and Nicaraguans into Costa Rica. This implied the regionalization, in Central American terms, of the flow of labor. However, on the other hand, labor was also imported from the Antilles, thereby making the labor market international. These phenomena had important repercussions in terms of the types of labor relations formed, as will be seen later on, due to the manner in which the ethnic (and more specifically, the racial) factor was used by the companies. Second, the wage worker condition of the labor force was unequivocal; thus, the bananas enclave was associated with clear processes of proletarianization. Third, the nature of the enclave meant that contrary to the coffee sector, job creation was limited. Finally, despite this image of less coercive labor relations than those of the coffee sector, mechanisms of economic violence operated within the banana plantations related to methods of pay that sought to keep a hold on the labor force and, therefore, captivate the respective labor market.

In more global terms and faced with the onset of the modernization process, it must be pointed out that neither type of production represented accumulative options capable of offering jobs to a large sector of the population. Thus, the coffee sector was known for the seasonal nature of its labor market, and the banana sector, as mentioned in the previous paragraph, for its very limited job creation dynamics. These constituted the basic structural factors influencing Central American labor markets around the middle of the twentieth century. Three traits, common to all the markets in the countries within the region, may be highlighted, based on the information available in the censuses carried out at that time. First, they were markedly masculine, with the possible exception of Honduras. Second, there was a significant presence of a young labor force, indicating its very low level of schooling. In addition, agricultural activities provided the highest level of employment, indicating a high sectorial concentration and implying that from a spatial point of view, labor markets were essentially rural. Costa Rica was the only exception, albeit relative, to these last two characteristics. Thus, as was to be expected, the employment structures did not show any significant signs of modernization. Costa Rica proved the only case that differed partially from this image, which was reflected most patently in Guatemala and, above all, in Honduras.

These differences within the region are in line with the concrete forms in which the main accumulative axes manifest themselves. Thus, the bananas enclave was more predominant in Honduras, implying that the majority of the labor force remained confined to traditional labor spheres. In regard to Guatemala, it must be remembered that in relation to the coffee sector, the formation of a labor market free from the extraeconomic coercion did not take place until the mid–1940s. Costa Rica shows a more widespread growth of the proletariat. This characteristic was also shared by El Salvador, although with two significant differences. On the one hand, the wage workers there, as will be discussed later, earned lower salaries, indicating a more precarious proletarianizing process. On the other hand, Costa Rica developed a peasant economy that was not relegated to subsistence but incorporated in coffee trading processes.

The predominance of the basic axes of the accumulative processes in the region within the coffee and banana sectors was questioned with the diversification of agroexports, introduced around the 1950s. Three new products that were more capable of establishing backward and forward linkages emerged: cotton, sugarcane, and beef. In this respect, one must bear in mind that due to their production logic (more advanced technology, increase in the capital/land ratio, and greater investment in inputs), these new products made the importance attached to land and work by the previous agroexports relative. This implied that in the case of cotton and sugarcane, employment was temporary, and the capacity of beef production to create jobs was very limited. Consequently, the onset of modernization, based on the diversification of agroexports that resulted in new accumulative axes, did not imply any significant change with regard to the region's labor market structural logics. However, this first impression is deceptive, as two important transformations took place.

In the first instance, it must be pointed out that the seasonal nature of the employment, a key factor, caused diverse flows of migration (to where the agroexports themselves were produced, to the cities or to agricultural frontier areas). The result was that the mobilization of the population became more acute, and consequently, labor markets began to shed their restricted territorial limits and project themselves on a more national level. In other words, national scale labor markets, which the ensuing urbanization tended to consolidate, were prefigured.

Second, the new agroexports highlighted the agrarian dualism, in terms of land ownership, imposing the well-known double equation: Export agriculture = large *fincas*, and agriculture for domestic use = small units. To this must be added the inevitable demographic growth that all modernizing processes are accompanied by and that meant increased pressure on land naturally affecting small properties the most. As a result, the majority of the Central American rural population found itself in the worst possible situation: Its peasant condition was deteriorating in economically viable terms, and the accumulative process, with its different agroexport variants, only permitted temporary wage labor. In other words, the rural population were neither true peasants nor true proletariats. Only the existence of an agricultural frontier in Nicaragua and Honduras (and, to a lesser extent, in Guatemala) was able to partially relieve these destructuring effects. The result was an impoverishment of the rural population, which was one of the principal causes of the political violence that was to break out in the following years.

The industrializing experience that began in the 1960s provided different perspectives due to the fact that this was supposedly a more self-centered and sustained accumulative process. In effect, jobs were created, and moreover, the empirical evidence available indicates that at that time, the handicraft sector was not significantly displaced, nor were these types of small scale producers subsequently proletarianized. However, perhaps the most relevant aspect of this new accumulative axis, in terms of employment, was the growth of urban jobs, especially tertiary jobs, it generated. Nonetheless, industrialization soon faced restrictions. These were the result of causes common to other Latin American experiences (dependence on exports, the value of which fell in the second half of the 1960s, for importing inputs) as well as specific factors (the framework of regional integration that did not succeed in achieving a uniform development between countries, and generated structural intraregional trade deficits). Furthermore, industrialization and subsequent urbanization had regressive effects on the distribution of income to the detriment of rural areas, thereby contributing to the process of impoverishment mentioned above. This deceleration in the industrializing process resulted in informality emerging, in the 1970s, in the Central American urban market sector as having a greater capacity for creating jobs. In this manner, the importance of this kind of employment, which became the main adjustment mechanism in these markets during the following decade that witnessed the crisis, was already prefigured.

Despite this series of effects on employment caused by the new accumulative axes that materialized starting in the second half of the twentieth century, it may be said that Central American labor markets underwent modernization during these three decades. The most dynamic aspects of these were those related to the formation of human capital and, to a lesser extent, the development of activities linked to services. However, urbanization and the generalization of wage labor were the most significant tendencies in this process of labor modernization. In contrast, the feminization of employment had poor results. Certain particular characteristics should be highlighted with regard to some countries: relatively low level of schooling in Guatemala, defeminization and rapid urbanization in Honduras, increased schooling and feminization in Nicaragua, and widespread wage labor and significant tertiarization in Costa Rica. In effect, around the mid-1970s, the latter country showed the highest level of modernization with regard to its employment structure, with Honduras and, to a lesser extent, Guatemala, representing the opposite end of the spectrum. Thus, it appears the intraregional contrasts identified back in 1950 had not undergone any significant changes during the decades of modernization.

Inevitably, the crisis in the 1980s had a considerable impact on employment. Several phenomena are worth highlighting in this respect. First, the different accumulative axes were already showing signs of difficulty in the 1970s regarding their capacity to absorb the labor force, and this tendency became more acute during the crisis. The result was that the secondary segments of the employment structure generated by the modernization process took on a more prominent occupational role. This implies that the jobs created were precarious, as will be argued further on. With regard to agricultural laborers, it must be pointed out that the fact that traditional agroexports had come to a standstill and new exports, with the exception of Costa Rica, showed little dynamism meant that the peasant sector had to absorb the increase in the labor force. However, this process led to a worsening of rural impoverishment and, more importantly, questioned the fact that the peasant economy should continue to take on the role of safety net for the underemployed rural work force in the future, especially in the countries where the agricultural frontier has disappeared. Regarding the urban environment, job creation took place in informal spheres. However, this growth in informal occupations occurred essentially in subsistence activities, which were the most common in respect to developments with accumulative capacity. In this sense, the differences within the urban context would help to explain different situations within the region. Thus, in northern cities (Guatemala City, San Salvador, Tegucigalpa, and Managua), the incidence of poverty in broad popular sectors induced the predominance of subsistence informality; in contrast, in San José, where there is a significant presence of middle sectors, it implied the far-from-inconsequential development of dynamic informal activities.

Second, the increase in open unemployment did not play a prominent role in the region in terms of a labor adjustment mechanism. The only exception to this was that of Costa Rica, where at the highest point in the recession (1982), a significant level of unemployment was reached, although it was soon absorbed by the economic recovery. This phenomenon implied that it was only in the region's most modernized economy, from a labor point of view, that this type of mechanism operated, albeit in a limited manner over the course of time. In the rest of the region, it was the increase in underemployment or other responses, such as migration in El Salvador's case, that affected the labor market, thereby indicating that its structures still maintained significant evidence of traditional factors.

Finally, it must be pointed out that the crisis paradoxically strengthened the modernizing tendency that had had poor results in previous decades: the feminization of employment. However, this increase in the number of women entering the labor market naturally took place in areas where jobs had been created—in other words, in precarious occupations. In addition, the relative decrease in wage labor must also be stressed, as it implied that the heterogeneity of the labor markets was reinforced.

Emphasis must be placed, above all, on the current formation of a new range of occupations as a result of the restructuring of production that followed the crisis and was promoted by the structural adjustment programs, which are being implemented in all the countries in the region. Within this heterogeneity, it is logics of globalization and accumulation that have the greatest capacity for formation. In this sense, old segmentations of the labor market would be redefined, especially in urban areas in terms of the formal/informal aspect. Three hypotheses have been formulated in this regard: emergence of a new sector of tradable goods that should not be classified as formal and that manifests itself in the form of activities such as the new export agriculture, the *maquila* and Free Trade Zones, or tourism; the decline of both private and public formal employment; and the shaping of a new informality with a different internal diversity than that of the previous period and new scenarios (economy of poverty, subordination to the tradable goods sector by means of subcontracting, and agglomerations of small dynamic firms).

Based on this emergence of this new occupational heterogeneity, two basic tendencies may be proposed in terms of employment. On the one hand, it may be argued that three types of developments exist according to the different occupational sectors identified in the previous paragraph. Thus, those sectors directly or indirectly involved in globalization are characterized by job creation. This would obviously be the case regarding the emerging tradable goods sector, but it would also apply to two types of neoinformality: subordinated, especially that of subcontracting with export firms; and that concerning agglomerations of small dynamic firms—in other words, the globalized community economies. However, one would have to bear in mind that this kind of job creation may fluctuate, as it not only involves cyclical factors of a technological nature but also the new volatile nature of the markets. In contrast, the previous formal sector would, both in its private and state variants, be subjected to job reduction tendencies resulting from more open markets and state reforms, respectively. Finally, the third type of neoinformality, the economy of poverty, would assume the role of adjusting the different flows of labor between these sectors; furthermore, it would absorb the new labor force that is unable to enter the globalizing process.

The second tendency that may be put forward concerns the spatial nature of the labor markets. Previous modernization to some extent set up national labor markets, establishing the urban sphere and especially that related to metropolitan centers as the central point of reference. This type of formation is changing due to two reasons. On the one hand, globalization to a certain extent implies internationalizing flows of labor. This is unquestionably manifest in the economic migration phenomenon that is relevant in the case of Nicaragua (in relation to Costa Rica), in Guatemala, and above all, in El Salvador (with respect to the north). On the other hand, the tendency to metropolize employment is being reverted. Although the reruralization of employment has not been proposed, it is suspected that the intermediate and lower levels of the urban systems are gaining ground, relatively speaking, within national employment structures. The following are prime examples of this redefinition: the location of Free Trade Zones in less prominent urban centers in the Valle del Sula in Honduras; the relocation, to rural areas, of *maquila* firms in Costa Rica, and in particular in Guatemala, where the large Korean firms are moving to the indigenous *Altiplano* in search of local labor markets; and the development of agglomerations of small dynamic firms that tend to establish themselves on the border between urban and rural areas.

Labor Precariousness Persists

As was to be expected, the shaping of labor relations in the case of the traditional coffee sector varied, as mentioned earlier, according to the modes of production of this crop. In situations where extraeconomic coercion was used, reference must be made to the importance of the system whereby labor was exchanged for payment of debts. The contraction of these on the part of the workers "legitimized" the landowners' exercising of this coercion. The former reacted by seeking monetary advances from several *fincas* and rejecting the fulfillment of their debts by abandoning their jobs. In this sense, state action played a crucial role. In Guatemala, the public system was more developed than in Nicaragua and was, therefore, more effective in keeping the population under control. The relevance of this system, in terms of labor relations, was that it meant paying the labor force wages that were lower than their subsistence costs. The result was that during the course of time, a labor reproduction crisis accumulated, and this undermined the logic of the system. Thus, in Guatemala an intermediate solution in the form of the implementation of vagrancy laws during the Ubico era was resorted to, although this did not totally eliminate extraeconomic coercion.

In the second type of situation, which corresponded to the use of proletarianized labor, two phenomena must be stressed in terms of labor conditions. On the one hand, El Salvador and Costa Rica's wage levels differed: These were considerably lower in the former country, where wages had to be complemented by payment in the form of foods. The difference was marked by the existence of an agricultural frontier in Costa Rica, implying that attracting the labor force demanded acceptable wages. On the other hand, reports have been made of the incidence of a gender logic in the coffee sector's labor process, with tasks being arranged according to sex. Moreover, reference has been made to the existence of wage practices that discriminate against women who carry out tasks similar to those undertaken by men.

Finally, with regard to the predominance of family production units, it is interesting to mention the "changing hands" system. This system had initially shown signs of solidarity with these types of producers, though it also tended to base itself on asymmetric relations due to the processes of peasant differentiation that affected this aspect of the coffee sector.

The bananas enclave witnessed three phenomena worth highlighting in terms of labor relations. First, it tended to form labor relations based on ethnic factors, and especially racial factors, despite the existence of classic proletarianization processes. The importance, already mentioned above, of importing contingents of Caribbean English-speaking workers meant they occupied intermediary positions, which was a crucial factor in mitigating labor disputes. In this manner, the firms were able to manage the labor force from a racial angle, which tended to impede class solidarity.

Second, the organization of the labor process itself within the enclave gave rise to three types of labor subjects: plantation workers (the most numerous), railway workers, and dockers. It was at the heart of these last two categories that a clearer awareness of the workers' conditions and the rights these entailed was developed.

Third, it is important to mention the initial periodical monthly payment of wages. This meant that all wage advances were paid in the form of interchangeable coupons for their full value only in the company stores. In this manner, the firms attempted to control the process of reproducing the labor force they employed. A strategy that was reinforced in terms of the other key reproductive aspect was housing. In effect, so-called company towns were set up where the workers were crowded into large huts. In this way, a separate social world was created in line with the logic of the banana plantation enclave, which has constituted a recurring theme in Central American literature, giving rise to novels protesting harsh living and working conditions.

This shaping of labor relations in the region's main accumulative axes during the first half of the twentieth century was very important in terms of capitalist modernization options. In short, the key question was whether the payment of labor incorporated in both axes was capable of establishing the basis of internal demand and, therefore, of a possible national market. The answer is easy. In the case of the banana sector, its condition as enclave implies that regardless of the level of wages, the labor force employed was very limited. Regarding the coffee sector, as already mentioned, its labor intensive nature limited—given the world market's price fluctuations—any policy of a sustained increase in wages. Consequently, Central American modernization took place based on a badly paid work force. This situation underwent no significant changes with the emergence of new accumulative axes, though greater technological development made the effect of salaries on costs more relative. As mentioned earlier, this modernization by means of diversifying agroexports made poverty in rural areas all the more acute.

Only the onset of the industrializing process, a substitute for imports, suggested that this perverse dynamic could be overcome. Nevertheless, it must be remembered that the limitations of this process were twofold: From a spatial point of view, its impact was urban and eminently metropolitan; and it was very short-lived. Thus, as early as the 1970s, the informal segment of the region's urban labor markets was already proving itself to be the most capable of absorbing labor, as pointed out earlier. Although no studies were done on this phenomenon in the 1970s, it would not be unreasonable to assume that subsistence informality, involving poor working conditions, prevailed then. As a result, the urban employment generated by industrialization was also marked by precariousness. Only public employment escaped this tendency, as it was conceived as part of state development in the industrializing process. This type of occupation reached its highest point in Costa Rica, and it is not unrelated to a significant development of social policies that implied a greater growth of the state system. Furthermore, the universal application of these policies in Costa Rica had a positive impact in terms of the reproduction of the work force, ensuring that precarious labor should not necessarily be synonymous with a decline in living conditions. This is why the levels of poverty in Costa Rica were considerably lower than in the rest of the region.

Wage labor, the form of labor that modernization had consolidated, did not escape precariousness. This phenomenon is manifest in two ways. On the one hand, when the impact of imported inflation resulting from the first oil crisis in the 1970s was being felt, real wages were exposed to an inevitable process of decline; only Costa Rica, where an active minimum wage policy was implemented, and Honduras managed to avoid this fall. On the other hand, there was no evidence of work relations being effectively regulated in the region. In this sense, one must bear in mind that the majority of labor legislation, such as that in Guatemala or Costa Rica, had been formulated in the 1940s within the framework of predominantly rural societies. The exception was Honduras, where its later enactment implied a less obsolete set of regulations; and moreover, the fact that this country's trade union movement was, relatively speaking, the strongest in the region (as will be seen later on) meant it achieved a greater recognition of its labor demands, especially during the military reformist experience in the 1970s. Generally speaking, it may be said that with the exception of public employment and isolated cases involving large firms, there was no true regulation of labor relations as such in the region as a result of the modernizing process. Moreover, one must bear in mind that the persistence of authoritarian regimes in the majority of the countries meant that the few regulations in existence were often not applied in practice. That is, it cannot be said that modernization generated rigid institutional norms for the labor market in Central America that the crisis in the 1980s and the structural adjustment processes had to eliminate.

As has been argued earlier, the crisis did not manifest itself—in terms of labor—as it had done in other areas of Latin America, which had experienced modernization at an earlier stage and with more far-reaching consequences in the form of an increase in unemployment. It was only when the crisis underwent a recessive period in Costa Rica that this labor adjustment mechanism became significant. It was, indeed, the growth of so-called underemployment, especially in its invisible mode, that constituted labor's main means of adjusting to the crisis. This implies that the precariousness of labor became more acute in the 1980s. This phenomenon was more apparent in urban areas because the crisis had a stronger impact on sectors that focused more on trade. In this sense, the most significant labor phenomenon of the 1980s was the importance acquired by urban informality, as mentioned earlier.

In terms of labor relations there are several aspects of this phenomenon worth highlighting and that empirical evidence concerning the region has clearly shown. First, its internal heterogeneity, which is the key to understanding this unique world of labor, implies that considerable differences in income exist within it and that informality cannot therefore be considered equivalent to poverty. Nevertheless, the predominance of subsistence informality in the region indicates that the income generated was insufficient both for making the corresponding establishment more dynamic and providing sufficient means of reproduction for the household. In this sense, the differences established by the urban context, as argued earlier, must be borne in mind. Second, the low productivity that characterized this occupational sector meant that economic feasibility was obtained by working very long hours. This implied the considerable exhaustion of the work force involved, beginning with the owner. Third, these labor processes are not ruled by Taylorist criteria. This has an important consequence that is twofold. On the one hand, informality emerges as an environment where labor knowledge may be transmitted. On the other hand, the social relations within the establishment are of a horizontal nature, giving rise to particular occupational identities. In many cases this fact is not unrelated to the use of family labor.

Another example of the precariousness induced by the crisis concerns the adjustment wage workers suffered in terms of the decline in wages during the course of the 1980s. This phenomenon reached its climax in Nicaragua. In contrast, in Costa Rica, where the tradition of an active minimum wage policy was sustained, it was possible to maintain the level of wages. With respect to that country, it must be pointed out that it was the first to implement a structural adjustment strategy in the region and, moreover, in a far-reaching manner, and that this had a positive impact on the labor market. Nonetheless, this strategy was far from being completed in the 1980s, and it is currently having to be continued in a geopolitical context that is no longer as favorable for Costa Rica, thereby raising questions as to its effects on labor.

It may be said that in light of the new occupational heterogeneity currently being generated by the restructuring of production, there is one characteristic the different sectors of labor have in common: the precariousness of their work relations. However, this expresses itself in different ways according to the occupational area.

Thus, in the old formal sector it could be said that the labor rights acquired in the previous period are beginning to wane. This phenomenon may even be observed in the case of public employment, the area favored by labor regulations during the decades of modernization. State reforms, which are a key element in the structural adjustment strategy, involve not only the reduction of public employment, as mentioned earlier, but also a redefinition of working conditions that to some extent questions the nature of the state occupations being regulated. However, decline is far more acute in the private sector, where the dilemma of reconversion or marginalization is confronted, implying that in the future, formal work will be synonymous with public employment.

In the emerging tradable goods and services sector, two types of tendencies may be referred to, depending on what accumulative course is being discussed. In the case of the productive reconversion of firms, the most likely outcome is a trade-off between work stability and other aspects on a downward trend, as seen in other parts of Latin America. With regard to new firms, the existing bibliography on the *maquilas* in

the region consistently demonstrates three facts. First, there is a high rotation of the work force—in other words, little occupational stability.
This phenomenon is a response to two causes: On the one hand, this is a
young work force lacking clearly defined labor orientations; on the
other hand, the poor quality of the work does not induce any particular
sense of identification with the same. Second, working days are long
and hard, causing the depletion of work capacity; this explains why age
is crucial to the labor force employed, as youth implies a higher level of
energy. Third, although the empirical evidence regarding wages is dis-
parate, it may be said that the income obtained was insufficient to guarantee the reproduction of the respective household and served more as
a complement.

The three modes of neoinformality coincided with regard to the precariousness of their labor relations. Nonetheless, the development of
these took on different guises. In the case of subsistence informality, its
evolvement did not follow that of the development of the area itself, as
the latter was marked by the logic of impoverishment that leaves no
room for growth or improvement. Therefore, this development is ultimately related to the problem of equity within society. Subordinate informality will perpetuate precariousness as long as it continues to maintain
its vertical and hierarchical subcontracting ties. The agglomerations of
small dynamic firms would be able to establish working conditions that
are not precarious if they could achieve the growth based on interaction
between competition and cooperation that has typified the development
of the so-called industrial districts of the north.

This new context of globalization poses a key question in terms of the
organization of the labor process. Together with the changes that have
taken place in the way markets operate (volatility, emphasis on quality,
etc.) and the development of a new technological revolution, it must be
pointed out that the new organizational innovations constitute one of the
fundamental elements of the new socioproductive order. This aspect is
crucial to the construction of labor relations in Central America and particularly for the emerging tradables sector, which is the most involved in
globalization tendencies.

Considering it was inherent in the previous modernizing process, the
Taylorist model is the point of reference for outlining changes in the organization of the labor process. It must be remembered that it could be described as sub-Taylorism in the sense that it was not fully implemented
due to the limitations that characterized the previous industrializing
model based on the substitution of imports for the regional market. The
limitations on demand, resulting from the continued unfair distribution
of income, meant that there was a high level of idle production capacity
that must have in turn implied that the work force was not being made

the best use of. Thus, it is suspected that Taylorist principles were not fully applied.

In contrast, in the tradables sector, and especially in the *maquila* industry, it may be argued that the changes that took place regarding the market produced a revival of the Taylorist model that is currently being fully implemented. In effect, the export industry involves markets with practically infinite demands for the existing production capacity; this explains why overtime and subcontracting are frequently resorted to. However, if globalization is seen to induce a revival of Taylorism, so too do the new markets prompt tendencies toward the principle of involvement that is typical of the model of flexible specialization. The volatile nature of the markets and, above all, the greater emphasis on quality, stimulate this tendency. In other words, one may formulate a hypothesis on the fact that in the case of the tradables sector, hybrid modes of organization of the labor process exist, but these are governed by the predominance of a revival of Taylorism.

The Frailty of Actors and Labor Identities

The types of labor relations typified by both the coffee and banana sectors meant that conditions were not particularly favorable for the development of worker organizations in the accumulative axes of the first half of the century.

With regard to the coffee sector, reactions tended to be individual in extraeconomic coercion contexts, where the fulfillment of debts incurred was resisted, as mentioned earlier. Regarding small family production, the ties that linked them to the local community and the dependence regarding the capital that controlled the profits and trading of the coffee made it possible for owners and nonfamily workers to share a similar world view, thus avoiding antagonistic interests. It was only in cases of widespread wage labor that conditions were less unfavorable for the rise of a collective labor actor. However, this type of coffee sector was marked—as was the case with the other two types—by the temporary nature of its employment, which explained how difficult it was for the world of coffee to construct a solid, stable labor identity.

Conditions in the bananas enclave differed. Typical processes of proletarianization had been produced, and therefore, wage relations were clearly established. Nonetheless, the rigid management of the labor force on the part of the companies made it very difficult for worker organizations to establish themselves. In this respect, two elements that have already been mentioned must be borne in mind. On the one hand, the use of foreign (and particularly English-speaking Caribbean) workers in intermediary positions clearly intended to ease conflicts. On the other hand, the control exerted by the companies was also extended to the reproductive sphere by means of the company stores and "company towns" that limited the workers' autonomy outside the plantations and confined them to the closed world of the enclave.

Consequently, as was to be expected, in situations of this kind the construction of a collective actor emerging from the labor environment took place in urban areas and focused on the handicraft sector. As in other parts of Latin America, the first organizations appeared in the form of *mutuales*. Several processes, already mentioned, were involved in the setting up of these entities: the construction of an urban-labor identity, the establishment of a popular basis for liberal projects, and the simultaneous creation of middle and working classes. These were, therefore, organizations that had a united objective; they sought the well-being of their members, particularly through savings, mutual aid, and education; and they had no clearly defined social interests, which left them open to political manipulation.

However, as early as the 1920s, *mutualismo* was undergoing reorientation processes, which gradually led to the shaping of true worker organizations. From this time until the mid–1940s, which constituted a significant moment for the incipient Central American trade unionism, three types of situations may be identified. The first deals with Nicaragua, where union development was minimal and would remain that way for decades. The second is represented by Guatemala and El Salvador, where trade unionism witnessed a forceful beginning in the 1920s, which was frustrated by the installation in the following decade of two authoritarian regimes that suppressed labor organizations. The third situation corresponded to Honduras and, in particular, Costa Rica, where union development was initially slower but became more dynamic in the 1930s. During those two and a half decades, labor action favored the strike as a conflict mechanism, thereby illustrating the move from *mutualismo* to trade unionism mentioned above. Improved wages and working conditions were, generally speaking, the most common demands made by organized Central American workers. Two situations must be pointed out in this respect. First, there is the case of the 1932 killings in the Salvadoran Izalcos coffee region, the outcome of which meant that the labor movement would require several years to recover, although the indigenous population had a higher price to pay because their ethnic condition was stigmatized as a result of it being associated with Communist leanings. The second situation is represented by the 1934 banana strike in the Costa Rican Atlantic region, which was symbolically significant for consolidating, under the auspices of the Communist party, that country's trade union movement, whose most solid social base was the cobblers' union. It is important to mention that both events were situated in the two prevailing accumulative axes (the coffee sector and the bananas enclave), thereby illustrating how, in the midst of their own crisis, it was impossible to continue suppressing social conflict as they had in the past.

In the majority of the countries in the region, the end of World War II gave rise, as mentioned above, to circumstances in which political expression was given to the crisis affecting the oligarchy, whose material foundations had already been shaken by the depression in the early 1930s. This moment in time was significant for the world of Central American labor for three reasons: An important phase of union organization development took place; political parties with working-class leanings appeared, allowing the workers to project themselves onto the political arena; and state recognition was given to the worker with the enactment of labor codes, among which the Guatemalan and Costa Rican were the most outstanding examples. Nevertheless, the end of the oligarchical crisis implied a weakening of the Central American trade union movement due to different causes. The most dramatic case was that of Guatemala: As of the 1944 revolution and, in particular, during the Arbenz government, there was an unprecedented rise of trade unions in the region, which also included agricultural laborers. The overthrowing of this government meant the suppression and involution of Guatemala's labor movement. However, there was an exception to Central American trade unionism's desolate panorama on the eve of the onset of modernization. In Honduras, a strike broke out in the bananas enclave in 1954 that prompted a show of solidarity from other sectors, marking the most important milestone in the history of that country's labor movement. Regardless of how the outcome of this conflict is assessed, it had a fundamental consequence that was twofold: On the one hand, it imposed the right of the workers to organize a union; on the other hand, it led, during the years immediately after it, to the approval of an entire series of decrees that would culminate in the enactment of a labor code. In this sense, it may be said that the Honduran labor movement was the only one in Central America able to face modernization from a more consolidated position. In other words, with the relative exception of this case, the workers did not appear as a consolidated actor capable of making an impact on the transformations of the region during the following decades.

However, the modernizing developments allowed for a revival, to a certain extent, of the trade union movement, which should be considered from an organizational angle as well as from the point of view of action.

With regard to the first perspective, there are two aspects worth highlighting. On the one hand, there is no doubt that during the course of these years, there was a tendency toward the growth of union organizations. Nonetheless, this growth should not obscure the fact that around the 1970s, the rates of trade union membership in Central American countries were very low: approximately 10 percent in Costa Rica and Honduras, with a greater presence of urban and state workers in the former, and rural workers in the latter; approximately 5 percent in El Salvador, with limited memberships in the cities; and lower in Guatemala and Nicaragua, the latter registering a mere 2 percent due to its late union development. On the other hand, it may be said that three ideological tendencies prevailed, their influence differing according to the country and the period. First, it must be pointed out that the weak state of the trade unions in the 1950s was taken advantage of by the governments who used them to create government-run movements. The ORIT, supported by the United States government in the new context of the cold war, played a fundamental role in this effort and became an external actor that exerted considerable influence on the Central American world of labor. Even the powerful Honduran SITRATERCO was initially involved in this type of tendency. However, in the second place, reference should be made to the failure of the Communist trend to die out. Although it was initially forced underground, in time it gained strength, and in the 1960s a Christian-orientated trade unionism burst forth. This played a key role in, for example, Guatemala, aiding the recovery of the labor movement, and it assumed a radical position in the 1970s.

Three phenomena should be highlighted in terms of trade union action. First, the strike was the most favored form of action in situations not suited to negotiation. In this manner, the previous model of action was given continuity, thereby reaffirming trade union identity. This confrontational method was intensified in the 1970s due to the decline in wages resulting from the inflation imported by the first oil crisis. Thus, light was shed on the absence of minimum wage state policies—with the exception of Costa Rica, where the state maintained its sense of social duty. Second, the increasingly radical stance adopted by union leaders must be mentioned for it reduced the scope of action carried out by official trade unionism. By the end of the 1970s, two countries, Guatemala and El Salvador, exemplified this tendency. This radical position represented a social precedent for the armed conflicts that were to take place in the following decade in both of these societies. However, it must be remembered that the central actors in this social upheaval were to be found in the rural environment. In El Salvador's case, the subject was the impoverished or subordinate peasant; Guatemala's case proves more complex due to the decisive intervention of the ethnic factor. In both cases, these actors formed the social basis of the rebel movements. The third phenomenon under consideration is that of the relation with the state. In this respect, it is important to point out the multiple reactions of the political power to this radicalization of labor and society in general. On the one hand, an attempt was made to apply minimum wage policies and extend social security coverage for urban workers. On the other hand, meanwhile, efforts were made to respond to agrarian workers' demands by proposing agrarian reform policies and promoting cooperativism. However, these did not question the historical political exclusion the peasantry had been subjected to within the region.

The emphases given to these actions varied from country to country, as did the success of their implementation. In this regard, two situations may be identified as a result of this dialectic. On the one hand, the relative success of the application of some of these measures meant that opportunities for negotiation arose, and consequently, conflicts were to a certain extent institutionalized. This was the case in Costa Rica, where historical factors (democratic stability and social obligation on the part of the state) played a decisive role. In addition, Honduras should be included in this category due to the effects of military reformism; though the situation tended to deteriorate in the second half of the 1970s, it did not sink to the levels of the second type of situation. The latter, on the other hand, includes the rest of the countries where the failure or mere lack of implementation of these measures intensified the radicalization of the labor conflicts that were inevitably etched on the logic of the armed conflict. The outcome for the respective trade union movements differed according to the country, as shall be seen in the following analysis.

The crisis in the 1980s presented two challenges for the Central American trade union movement: on the one hand, the challenge of how it would respond to the economic effects of the crisis and the onset of the implementation of structural adjustment measures; and on the other hand, as referred to in the former paragraph, how it would adapt to a change in its relations with the state, especially in situations where conflicts had intensified and, in several countries, reached a state of war. The first challenge was most clearly expressed in Costa Rica, whereas the second proved central to the Guatemalan, Salvadoran, and Nicaraguan contexts. Honduras found itself in an intermediary position.

With regard to Costa Rica, two key phenomena that influenced the development of union action and organization during the 1980s must be mentioned. First, it was in this country, as mentioned earlier, that structural adjustment measures were applied at an earlier date and in a more far-reaching manner. However, the most important aspect is the gradual manner in which this took place. Thus, as there were none of the well-known stabilizing measure *paquetazos* (barrage of packages) common to other areas of Latin America, no major social conflicts arose; however, a sector of the population was mobilized in response to the increase in electricity rates, although the unions did not play a central role in this. This gradual implementation neutralized the trade union movement. In the second instance, and more importantly, *solidarismo* underwent spectacular development in the private sector. This gave rise to a labor consensus that clearly favored management interests. This movement has attempted to establish itself in other countries in the region, but its influence has not reached the level it has achieved in Costa Rica. In this respect, one must bear in mind that in Costa Rica a tradition of consensus prevails, in contrast to the rest of Central America, where historically speaking, the logic of confrontation has predominated.

For its part, in Honduras, as discussed above, the trade union movement found itself facing both challenges. Perhaps the most significant aspect of this period was the central role taken on by state employees: The large majority of the labor conflicts that took place during these years occurred in the public sector.

In the remaining countries, which were each marked by armed conflict, the main problem has been the relation with the state, with results varying in each case. In Guatemala, suppression forced the trade union movement underground, and the logic of armed conflict led to its destruction as a social movement, especially in the case of the CUC. This same type of situation occurred in El Salvador. However, in late 1983 this situation took an about-turn due to a combination of three factors: the involvement of state employees in the popular struggles; the successful setting up of the most important unifying trade union entity in the country's history, the UNTS; and the inclusion on the union platform of demands related to the war (human rights and peacekeeping). Thus, in contrast to the Guatemalan situation, El Salvador's trade unionism was fortified. We consider the major difference between these two contexts to have been determined by the development of the armed conflict: Whereas in Guatemala the army imposed itself, from a strategic point of view, in El Salvador neither side overcame the other.

Although affected by the armed conflict, Nicaragua presented a series of peculiarities, given the overthrow of the Somoza dictatorship and the installation of the *Sandinista* government. Three aspects are worth mentioning. First, the new political situation created an unprecedented upsurge of trade union organizations in the country, which was historically lagging behind the rest of Central America. Second, two tendencies may be identified within the Nicaraguan labor movement: On the one hand, there were the previous organizations that essentially proposed corporative demands; on the other hand were the *Sandinista* organizations that placed these demands after the revolutionary project. However, even within the latter, distinctions must be made, for national and grass-roots management differed; these differences became more pointed with the increase in economic hardships. Third, the labor policy implemented by the *Sandinista* regime was marked by serious problems as a result of the decline in the country's situation. Thus, following a variety of experiments, wages in kind were resorted to in terms of wage policy. This form of remuneration led to a lack of labor discipline and forced wage workers into informal trade circuits where they sold the majority of this type of salary. In this manner, the condition of the worker as such was distorted, created identity crises. In addition, the *Sandinista* government found itself having to cut back on public employment by applying the so-called *política de compactación* (streamlining policy) due to the need to impose stabilizing measures.

Consequently, the trade union movement in Central America emerged from the crisis of the 1980s in a weakened state, both from a corporative and political point of view, and thus faced the restructuring of production that began to be implemented in the 1990s. The rise of new activities such as the *maquila* industry, involving the hiring of a new labor force with little experience of trade unions and strong opposition on the part of the employers to any form of union organization, or state reforms with their subsequent cutbacks in public employment, have immersed the labor movement in a defensive position.

This situation may currently be observed in the formal sector, including the public sector, which in effect represents the main basis of union memberships. However, as mentioned earlier, the structural adjustment strategies that are already being implemented throughout the region and that place greater emphasis on far-reaching transformations also affect this occupational environment by means of state reforms. This phenomenon has, to date, been manifest most blatantly by the Nicaraguan context due to the fact that the dismantling of the state mechanism set up by the *Sandinista* regime has been added to calls for adjustment. Another case that should be kept in mind is that of Costa Rica, because it is the state that has traditionally been developed the most in the region.

With regard to the new tradables sector, the existence of three possible situations may be considered, taking into account the shaping of a new occupational heterogeneity. The first and foremost is that of fragmentation. That is to say, in this sector the construction of collective identities is a complex one. As already mentioned, the evidence available regarding the *maquila* industry demonstrates the presence of a very young work force with little likelihood of having defined its occupational orientations; furthermore, it does not appear to identify itself with its employment due to the poor quality of the same. Second, the Costa Rican experience reflects the presence of *solidarista* organizations that the employers themselves consider the ideal model for worker representation. Nonetheless, as argued above, in light of the prevailing tradition of negotiation and consensus particular to Costa Rican society, this labor movement does not appear to have enjoyed the same success in other Central American countries. Third, the possibility of a trade union presence such as reconverted firms that already had union organizations is being proposed. However, the changes being brought about by globalization imply that trade union action would undergo a process of redefinition. In this sense, the firm itself, rather than the state, as in the past, would be the point of reference.

Of the three types of informality, subordinate informality would be the most precarious in terms of producing actors. The dividing logic of subcontracting implies that fragmentation should be the prevailing tendency. In contrast, within the context of subsistence informality, the construction of certain actors may be considered. On the one hand, there is circumstantial construction, as in the case of the street vendor in conflict with the municipal authorities regarding territorial control. On the other hand, within this environment of exclusion, other social references, such as spatial factors, may allow for the construction of actors in terms of neighborhood or other types of organizations. In effect, this phenomenon was already observed in the previous modernization process where, faced with the high level of precarious labor, the actors found opportunities in nonproductive areas. With regard to agglomerations of small dynamic firms, it seems obvious that the actor would, above all, take on a local form. In this respect, it is important to mention that activating social capital in this scenario tends to reinforce community identities. That is, in this type of context the fragmenting effects of globalization may be reversed in order that society be strengthened.

Consequently, the current situation does not imply the emergence, from the point of view of the Central American world of labor, of actors involved in and, above all, affecting the globalization process. In fact, the labor subjects observed were seen to have a fragile constitution. However, this frailty is not a new phenomenon. It was present in the coffee and banana sectors and in the agroexport diversification that began halfway through the twentieth century. These accumulative developments gave rise, in general terms, to a labor subject caught between peasant impoverishment and temporary wage labor. Likewise, import-substituting industrialization failed to construct a solid proletariat. In the end, it was the informal world that became the main point of reference for urban labor in the region. Public employees were the only ones that succeeded in consolidating themselves from a labor perspective. Thus, it is hardly surprising that the influence of the trade union movement on the work force as a whole was limited and that it has, in effect, become most firmly rooted in the realm of public employment. The crisis in the 1980s affected the workers both from an economic and political point of view, shedding light on their social vulnerability, which has, due to the current restructuring of production, become more acute as a result of the exclusion tendencies of the new accumulative model.

However, this tendency of labor subjects toward weakness is not unrelated to the other two tendencies analyzed in this last chapter: insufficient job creation and the precariousness of labor. In effect, both of these have contributed to setting up the situation framework in which this frailty of society has been reproduced to this day. Therefore, the traditional world of labor, which was linked to the coffee sector and the bananas enclave, was typified by the temporary nature of the work or by the limited amount of labor employed. Insufficient pay and other inadequate working conditions completed the picture, which was, by and large, maintained during the period of agroexport diversification that followed. The best example of this labor situation is the widespread and deep-rooted process of impoverishment that Central American agricultural laborers were subjected to. Urbanization, introduced by industrialization, opened the way to increased job creation and less precariousness. However, this new accumulative axis was not dynamic enough and resulted in the development of informal urban labor. The crisis intensified precarious labor and the current restructuring of production does not appear to show globalization as being accompanied by more sustained employment dynamics. Its clearest examples tend, rather, to illustrate the extent of the absorbed work force is limited and that working conditions are set within flexible tendencies.

Thus, insufficient job creation, precarious labor, and fragile labor subjects and actors emerge as the three main historical logics that have—in a vulnerable manner—constructed the world of labor in Central America. Examples of these have undoubtedly varied in time, as demonstrated by the analysis carried out in each chapter, where specific factors regarding each period have been discussed. In this sense, modernization has, it must be said, made changes with regard to labor. However, the structuring logic behind these basic tendencies has, reticently, remained the same during the course of these decades. There was no break with modernization or the crisis in the 1980s, and it seems this will be the case regarding the new emerging accumulative model. Thus, it should come as no surprise that the accounts of Rigoberta Menchú and Lesly Rodríguez, which opened this text, are interchangeable despite the fact they were written thirty years apart and are supposedly referring to different labor situations. It appears that time has come to a standstill for Central American workers in their transition from the *finca* to the *maquila*.

References

Aburto, R. "El boom de la economía informal en Nicaragua," *Boletín Socio-Económico*, 8, 1998.

Achío, M. "Crisis y reproducción de la fuerza de trabajo industrial en Costa Rica," *Ciencias Sociales*, 37–38, 1987.

ACI. "Las cooperativas en el desarrollo rural," *Documentos de investigación*. San José: Alianza Cooperativa Internacional, 1991.

Acuña Ortega, V. H. *Los orígenes de la clase obrera en Costa Rica: las huelgas de 1920 por la jornada de ocho horas*. San José: CENAP/CEPAS, 1986a.

_____. "Patrones del conflicto social en la economía cafetalera costarricense (1940–1948)," *Revista de Ciencias Sociales*, 31, 1986b.

_____. "Clases subalternas y movimientos sociales en Centroamérica (1870–1930)," in V. H. Acuña Ortega (ed.), *Historia General de Centroamérica: Las repúblicas agroexportadoras (1870–1945)*. Madrid: FLACSO/Sociedad Estatal Quinto Centenario, 1993.

Acuña Ortega, V. H. and I. Molina Jiménez. *Historia económica social de Costa Rica (1750–1950)*. San José: Editorial Porvenir, 1991.

Adams, R. N. "Etnias y sociedades (1930–1979)," in H. Pérez Brignoli (ed.), *Historia General de Centroamérica: De la postguerra a la crisis (1945–1979)*. Madrid: FLACSO/Sociedad Estatal Quinto Centenario, 1993.

Aguilar, M. *Clase trabajadora y organización sindical en Costa Rica, 1943–1971*. San José: ICES/Porvenir/FLACSO, 1989.

Altenburg, T. "Estudio sobre efectos multiplicadores de las Zonas Francas de Exportación sobre el desarrollo nacional," *report* for Corporación de la Zona Franca de Exportación, S.A., 1993.

Aquino, L. A. "Reforma agraria y empleo en El Salvador," in PREALC, Centroamérica: acerca del empleo, la estructura y en cambio agrarios," *Cuadernos de Ciencias Sociales*, 23, San José: FLACSO, 1989.

Arends, M. "Female Labor Force Participation and Earnings in Guatemala," in G. Psacharopoulos and Z. Tzannatos (eds.), *Case Studies on Women´s Employment and Pay in Latin America*. Washington, D.C.: The World Bank, 1992.

Arévalo, R. and J. Arriola. "Estudios de casos y educación obrera en zonas francas y empresas maquiladoras del Istmo Centroamericano y República Dominicana." El caso de El Salvador, *informe*, San José: OIT, 1995.

Arias, A. "El movimiento indígena en Guatemala: 1970–1983," in D. Camacho and R. Menjívar (coords.), *Movimientos populares en Centroamérica*. San José: EDUCA, 1985.

Arriola, J. "Los procesos de trabajo en la Zona Franca de San Bartolo," *Documentos de Trabajo*, 93–2, San Salvador: IIES-UCA, 1993.

168   *References*

AVANCSO. "El significado de la maquila en Guatemala: Elementos para su comprensión," *Cuadernos de Investigación*, 10, Guatemala: AVANCSO, 1994.
Balcárcel, J. L. "El movimiento obrero in Guatemala," in P. González Casanova (coord.), *Historia del movimiento obrero en América Latina*, 2. México: Siglo XXI, 1985.
Bastos, S. and M. Camus. "Indígenas en la Ciudad de Guatemala: subsistencia y cambio étnico," *Debate*, 6, Guatemala: FLACSO, 1989.
_____. "Establecimiento y hogar en Ciudad de Guatemala: un enfoque de género," in R. Menjívar Larín and J. P. Pérez Sáinz (coords.), *Ni héroes ni villanas. Género e informalidad urbana en Centroamérica*. San José: FLACSO, 1993a.
_____. *Quebrando el silencio: Organizaciones del pueblo maya y sus demandas (1986–1992)*. Guatemala: FLACSO, 1993b.
Baumeister, E. "La agricultura centroamericana en los ochenta," *Polémica*, 14–15, 1991.
_____. "Guatemala: Los trabajadores temporales en la agricultura," in S. Gómez and E. Klein (eds.), *Los Pobres del campo: El trabajador eventual*. Santiago: FLACSO/PREALC, 1993.
_____. "El café en Honduras," in H. Pérez Brignoli and M. Samper (comps.), *Tierra, café y sociedad: Ensayos sobre la historia agraria centroamericana*. San José: FLACSO, 1994.
BCH. "Actividad económica de las Zonas Libres y de las Zonas de Procesamiento Industrial," *informe*, Tegucigalpa: Banco Central de Honduras, 1993.
Brenes, J. "Las centrales sindicales ante la política económica," *Boletín socioeconómico*, 5, 1987.
Briones, C. "Un ensayo de descripción de las características del sector informal urbano salvadoreño," *Boletín de Ciencias Económicas y Sociales*, 4, 1987.
_____. "Economía informal en el Gran San Salvador," in J. P. Pérez Sáinz and R. Menjívar Larín (coords.), *Informalidad Urbana en Centroamérica: Entre la acumulación y la subsistencia*. Caracas: FLACSO/Nueva Sociedad, 1991.
Bodson, P., A. Cordero, and J. P. Pérez Sáinz. *Las nuevas caras del empleo*. San José: FLACSO, 1995.
Bourgois, C. *Banano, etnia y lucha social en Centroamérica*. San José: DEI, 1994.
Browning, D. *El Salvador: La tierra y el hombre*. San Salvador: Ministerio de Educación, 1975.
Bulmer-Thomas, V. *La economía política de Centroamérica desde 1920*. Tegucigalpa: Banco Centroamericano de Integración Económica, 1989.
_____. "La crisis de la economía de agroexportación (1930–1945)," in V. H. Acuña Ortega (ed.), *Historia General de Centroamérica: Las repúblicas agroexportadoras (1870–1945)*. Madrid: FLACSO/Sociedad Estatal Quinto Centenario, 1993.
Burgos, E. *Me llamo Rigoberta Menchú y así me nació la conciencia*. Mexico: Siglo XXI, 1991.
Caballero, E. L. and C. Sánchez Lam. "Sondeo sobre las condiciones de trabajo y contratación de las mujeres que laboran en la maquila de Puerto Cortés, Honduras," *informe de investigación*, Tegucigalpa: UnoUno Consultoras, 1992.
Camus, M. "La maquila en Guatemala: un acercamiento a las relaciones laborales," in J. P. Pérez Sáinz (coord.), *Globalización y fuerza laboral en Centroamérica*. San José: FLACSO, 1994.

Carmack, R. M. "The Story of Santa Cruz Quiché," in R. M. Carmack (ed.), *Harvest of Violence: The Maya Indians and the Guatemalan Crisis*. Norman: University of Oklahoma Press, 1988.

Castellanos Cambranes, J. *Café y campesinos en Guatemala, 1853–1897*. Guatemala: Editorial Universitaria, 1985.

CEPAL. "Centroamérica: el empleo femenino en la industria maquiladora de exportación," *documento*, México: CEPAL, 1994.

CETRA. "El sector informal urbano en Managua," *informe*, Managua: CETRA, 1987.

Chamorro, A., M. Chávez, and M. Membreño. "El sector informal en Nicaragua," in J. P. Pérez Sáinz and R. Menjívar Larín (coords.), *Informalidad Urbana en Centroamérica: Entre la acumulación y la subsistencia*. Caracas: FLACSO/Nueva Sociedad, 1991.

CITGUA. "El movimiento sindical en Guatemala (1975–1985)," *documento*, México: CITGUA, 1989.

_____. "La maquila en Guatemala," *documento*, México: CITGUA, 1991.

Ciudad, A. "La administración e inspección del trabajo y las empresas de maquila y zonas francas en Centroamérica, Panamá y República dominicana," *mimeo*, 1995.

Cordero, A. "¿Hay un nuevo modelo de producción en la industria costarricense?" in J. P. Pérez Sáinz (coord.), *Globalización y fuerza laboral en Centroamérica*. San José: FLACSO, 1994.

Cruz, M. "El mercado informal de trabajo y su imbricación con las grandes empresas," *Boletín de Ciencias Económicas y Sociales*, 2, 1984.

Cuevas, F. "Impacto socio-económico de las maquilas y las zonas francas en Costa Rica," *informe*, San José: OIT, 1995.

Dary Fuentes, C. *Mujeres tradicionales y nuevos cultivos*. Guatemala: FLACSO, 1991.

Del-Cid, R. "El sector informal en dos ciudades de Honduras," in J. P. Pérez Sáinz and R. Menjívar Larín (coords.), *Informalidad Urbana en Centroamérica: Entre la acumulación y la subsistencia*. Caracas: FLACSO/Nueva Sociedad, 1991.

DGEC. *Censo General de Población de 1950*. Tegucigalpa: Dirección General de Estadística y Censos, 1952.

_____. *Censo General de Población de la República de Nicaragua*, 1950. Managua: Dirección General de Estadísticas y Censos, 1954.

_____. *Censo de Población*, 1961. Tegucigalpa: Dirección General de Estadísticas y Censos, 1963.

_____. *Censo de Población*, 1974. Tegucigalpa: Dirección General de Estadísticas y Censos, 1975.

_____. *Censos Nacionales*, 1963. Managua: Dirección General de Estadísticas y Censos, 1967.

_____. *Censos Nacionales*, 1971. Managua: Dirección General de Estadísticas y Censos, 1974.

_____. *Censos de Población de Costa Rica*, 1950. San José: Dirección General de Estadísticas y Censos, 1953.

_____. *Censos de Población de Costa Rica*. 1963, San José: Dirección General de Estadísticas y Censos, 1966.

_____. *Censos de Población de Costa Rica,* 1973. San José: Dirección General de Estadísticas y Censos, 1974.

_____. *Cuarto Censo de Población,* 1971. San Salvador: Dirección General de Estadísticas y Censos, 1977.

_____. *Encuesta nacional de hogares empleo y desempleo.* San José: Dirección General de Estadísticas y Censos, 1980, 1985, 1989.

_____. *Encuesta permanente de hogares de propósitos múltiples.* Tegucigalpa: Dirección General de Estadística y Censos, 1988.

_____. *Segundo Censo de Población, 1950.* San Salvador: Dirección General de Estadísticas y Censos, 1953.

_____. *Tercer Censo de Población,* 1961. San Salvador: Dirección General de Estadísticas y Censos, 1965.

_____. *VI Censo de Población,* 1950. Guatemala: Dirección General de Estadísticas y Censos, 1957.

_____. *VII Censo de Población,* 1964. Guatemala: Dirección General de Estadísticas y Censos, 1971.

_____. *VIII Censo de Población,* 1973. Guatemala: Dirección General de Estadísticas y Censos, 1975.

Dierckxsens, W. "Mujer y fuerza de trabajo en Centroamérica," *Cuadernos de Ciencias Sociales,* 28, San José, FLACSO, 1990.

Donato, E. and C. Castro. "El movimiento sindical en Costa Rica ante la crisis y los cambios en el Estado (1980–1988)," in CAAS-CEPAS, *El sindicalismo y la crisis centroamericana.* Heredia: CAAS-CEPAS, 1990.

Donato, E. and M. Rojas. *Sindicatos, política y economía, 1972–1986.* San José: Alma Mater, 1987.

Dore, E. "La producción cafetalera nicaragüense, 1860–1960: transformaciones estructurales," in H. Pérez Brignoli and M. Samper (comps.), *Tierra, café y sociedad: Ensayos sobre la historia agraria centroamericana.* San José: FLACSO, 1994.

Duarte, A. and S. Quintanilla. "Condiciones socio-laborales de las obreras en la maquila textil: Costa Rica años 1980–1990," *Tesis de Licenciatura,* Heredia: Escuela de Sociología/UNA, 1991.

Ellis, F. *Las transnacionales del banano en Centroamérica.* San José: EDUCA, 1983.

Enríquez, C. A. "El movimiento sindical guatemalteco en la década de los ochenta (una periodización y cuatro tesis para comprender)," in CAAS-CEPAS, *El sindicalismo y la crisis centroamericana.* Heredia: CAAS-CEPAS, 1990.

Evans, T. "Ajuste estructural y sector público en Nicaragua," in T. Evans (coord.), *La transformación neoliberal del sector público: Ajuste estructural y sector público en Centroamérica y El Caribe.* Managua: Latino Editores, 1995.

FADES. "El sector informal: Estudio sobre el sector informal de producción y servicios en el Area Urbana Central de Guatemala," *informe,* Guatemala: FADES, 1987.

FLACSO. *Centroamérica en cifras 1980–1992.* San José: FLACSO, 1995.

Flores Macal, M. "El movimiento sindical salvadoreño: Características principales," *Anuario de Estudios Centroamericanos,* 6, 1980.

Frundt, H. "The Effectiveness of National Labor Codes in Central America," *ponencia* presented at the Latin American Studies Association, Washington, D.C.: September 30, 1995.

Fundación Arias. "Mujer y secator informal urbano en Centroamérica," *documento*, San José: Fundación Arias, 1992.

Funkhouser, E. "Mass Emigration, Remittances and Economic Adjustment: The Case of El Salvador in the 1980s," in R. Freeman and G. Borjas (eds.), *The Economic Effects of Inmigration in Source and Receiving Countries.* Chicago: University of Chicago Press, 1992a.

_____. "Migration from Managua: Some Recent Evidence," *World Development*, 20, 8, 1992b.

_____. "Wage Structure in Guatemala," *manuscrito*, 1993.

_____. "Central American Labor Markets: What Do We Know?" *ponencia* presented at the Latin American Studies Association conference, Atlanta, Ga.: March 12, 1994a.

_____. "Labor Market Adjustments to Political Conflict: Changes in El Salvador During the 1980s," *manuscrito*, 1994b.

_____. "The Urban Informal Sector in Central America: Household Survey Evidence," *manuscrito*, 1994c.

FUSADES. "Zonas francas en El Salvador," *Boletín Económico Social*, 64, 1991.

Gallardo, M. and J. R. López. *Centroamérica: La crisis en cifras.* San José: FLACSO/IICA, 1986.

García, A. I. and E. Gómariz. *Mujeres centroamericanas.* San José: FLACSO, Tomo Y, 1989.

García, N. E. *Ajuste, reformas y mercado laboral: Costa Rica (1980–1990), Chile (1973–1992), México (1981–1991).* Santiago: PREALC, 1993.

García-Huidobro, G. "Política económica de ajuste y mercado de trabajo: el caso de Costa Rica 1982–1986," *Documento de Trabajo*, 310, Santiago: PREALC, 1987.

_____. "Empleo femenino en Centroamérica," *documento*, Panamá: PNUD/OIT/PREALC, 1989.

Ghidinelli, A. "Aspectos económicos de la cultura los Caribes Negros del municipio de Livinstong," *Guatemala Indígena*, 7, 4, 1972.

Gindling, T. H. "¿Existe segmentación en el mercado de trabajo urbano de Costa Rica?" *Documento de Trabajo*, 92, San José: Instituto de Investigaciones en Ciencias Económicas, 1986.

_____. "Crisis económica y segmentación del mercado en el área urbana de Costa Rica," *Ciencias Económicas*, 9, 12, 1989.

_____. "Why Women Earn Less than Men in Costa Rica," in G. Psacharopoulos and Z. Tzannatos (eds.), *Case Studies on Women´s Employment and Pay in Latin America.* Washington, D.C.: The World Bank, 1992.

Goldenberg, O. "Informalidad urbana y género en Costa Rica," in R. Menjívar Larín and J. P. Pérez Sáinz (coords.), *Ni héroes ni villanas: Género e informalidad urbana en Centroamérica.* San José: FLACSO, 1993.

González, J. F. "Impacto socio-económico de las maquilas y las zonas francas en El Salvador," *informe*, San José: OIT, 1995.

González, M. A. "El desarrollo de la industria maquila en Guatemala: Estudio de casos de la ocupación de la mano de obra femenina," *informe de investigación*, Guatemala: FLACSO, 1991.

Gould, J. "Amigos peligrosos, enemigos mortales: un análisis del movimiento obrero nicaragüense y Somoza, 1944–1946," *Revista de Historia*, 11–12, 1986.

_____. "Estábamos principiando: un estudio sobre el movimiento obrero en Chinandega, Nicaragua (1920–1949)," *Revista de Historia*, 18, 1988.

_____."El café, el trabajo y la comunidad indígena de Matagalpa, 1880–1925," in H. Pérez Brignoli and M. Samper (comps.), *Tierra, café y sociedad: Ensayos sobre la historia agraria centroamericana*. San José: FLACSO, 1994.

Gudmundson, L. "Peasant, Farmer, Proletarian: Class Formation in a Smallholder Coffee Economy, 1850–1950," in W. Roseberry, L. Gudmundson, and M. Samper (eds.), *Coffee, Society and Power in Latin America*. Baltimore: Johns Hopkins University Press, 1995.

Guerra-Borges, A. "El desarrollo económico," in H. Pérez Brignoli (ed.), *Historia General de Centroamérica: De la postguerra a la crisis (1945–1979)*. Madrid: FLACSO/Sociedad Estatal Quinto Centenario, 1993.

Guido Béjar, R. "El movimiento sindical post-II Guerra Mundial en El Salvador," in CAAS-CEPAS, *El sindicalismo y la crisis centroamericana*. Heredia: CAAS-CEPAS, 1990.

Gutiérrez López, O. "Las zonas francas industriales de exportación: efectos económicos e impacto sobre el empleo en Nicaragua," *informe*, San José: OIT, 1994.

Gutiérrez Mayorga, G. "Historia del movimiento obrero de Nicaragua (1900–1977)," in P. González Casanova (coord.), *Historia del movimiento obrero en América Latina* 2. México: Siglo XXI, 1985.

Gutiérrez Quintero, M. "Estudio comparativo sobre algunos aspectos de la legislación del trabajo y la seguridad social en la región de Centro América y Panamá aplicables en las zonas francas y a las empresas maquiladoras," *mimeo*, n.d.

Haan, H. "Costa Rica: características de las microempresas y sus dueños," *Documento de Trabajo*, 253, Santiago: PREALC, 1984.

_____. "El sector informal en Centroamérica," *Investigaciones sobre empleo*, 26, Santiago: PREALC, 1985.

Hintermeister, A. "Modernización de la agricultura y pobreza rural en Guatemala," *Trabajo Ocasional*, 45, Santiago: PREALC, 1982.

INE. *IX Censo de Población*. Guatemala: Instituto Nacional de Estadística, 1985.

_____. *Encuesta nacional socio-demográfica: Empleo, Total República*. Guatemala: Instituto Nacional de Estadística, 1987, 1990.

INEC. *Tabulaciones básicas volumen VII: características económicas de la población de 10 años y más*. Managua: Instituto Nacional de Estadísticas y Censos, 1985.

Jiménez, D. "El movimiento campesino en Guatemala: 1969–1980," in D. Camacho and R. Menjívar (coords.), *Movimientos populares en Centroamérica*. San José: EDUCA, 1985.

Jonas, S. *The Battle for Guatemala: Rebels, Death Squads, and U.S. Power*. Boulder: Westview Press, 1991.

Lazo, F. and J. Herrera. "El movimiento sindical salvadoreño, 1980–1984, en CINAS: El movimiento sindical salvadoreño, 1979–1984," *Cuaderno de Trabajo*, 5, México: CINAS, 1985.

Le Bot, Y. *La guerre en terre maya: Communauté, violence et modernité au Guatemala*. París: Karthala, 1992.

Levinson-Estrada, D. *Trade Unionist Against Terror: Guatemala City, 1954–1985*. Chapel Hill: University of North Carolina Press, 1994.

López, F., J. Brenes, and C. A. Jiménez. "Consideraciones sobre el movimiento obrero nicaragüense," in CAAS-CEPAS, *El sindicalismo y la crisis centroamericana.* Heredia: CAAS-CEPAS, 1990.

Lungo, M. *La lucha de masas en El Salvador.* San Salvador: UCA Editores, 1987.

_____. "Movimiento popular y movimiento sindical en El Salvador en los años ochenta," in CAAS-CEPAS, *El sindicalismo y la crisis centroamericana.* Heredia: CAAS-CEPAS, 1990.

Martínez, D. "Pobreza y mercado de trabajo rural en el Istmo centroamericano," in PREALC, *¿Maíz o melón? Las respuestas del agro centroamericano a los cambios de las políticas económicas.* Panamá: PREALC, 1993.

McCreery, D. "State Power, Indigineous Communities, and Land in Nineteenth-Century Guatemala, 1820–1920," in C. A. Smith (ed.), *Guatemalan Indians and the State, 1540 to 1988.* Austin: University of Texas Press, 1990.

_____."El impacto del café en las tierras de las comunidades indígenas: Guatemala, 1870–1930," in H. Pérez Brignoli and M. Samper (comps.), *Tierra, café y sociedad: Ensayos sobre la historia agraria centroamericana.* San José: FLACSO, 1994.

_____. *Rural Guatemala, 1760–1940.* Stanford: Stanford University Press, 1994b.

_____. "Wage Labor, Free Labor and Vagrancy Laws: The Transition to Capitalism in Guatemala, 1920–1945, in W. Roseberry, L. Gudmundson, and M. Samper (eds.), *Coffee, Society and Power in Latin America.* Baltimore: Johns Hopkins University Press, 1995.

Membreño, R. and E. Guerrero. *Maquila y organización sindical en Centroamérica.* Managua: Centro de Estudios y Análisis Sociolaborales, 1994.

Menjívar, R. *Acumulación originaria y desarrollo del capitalismo en El Salvador.* San José: EDUCA., 1980.

_____. *Formación y lucha del proletariado industrial salvadoreño.* San José: EDUCA., 1982.

_____. "Notas sobre el movimiento obrero salvadoreño," in P. González Casanova (coord.), *Historia del movimiento obrero en América Latina* 2. México: Siglo XXI, 1985.

Menjívar, R., S. M. Li Kam, and V. Portuguéz. "El movimiento campesino en Costa Rica," in D. Camacho and R. Menjívar (coords.), *Movimientos populares en Centroamérica.* San José: EDUCA, 1985.

Menjívar, R. and J. D. Trejos. *La pobreza en América Central.* San José: FLACSO, 1992.

Menjívar Larín, R. and J. P. Pérez Sáinz (coords.). *Ni héroes ni villanas: Género e informalidad urbana en Centroamérica.* San José: FLACSO, 1993.

Meza, V. *Historia del movimiento obrero hondureño.* Tegucigalpa: CEDOH, 1991.

Meza Pineda, L. "Las relaciones del Estado hondureño con el sindicalismo en la década del ochenta: el caso del sector público," in CAAS-CEPAS, *El sindicalismo y la crisis centroamericana.* Heredia: CAAS-CEPAS, 1990.

MIPLADES. *Encuesta de hogares de propósitos multiples, urbano y rural 1985.* San Salvador: Ministerio de Planificación y Coordinación del Desarrollo Economico y Social, 1985.

MIPLAN. *Encuesta de hogares de propósitos múltiples 1985.* San Salvador: Ministerio de Planificación, Coordinación y Presupuesto, 1985.

Moller, M. "Segmentación del mercado de trabajo en el Area Metropolitana de San José," *documento*, San José: MIDEPLAN, 1985.

Monzón, A. S. "Condiciones de vida de la mujer asalariada en las plantas maquiladoras de confección: Area Metropolitana de Guatemala," *Tesis de Licenciatura*, Guatemala: Escuela de Ciencias Políticas/USAC, 1992.

Mora, J. *Cooperativismo y desarrollo agrario*. San José: Universidad Nacional a Distancia, 1987.

_____. "Movimientos campesinos en Costa Rica," *Cuadernos de Ciencias Sociales*, 53, 1992.

Murillo, C., R. Martínez, J. Ramírez, and D. Villalobos. "Diagnóstico socioeconómico de los vendedores informales en la ciudad de San José," *informe de investigación*, San José: CECADE, 1984.

Nash, M. *Los mayas en la era de la máquina*. Guatemala: Seminario de Integración Social Guatemalteca, 1970.

Negreros, S. "Características básicas del empleo femenino en Guatemala," *documento*, Guatemala: PNUD/Ministerio de Trabajo y Previsión Social, 1989a.

_____. "Estacionalidad agrícola, salarios y empleo temporal en Guatemala," in PREALC, "Centroamérica: acerca del empleo, la estructura y en cambio agrarios," *Cuadernos de Ciencias Sociales*, 23, San José: FLACSO, 1989b.

Nowalski, J., P. Morales, and G. Berliavsky. "Impacto de la maquila en la economía costarricense," *mimeo*, San José: Fundación Ebert, 1993.

OIT. "Estudios de casos y educación obrera en zonas francas y empresas maquiladoras en países del Istmo centroamericano y República Dominicana," *Documentos de Trabajo*, San José: OIT, 1995.

Oliva Medina, M. *Artesano y obreros costarricenses, 1880–1914*. San José: Editorial Costa Rica, 1985.

Pávez, G. "Industrias de maquila, zonas procesadoras de exportación y empresas multinacionales en Costa Rica y El Salvador," *Documentos de Trabajo*, 48, Programa de Empresas Multinacionales, Ginebra: OIT, 1987.

Pérez, N. and C. A. Varela. "Impacto socioeconómico de las maquiladoras y las zonas libres en Honduras," *informe*, San José: OIT, 1995.

Pérez Brignoli, H. "Crecimiento agroexportador y regímenes políticos en Centroamérica: Un ensayo de historia comparada," in H. Pérez Brignoli and M. Samper (comps.), *Tierra, café y sociedad: Ensayos sobre la historia agraria centroamericana*. San José: FLACSO, 1994a.

_____. "Economía política del café en Costa Rica (1850–1950)," in H. Pérez Brignoli and M. Samper (comps.), *Tierra, café y sociedad: Ensayos sobre la historia agraria centroamericana*. San José: FLACSO, 1994b.

Pérez Sáinz, J. P. "Ciudad de Guatemala en la década de los ochenta: crisis y urbanización," in A. Portes and M. Lungo (coords.), *Urbanización en Centroamérica*. San José: FLACSO, 1992.

_____. *El dilema del nahual. Globalización, exclusión y trabajo en Centroamérica*. San José: FLACSO, 1994a.

_____. "La reflexión sobre temas laborales en Centroamérica : de la década de la crisis a los tiempos de la globalización," *Economía y Sociología del Trabajo*, 23–24, 1994b.

_____. "Reestructuración industrial y gestión de la fuerza laboral en Centroamérica: un análisis regional," in J. P. Pérez Sáinz (coord.), *Globalización y fuerza laboral en Centroamérica*. San José: FLACSO, 1994c.

_____. "Actores y cultura laboral en la industria de exportación: una comparación entre Costa Rica y República Dominicana," *Documentos de Trabajo*, 6, San José: OIT, 1995a.

_____. "Impacto socio-laboral de maquilas y zonas francas en Centroamérica y República Dominicana," *Documentos de Trabajo*, 6, San José: OIT, 1995b.

_____. *Neoinformalidad en Centroamérica*. San José: FLACSO, 1996.

_____. "The New Faces of Informality in Central America," *Journal of Latin American Studies*, 30 (part 1), 1998.

Pérez Sáinz, J. P. and E. Castellanos de Ponciano. *Mujeres y empleo en la Ciudad de Guatemala*. Guatemala: FLACSO, 1991.

Pérez Sáinz, J. P. and R. Menjívar Larín (coords.). *Informalidad Urbana en Centroamérica: Entre la acumulación y la subsistencia*. Caracas: FLACSO/Nueva Sociedad, 1991.

Pérez Sáinz, J. P., M. Camus, and S. Bastos. . . . *todito, todito es trabajo. Indígenas y empleo en Ciudad de Guatemala*. Guatemala: FLACSO, 1992.

Pérez Sáinz, J. P. and A. Leal. "Pequeña empresa, capital social y etnicidad: el caso de San Pedro Sacatepéquez," *Debate*, 17, Guatemala: FLACSO, 1992.

Pérez Sáinz, J. P. and A. Cordero. "Los nuevos escenarios laborales en Centroamérica: una propuesta de análisis," *Anuario de Estudios Centroamericanos*, 20, 2, 1994a.

_____. *Sarchí: Artesanía y capital social en Sarchí*. San José: FLACSO, 1994b.

Petersen, K. *The Maquiladora Revolution in Guatemala*. Occasional Paper Series, 2, Orville H. Schell, Jr., Center for International Human Rights, Yale Law School, 1992.

Piel, J. *El departamento del Quiché bajo la dictadura liberal (1880–1920)*. Guatemala: FLACSO, 1995.

Poitevin, R. *El proceso de industrialización en Guatemala*. San José: EDUCA, 1977.

Posas, M. *Las sociedades artesanales y los orígenes del movimiento obrero hondureño*. Tegucigalpa, Esp L4 Editorial, 1977.

_____. "Reforma agraria y empleo rural en Honduras," in PREALC, "Centroamérica: acerca del empleo, la estructura y en cambio agrarios," *Cuadernos de Ciencias Sociales*, 23, San José: FLACSO, 1989.

_____. "El movimiento sindical hondureño durante la década de los ochenta," in CAAS-CEPAS, *El sindicalismo y la crisis centroamericana*. Heredia: CAAS-CEPAS, 1990.

_____. "La plantación bananera en Centroamérica (1870–1929)," in V. H. Acuña Ortega (ed.), *Historia General de Centroamérica: Las repúblicas agroexportadoras (1870–1945)*. Madrid: FLACSO/Sociedad Estatal Quinto Centenario, 1993.

PREALC. *Situación y perspectivas del empleo en El Salvador*. Santiago: PREALC, 1977.

_____. "Empleo y salarios en Nicaragua," *Documentos de Trabajo*, 194, Santiago: PREALC, 1980a.

_____. "Guatemala: estacionalidad y subempleo en el sector agropecuario," *Documentos de Trabajo*, 207, Santiago: PREALC, 1980b.

_____. *Cambio y polarización ocupacional den Centroamérica*. San José: EDUCA/ PREALC, 1986.

_____. "Pobreza y empleo en Centroamérica y Panamá," *documento*, Panamá: PNUD/OIT/PREALC, 1992.

Price Waterhouse. "Estudio de base de la población afectada por las Zonas Industriales de Procesamiento," *informe*, Tegucigalpa, 1992.

_____. "Actualización del estudio de base sobre las Zonas Industriales de Procesamiento en Honduras," *informe*, Tegucigalpa, 1993.

Redondo, A. and M. Juárez. "Las vendedoras de los mercados y su conciencia feminista," *Cuadernos de Investigación*, Managua: INIES, 1987.

Rodríguez, C. "Causas del desarrollo solidarista en Costa Rica y Centroamérica," in ASEPROLA/CEDAL, *El problema solidarista y la respuesta sindical en Centroamérica*. San José: ASEPROLA/CEDAL, 1989.

Rodríguez, C. R. *Tierra de Labriegos*. San José: FLACSO, 1993.

Rodríguez García, C. "El auge del Solidarismo en la década de los ochenta en Costa Rica," in CAAS-CEPAS, *El sindicalismo y la crisis centroamericana*. Heredia: CAAS-CEPAS, 1990.

Rojas, M. and Y. Román. "Agricultura de exportación y pequeños productores," *Cuadernos de Ciencias Sociales*, 61, 1993.

Rojas Bolaños, M. "Costa Rica: el movimiento obrero y popular en el contexto de una crisis," *Anuario de Estudios Centroamericanos*, 6, 1980.

_____. "El movimiento obrero en Costa Rica (reseña histórica)," in P. González Casanova (coord.), *Historia del movimiento obrero en América Latina* 2. México: Siglo XXI, 1985.

_____. "El sindicalismo centroamericano en la crisis." Una perspectiva comparativa, ponencia presentada al VIII Congreso Centroamericano de Sociología, Guatemala, 1988.

Samper, M. "Café, trabajo y sociedad en Centroamérica, (1870–1930): una historia común y divergente," in V. H. Acuña Ortega (ed.), *Historia General de Centroamérica: Las repúblicas agroexportadoras (1870–1945)*. Madrid: FLACSO/Sociedad Estatal Quinto Centenario, 1993.

_____. "El significado social de la caficultura costarricense y salvadoreña: análisis histórico comparado a partir de los censos cafetaleros," in H. Pérez Brignoli and M. Samper (comps.), *Tierra, café y sociedad: Ensayos sobre la historia agraria centroamericana*. San José: FLACSO, 1994a.

_____. "Los paisajes sociales del café: Reflexiones comparadas," in H. Pérez Brignoli and M. Samper (comps.), *Tierra, café y sociedad: Ensayos sobre la historia agraria centroamericana*. San José: FLACSO, 1994b.

Schoepfle, K. and J. Pérez-López. *Assembly Operations in Central America*. unpublished manuscript, 1992.

Smith, C. A. "Origins of the National Question in Guatemala: A Hypothesis," in C. A. Smith (ed.), *Guatemalan Indians and the State, 1540 to 1988*, Austin: University of Texas Press, 1990.

Solórzano, V. *El relato de Juan Tayún: La vida de un indio guatemalteco*. México: Costa-Amic, 1985.

Taracena Arriola, A. "Presencia anarquista en Guatemala," *Mesoamérica*, 15, 1988.

Tardanico, R. "Crisis económica y ajuse estructural: el mercado laboral en San José, Costa Rica," *Anuario de Estudios Centroamericanos*, 16(2) and 17(1), 1991–1992.

Tardanico, R. and M. Lungo. "Local dimensions of global restructuring: changing labour-market contours in urban Costa Rica," *International Journal of Urban and Regional Research*, 19, 2, 1995.

Torres-Rivas, E. *Interpretación del desarrollo social centroamericano*. San José: FLACSO, 1989. "¿Quién destapó la caja de Pandora?" in D. Camacho and M. Rojas, eds., *La crisis centroamericana*. San José: EDUCA/FLASCO, 1984.

_____. "Sobre la teoría de las dos crisis en Centroamérica," in E. Torres-Rivas, *Centroamérica: la democracia posible*. San José: EDUCA/FLASCO, 1987.

_____. Interpretación del desarrollo social centroamericano. San José: FLASCO, 1989.

Trejos, M. E. "Procesos de Trabajo en la Industria Exportadora Costarricense," *Aportes al Debate*, 1, Heredia: UNA, 1992.

Uthoff, A. and M. Pollack. "Análisis microeconómico del ajuste del mercado de trabajo en Costa Rica 1979–1982," *Revista Ciencias Económicas*, 5, 1, 1985.

Valverde, J. M., M. E. Trejos, and M. Mora. *La movilidad laboral al descubierto: Impacto socio-laboral del Plan de Movilidad Laboral en Costa Rica*. San José: ANEP/ASEPROLA, 1993.

Vega, V. "La ideología solidarista," in ASEPROLA/CEDAL, *El problema solidarista y la respuesta sindical en Centroamérica*. San José: ASEPROLA/CEDAL, 1989.

Vilas, C. M. *Transición desde el subdesarrollo: Revolución y reforma en la periferia*. Caracas: Nueva Sociedad, 1989.

_____. *Mercado, estados y revoluciones: Centroamérica 1950–1990*. México: Centro de Investigaciones Interdisciplinarias en Humanidades/UNAM, 1994.

Villagra, W. "Las posiciones políticas de las corrientes sindicales nicaragüenses," *Anuario de Estudios Centroamericanos*, 6, 1980.

Walker, I. and R. Gómez Zúñiga. "La industria de maquila y la organización laboral: El caso de Honduras," in J. P. Pérez Sáinz (coord.), *Globalización y fuerza laboral en Centroamérica*. San José: FLACSO, 1994c.

Weller, J. "Las exportaciones agrícolas no tradicionales en Costa Rica, Honduras y Panamá: la generación de empleo e ingresos y las perspectivas de los pequeños productores," *Documentos de Trabajo*, 370, Panamá: PREALC, 1992.

_____. "El empleo rural en el Istmo centroamericano: evolución reciente y perspectivas," *ponencia* presentada al Seminario "Mercado de trabajo, ajuste y globalización : cambios recientes y perspectivas hacia el 2,000," San José; June 9–10, 1994a.

_____. "Los mercados de trabajo centroamericanos durante la década de 1980 e inicios de la de 1990: efectos de la crisis y del ajuste estructural," *ponencia* presented at the seminar "Mercado de trabajo, ajuste y globalización: cambios recientes y perspectivas hacia el 2,000," San José, June 9–10, 1994b.

Williams, R. G. *Export Agriculture and the Crisis in Central America*. Chapel Hill: University of North Carolina Press, 1986.

_____. *States and Social Evolution: Coffee and the Rise of National Governments in Central America*. Chapel Hill: University of North Carolina Press, 1994.

Winter, C. and T. H. Gindling. "Women's Labor Force and Earnings in Honduras," in G. Psacharopoulos and Z. Tzannatos (eds.), *Case Studies on Women's Employment and Pay in Latin America.* Washington, D.C.: The World Bank, 1992.

Witzel, R. *Más de 100 años del movimiento obrero urbano en Guatemala: Artesanos y obreros en el período liberal (1877–1944).* Guatemala: ASIES, Tomo II, 1991.

_____. *Más de 100 años del movimiento obrero urbano en Guatemala: El protagonismo sindical en la construcción de la democracia (1944–1954).* Guatemala: ASIES, Tomo II, 1992.

_____. *Más de 100 años del movimiento obrero urbano en Guatemala. Reorganización, auge y desarticulación del movimiento sindical (1954–1982).* Guatemala: ASIES, Tomo III, n.d.

Yang, H. "Female Labor Participation and Earnings Differentials in Costa Rica," in G. Psacharapoulos and Z. Tzannatos (eds.), *Case Studies on Women's Employment and Pay in Latin America.* Washington, D.C.: The World Bank, 1992.

Index

Academic nature, 5
Acción Catolica (Catholic Action), 67
Accumulation process, 94, 115, 129, 133, 148–150, 164
Actors, 157–164
  shaping, 143
Agrarian reform, 66, 68, 72(n35), 147, 161
  implementation of, 89
  modification of, 67
Agricultural sector, 18, 19
  employment in, 19(table), 20, 46, 47, 89
  modernization of, 45, 52, 54
  proletarianization in, 66
  surplus labor in, 107
Agriculture
  diversification in, 47–48, 50–56, 58, 86
  for domestic use, 52, 53, 147
  See also Subsistence agriculture
Agroexports, 52, 53, 89, 118, 149, 150, 153
  diversification of, 35, 147
  globalization and, 164
  labor for, 148
  urbanization and, 6
Alliance for Progress, 55, 67–68
American Foundation of Labor, Interamerican Workers Confederation and, 59
American Institute for the Development of Free Trade Unionism (IADSL), 105
ANACH. *See* National Peasants' Association of Honduras
Aparcería, 53

Arbenz, Juan Jacobo, 28, 30
  cooperativism and, 67
  labor rights and, 60
  trade unions and, 102, 103, 109, 159
Area of the Property of the People, 117
Armed conflicts, economic crisis and, 101–102
Assassinations, 102–103
ATC. *See* Rural Workers Association
Authentic Democratic Workers Confederation (CATD), 62, 107
Authoritarian regimes, 27, 36–37, 76
  persistence of, 154
  state terrorism and, 4
  See also Oligarchic system
Autonomous Trade Union Federation (FAS), 28
AVANCSO, 119

Banana sector, 3, 6, 31(n13), 35, 51, 147
  conditions in, 157–158
  economic crisis and, 15
  globalization and, 164
  labor and, 9–16, 146, 165
  labor relations in, 29, 143, 152, 153, 157
  modernization and, 50
  predominance of, 4, 9
  proletarianization in, 146
  strike in, 24, 25, 29, 30, 59, 61, 99–100, 158, 159
  trade unions and, 34(n38), 63–64, 99
  transnational capital in, 35
  wages in, 21, 124
Bribris, 13, 31(n15)